Politikos

The sovereigns and courts of Europe

Politikos

The sovereigns and courts of Europe

ISBN/EAN: 9783743311305

Manufactured in Europe, USA, Canada, Australia, Japa

Cover: Foto ©ninafisch / pixelio.de

Manufactured and distributed by brebook publishing software (www.brebook.com)

Politikos

The sovereigns and courts of Europe

THE QUEEN OF ENGLAND.
(*From a recent Photograph.*)

THE SOVEREIGNS
AND COURTS OF EUROPE

BY
"POLITIKOS"

WITH PORTRAITS

NEW YORK
D. APPLETON AND COMPANY
1894

PREFACE.

HISTORY has ceased to be written in the names of kings and princes. Historians have learnt to recognize that it is the people who make history; that the narrative of the world's progress must consist of the story of the march of the nations, not of the biography of one individual, even though that individual be the leader of the same people. Unless the leader be followed, he leadeth in vain, and however tyrannical and oppressive the rule of a monarch, experience has proved that the victory rests with the majority, even though that victory be slow and delayed. That every people has the government it deserves is a dictum most emphatically true. The new historical method, therefore, strives to present the thoughts, aspirations, and deeds of the nations, and only that portion of the rulers' lives and characters which reflect and influence these.

Every era has its prominent men, who, with the

government, though not infrequently in opposition to it, help towards the march of events. The Victorian era in England is in itself a striking illustration of the way in which men of every grade combine in diversity of action to make a great epoch. "The divinity that doth hedge a king" is but little regarded in these post-revolutionary days, when the deeds of men are weighed in the same balances and judged by the same standards. Still, so long as kings remain, they must have a certain measure of influence upon their peoples and surroundings. Nor can the measure of this influence be defined by the letter of constitutions. Personal character and traditions exert a sway, conscious or unconscious. Hence, while men have learnt to recognize that history includes the masses, and does not mean merely the deeds or misdeeds of a few persons placed by the accident of birth in a certain marked position, kings still continue, and must continue for a while, to play a part in the making of the history of their times. It is with the view of enabling the general public better to know the men who hold the reins of office, and hence better to appreciate the course of modern politics, that the following chapters have been written. This series of biographies of reigning sovereigns endeavours to present, besides biographies, chapters of contemporary history. They have been carefully prepared from special and authoritative sources, and while speaking with the reserve due to individual privacy, also strive to speak with the fulness truth requires for the proper understanding of character. Of these sovereigns of Europe, it will generally be found to their honour, especially among the younger generation, that they are penetrated with the gravity of their responsibilities, and strive to do their duty according to their lights, even though some of these lights are but dim.

CONTENTS.

	PAGE
THE SULTAN OF TURKEY	3
THE CZAR OF RUSSIA	27
THE EMPEROR OF AUSTRIA	67
WILLIAM II., EMPEROR OF GERMANY	107
THE KING OF ITALY	165
THE KING OF SPAIN	193
THE REIGNING FAMILY OF PORTUGAL	221
GEORGE I., KING OF THE HELLENES	241
THE KING OF HOLLAND	259
THE KING OF THE BELGIANS	271
THE ROYAL FAMILY OF DENMARK	289

CONTENTS.

	PAGE
THE KING OF SWEDEN	307
THE ROYAL COUPLE OF ROUMANIA	327
THE KING OF SERVIA	351
THE KING OF SAXONY	369
THE MINOR GERMAN SOVEREIGNS	377
QUEEN VICTORIA OF ENGLAND	393

LIST OF ILLUSTRATIONS.

THE QUEEN OF ENGLAND .	. . .	*Frontispiece*
THE SULTAN OF TURKEY	. . .	*Facing page* 15
THE CZAR OF RUSSIA	. . . . ,,	,, 27
THE EMPEROR OF AUSTRIA	. . . ,,	,, 67
THE EMPEROR OF GERMANY	. . . ,,	,, 107
THE KING OF ITALY	. . . . ,,	,, 165
THE KING OF PORTUGAL .	. . ,,	,, 221
THE KING OF GREECE .	. . . ,,	,, 241
THE KING OF HOLLAND	. . . ,,	,, 259
THE KING OF THE BELGIANS	. . ,,	,, 271
THE KING OF DENMARK .	. . . ,,	,, 289
THE KING OF SWEDEN .	. . . ,,	,, 307
THE QUEEN OF ROUMANIA	. . . ,,	,, 327
THE KING OF ROUMANIA	. . . ,,	,, 341

THE SULTAN OF TURKEY.

THE SULTAN OF TURKEY.

ON Whit-Sunday, 1876, there occurred in a fair palace overlooking the Bosphorus one of those romantic tragedies which are but too common in the history of the Crescent. What happened exactly will perchance never be known, since truth and news are as carefully hushed up in Turkey as they are propagated in more civilized lands, and the mystery may never be solved whether Abdul Aziz committed suicide or was assassinated. The probabilities, however, all point to foul play. A palace plot is no uncommon thing in the Ottoman Empire, and in the history of its rulers. Certain it is that the ex-Sultan was found dead in his room, with a mortal gash in his arm, five days after he had been deposed, on the plea of insanity, to make way for his nephew, Sultan Mourad V. That the monarch was broken in health and mind is beyond question, and that hence he was not able to resist with sufficient energy the Muscovite pressure brought to bear upon him, which threatened to degrade Turkey into the position of a Russian province. That he was mad enough to commit suicide is far from proved. But his deposition was a political necessity, and hence insanity was used as a plea to make the act plausible to the world at large. It was hoped that Mourad would prove a wiser ruler. He had not been many weeks upon the throne when it became evident that he, too, was a man unable to meet the heavy strain which had to be borne by a Turkish sovereign in those difficult times. The ministers therefore resolved that this ruler, too, must be deposed, and with the consent of the Sheik-ul-Islam, the spiritual head of the Faith, Sultan Mourad also was quietly uncrowned. It was then decided in Council to offer the vacant throne to the younger brother of Mourad —Abdul Hamid—with the request that in the interests of the Empire he would assume the throne of Turkey, and be girt with the sword of Othman. The offer was by no means welcome to the man to whom it was made. Abdul Hamid had lived for years in retirement; he was not ambitious, and he had no desire to exchange his seclusion for a crown of thorns. He urged that his brother should be accorded a further trial, that his incapacity to rule should be further proved. When at last this was placed beyond doubt, reluctantly he yielded to the appeal made to him, and on the 31st of August, 1876, ascended the throne of his fathers to become one of the best sovereigns that had for long ruled the Empire of the Crescent.

Abdul Hamid, whose name means Servant of the Praiseworthy, was born in 1842, the son of a Circassian, who died shortly after the birth of her babe. The child's education was consequently entrusted to another wife of Abdul Medjid, herself childless. She was a wise, upright woman, who devoted herself with love to the motherless boy, and who guarded him with the most tender, judicious care. His first master was the Court mollah, Mustafa Efendi, and his later tutor Kemal Efendi, the latter a man of European culture, who gave him a good Oriental education, combined with Occidental ideas. The boy learnt Arabic and Persian, and studied history and geography with zeal and interest. But in all European languages, and above all in French, he made little progress, so that even to-day he understands them but indifferently, and does not speak them at all. It is this that renders intercourse with Europeans so difficult with him. From his babyhood he evinced signs of a weakly constitution, and was noted for his timidity and shyness. But all the more remarkable were his thoughtful bearing and his shrewdness of perception and comprehension. Never having known a mother's love, a mother's caressing care, rarely noticed by his father, he led almost from his childhood a retired life, keeping apart from all recreations. As a youth, too, he never joined in amusements, and was so careful of his means that when he ascended the throne he had amassed a capital of 60,000 Turkish pounds. In 1868 he travelled in Europe, in the company of his uncle, the then Sultan Abdul Aziz. According to his own showing, his sojourns in Paris, London, and Vienna, helped greatly to enlarge his mental vision and to increase his knowledge. On his return to Constantinople he was fired with a desire to fill up the lacunæ in his education, and set himself to reading industriously. He also occupied himself much with music. As before, he avoided all social recreations, and did not even hunt or shoot, that common pastime of princes. When the palace revolution occurred that ended in the violent death of Abdul Aziz, he was profoundly moved and impressed, and when his brother Mourad ascended the throne Abdul Hamid was the first to lay his obedient homage at his feet. It was not until Mourad had been declared weak of intellect, and that he himself was called upon to take his place, that Abdul Hamid revealed all the force of character that lay within him. Perchance he himself was unconscious of it, and that it needed circumstances to call it forth. For hardly in power, this quiet, studious recluse suddenly showed an energy that surprised even those who knew him most intimately.

He had been called to govern in a dark moment of Turkish history. The State had recently declared herself bankrupt, the finances were in a state of chaos; Russian agents were busy in every town and village stirring up the natives to rebellion by means of fair promises and clinking gold; Servia had declared war on Turkey, the army was disorganized and discontented, because unpaid. The Sultan met all these difficulties with a cool judgment, a diplomacy, that amazed Europe and displeased greatly the ruler on the banks of the Neva, who certainly did not desire to see Turkey recover from her position of European sick man. Great self-control, great patience, did Abdul Hamid show, and also great astuteness. He recognized the power that his chief minister, Midhat Pasha, held in hand, and he feigned for a period an entire submission to his will and to that of other influential ministers, while all the time carefully laying his own schemes and preparing to govern his country in accordance with his own ideas.

In April, 1877, Czar Alexander II. at last declared open war on Turkey in place of the secret one he had been carrying on for some time. His purpose, to quote his own words, was to give expression "to the intense anxiety felt by the whole Russian nation to effect an amelioration in the position of the Christians in the East." How the Czar managed to be so well acquainted with the intensest feelings of his subjects, seeing that the expression of popular opinion in Russia is gagged on press and platform, does not appear; but in any case, he considered himself obliged, in view of "the haughty obstinacy of Turkey," to draw the sword; and he ended his marvellous declaration by invoking the blessing of Heaven upon his army, called out to fight in so holy a cause.

How valiantly the Ottomans fought, how gallantly they defended their country, is matter of history; and though the Turks were often beaten, so too were the Russians. Finally, in March, 1878, was signed the famous Treaty of San Stefano, a treaty so grasping on the part of Russia that the moment its provisions were known in Europe it was manifest, from the excitement it created, that the other Powers would never permit it to be carried into effect. In consequence the famous Berlin Congress was summoned.

The result of this Congress, as all the world knows, was the practical tearing up of the Treaty of San Stefano. Lord Beaconsfield returned to London emitting the famous phrase, "Peace with honour"; the Russians went back to St. Petersburg to scheme further pretexts for interfering in the affairs of the Sublime Porte, and the Turkish representatives got home to Constantinople in time to assist at those councils whose end was revivification and reform.

For, the war over, Abdul Hamid showed his hand. He now felt that he was indeed firmly seated upon his throne, and his resolve was to restore prosperity and happiness to his distracted kingdom. But the first thing of all to do was to punish sternly the king-maker, the disturber of the internal peace. The Constitution drawn up by Midhat Pasha, to which the Sultan had been forced to give his consent, was revoked, Abdul Hamid rightly apprehending that the people on whom it had been thrust had not yet reached that phase of political development in which alone constitutions of any kind are workable. And, moreover, ready-made constitutions, constitutions that have not come naturally into being, are rarely of much value. After all, government is a question of climate and ethnology; and no fair-minded thinker can doubt, seeing the present low state of general culture in Turkey, and the absolute inaptitude for self-government, that direct rule remains for the Turks the best mode of government for the present. And the more so if this rule is wisely exercised. That Abdul Hamid was severely criticized for his step goes without saying. In Europe especially arose the cry that he was crushing the dawning freedom of his country, that he was pursuing a policy of reaction and obscurantism. It marks the Sultan's intellectual superiority that he so clearly saw through forms to facts, that he recognized that even well-meant innovations may be hurtful if premature, and that he continued his course unhindered by adverse criticism and by the counsels of candid foreign friends, themselves ignorant of the affairs of Turkey, of its internal state, its needs, its tastes. Undaunted, he pursued his path, showing great personal courage. At the same time the dread of a counter revolution did not let him rest; and as time went on, and he found himself deceived in some of his dearest hopes, deceived above all in the persons in whom he had put trust, whom he had raised to eminence, he began more and more to retreat personally from public life, though never abandoning State affairs. The Palace of Yildiz, a little outside Constantinople, grew to be his favourite residence; and he now rarely quits that spot. An eye-witness of Abdul Hamid's conduct at the end of the first month of his reign wrote as follows:

"In all matters of public importance the personal

views of the Sultan Hamid have exercised a most decisive influence, and this influence is growing every day; but it is altogether of a different kind from that of his predecessors. It is not that capricious interference, the result of momentary whims and covert advice or influence, but it is a systematic effort on the Sultan's part to master the affairs of State by seeking for information, and on the strength of this forming his judgment. . . . According to the etiquette of centuries, the Sultan came as little into contact with his ministers socially as with the rest of the world. The present Sultan has broken through the barriers of this isolation. He allows them to be seated in his presence and discusses affairs in council. He has already spoken earnestly of his strong wish to encourage trade and industry, to open agricultural schools, and to introduce model farms. In his choice of officers to attend about his person he has specially selected those who have received a European education and have become conversant not only with the languages but with the leading ideas of the civilized countries of Europe."

His wishes in respect of internal reforms have all been carried into effect. The first thing to do was to put the finances straight, for these were simply in confusion. As has been well said, never since Necker seized the purse-strings of revolutionary France, had an apparently more hopeless outlook to be faced by mortal financier. The official inquiry instituted at the request of the Sultan revealed a state of corruption and dishonesty which had assumed proportions surpassing all that even an Oriental country can show in the matter of peculation and trickery. A more enlightened financial policy was at once inaugurated, to whose wisdom and merit the improved state of Turkish finances and of the whole condition of the empire now bears witness. The next thing to do was to put down brigandage, one of the greatest curses of the Turkish empire, affording a lucrative if irregular method of gaining a livelihood to thousands, and exercising a rule of pressure and terrorism over all dutiful subjects. In this matter, too, Abdul Hamid showed that he had a resolute hand and decided views ; and the good results achieved already make themselves manifest. The work of exterminating brigandage goes on vigorously, to the decided advantage of Turkish finances and Turkish prosperity.

Nor are these the only marked improvements that have taken place since Abdul Hamid came into power. Under his personal initiative the school system has been much enlarged and perfected, and not only for males, but also for females, the schools for the latter especially being under the direct patronage of the Sultan, who is truly interested in the welfare and progress of his female subjects. The strides made in women's education under his reign are little short of marvellous. Among other changes, primary education has been made obligatory, and each commune must possess a school where children are taught gratuitously, and where instruction does not consist merely in the reading of the Koran, as in former times, but where more useful and more modern attainments can be acquired. It is perhaps needless to say that in initiating this reform Abdul Hamid has had to encounter much active and latent opposition, and that the latter, especially in the country districts and those remote from the capital, often hinders the more rapid spread of his good work. It is exceedingly difficult to impose reforms upon the Turk, who, after all, it must never be forgotten, is an Asiatic and a Mussulman. The press, too, has been taken under the Sultan's protection, and though one could scarely look for press freedom in an Oriental land, yet by Imperial command all the most important literary and scientific works of Europe are issued in translations from the Government printing office, a practice that would not have been tolerated under previous reigns. But one of Abdul Hamid's constant cares is to raise the intellectual status of his subjects.

Nor do Abdul Hamid's reforms stop here. The army had also to be reorganized and better disciplined; and from the Sultan devoting himself to this with the same energy that he had shown in other departments, the result is that the military system of the land is now far from despicable; indeed, is so good as to have won praises from that great authority on all that is soldierly, the Emperor William II. Further, the railroad system has been much extended, and new lines are be constructed in Asia.

And in all these matters it must never be forgotten

that Abdul Hamid himself is the active and reforming force, his ministers being merely subordinate officers who carry out his behests and directions, often belonging themselves to the old Turkish retrograde faction. And this is the Sultan's misfortune: while Abdul Hamid is thus sincerely enthusiastic for the welfare of his people, he is not seconded by his subordinates, who have neither his zeal nor his uprightness; so that in the interior the advance in culture and civilization is not yet so marked as nearer to the Sultan's direct supervision. That he himself is a humane sovereign is beyond doubt; nor is he in anywise responsible for the atrocities that but too often occur in his dominions, and shock the feelings of Europe. Thus it is a fact that he has not signed more than one death warrant since his accession. Indeed, capital punishment has been practically abolished by him, for it is he in person who has to decide the fate of criminals.

It is beyond doubt that Turkey, whatever its shortcomings — and these no doubt are great — has also suffered much from misrepresentation. All that occurs there reaches the outside world in a distorted shape; the good is depreciated, the evil is exaggerated. Indeed, the common notion seems to be, "Can any good thing come out of Turkey?" Thus it is always assumed without question that a Sultan gives himself up to luxurious and licentious living, and does not trouble himself with the affairs of the State. That the present Sultan is a serious man, whose entire energy and ability are devoted to the affairs of government, the reforms he has instituted prove. That his private life resembles much more that of an English gentleman than the popular idea of an Oriental prince, is familiar to all who reside at Constantinople. Among other financial reforms, he has consistently discouraged the expenditure on the harem. He himself is practically a monogamist, and has no more legal wives than four, the number obligatory upon a Sultan, and to none does he show special favour. That his harem is nevertheless largely populated arises from the customs of his land and of his dynasty. He personally would be glad enough to be rid of his three hundred brevet spouses, who merely cost him money, and often are the causes of those palace revolutions too common in Oriental lands. But, as we all know, the force of custom is not so easily broken. Thus, on his birthday, and on twenty other days in the year the Sultan invariably receives from his adopted mother the present of a beautiful slave, and this young lady has forthwith to be transferred to his establishment in the capacity of harem dame, with a household of her own, consisting of at least four eunuchs and six female servants, to say nothing of horses, carriages, and grooms. Multiply the number of these establishments by three hundred, and it ceases to be astonishing that the expenditure on the Sultan's Civil List should amount to £4,000,000 sterling a year. A large item in this sum represents the dowers which the Sultan pays to his slaves when he marries them to favourite officials. About one hundred are

THE SULTAN OF TURKEY.

married from the palace annually, and each of them is entitled to receive £10,000. Unfortunately, the bridegroom who takes a wife from the Sultan's hands must at his earliest convenience make a present of a slave to keep the staff of the Imperial seraglio up to its proper figure. The Sultan — those who know him affirm — loathes the whole thing; but there are too many vested interests engaged in keeping the Imperial harem supplied with wives, and if the Sultan were to cashier his entire female establishment, he would certainly be deposed or murdered. Sir William White is said to have advised his Majesty to reduce his establishment by not filling up vacancies, but this is not easy, seeing that every Cabinet Minister and Pasha of note looks to passing his daughter through the Sultan's harem as a simple means of securing her a marriage portion, with the title of "validé," which may be construed as princess.

That so huge a household must cost much is self-evident, and yet Abdul Hamid does his best to check reckless expenditure. Still, it is estimated that over six thousand persons are fed daily at his Dolma Bagtche Palace when he is there. Perhaps this is another reason why he prefers the smaller Yildiz Kiosk. One who is well informed gives a graphic picture of the Sultan's housekeeping. He admits that it is clear that there is good executive ability in the management of this enormous household, for there is scarcely ever a jar or hitch, even under the impulse of the most untimely demands. Every different department is under the control of a person who is directly responsible for that, and he has a corps of servants and slaves under his orders, who obey him only, and he is subject to the Treasurer of the Household. Women have no voice whatever in the management of anything in any department. Their sole occupation is to wait upon their respective mistresses, or to serve the Sultan in some specified capacity; and the labour about the palace is so sub-divided that no one works very hard except the Lord High Chamberlain and Treasurer of the Household.

The Chamberlain is mostly occupied in administering to the wants and caprices of the Sultan, and is in almost constant attendance upon him; so the Treasurer of the Household has the burden of the housekeeping on his burly shoulders. He has an organized force of buyers, who are each charged with the purchase of certain supplies for their individual departments, each having his helpers, servants, and slaves.

One man is charged with the duty of supplying all the fish, and as to furnish fish for six thousand persons is no light undertaking in a place where there are no great markets such as there are in all other large cities, he must have about twenty men to scour the various small markets and buy of the fishermen, and each of these men has two others to carry the fish they buy. The palace requires about ten tons of fish a week.

There are nearly eighteen thousand pounds of bread eaten daily, for the Turks are large bread eaters, and this is all baked in the enormous ovens situated at some distance from the palace. The kitchens are detached from all the palaces and kiosks. It requires a large force of bakers to bake the bread and another to bring it to the palace, and another force of buyers who purchase the flour and fuel. The bringing of the most of the wood and charcoal is done by camels, who carry it on their backs. The rest comes in caïques. The Turkish bread is baked in large loaves, and is light, moist, and sweet—delicious bread in every way, particularly that which is made of rye.

The food for the Sultan is prepared by one man and his aids, and none others touch it. It is cooked in silver vessels, and when done each kettle is sealed by a slip of paper and a stamp, and this is broken in the presence of the Sultan by the High Chamberlain, who takes one spoonful of each separate kettle before the Sultan tastes it. This is to prevent the Sultan from being poisoned. The food is almost always served up to the Sultan in the same vessels in which it was cooked, and these are often of gold, but when of baser metal the kettle is set into a rich golden bell-shaped holder, the handle of which is held by a slave while the Sultan eats. Each kettle is a course, and is served with bread and a kind of pancake, which is held on a golden tray by another slave.

It requires just twice as many slaves as there are courses to serve the Sultan's dinner. He usually sits on a divan near a window, which looks over the Bosphorus, and takes his ease in a loose *pembazar* and *gegelik* with his sleeves turned up. After he has eaten all he wants, the Sultan takes his coffee and his chibouk and lies back in an ecstasy of enjoyment and quiet reverie which he calls taking his *kief.* Woe to him who comes to disturb it!

The Sultan never uses a plate. He takes all his food direct from the little kettles, and never uses a table and rarely a knife or fork. A spoon, his bread, pancake, or fingers are far handier. The whole household is at liberty to take meals where it suits him or her best, and thus every one is served with a small tray, with a spoon and a great chunk of bread. The higher officers only get the pancakes.

Nearly one ton of rice per day is required for the inevitable *pillaff,* six hundred pounds of sugar, as much coffee, to say nothing of the other groceries, fruit, vegetables, and meat. Rice, mutton and bread form the greater part of the fare for the majority of Turks, together with fish, sweetmeats, confectionery, nuts, and dried and fresh fruits.

That there is enormous waste and extravagance in the kitchens is obvious, and it is said that enough is thrown away daily to maintain a hundred families; but such waste is perhaps not confined to a Turkish royal household, and might also be found in kitchens nearer home. The surplus is gathered up by the beggars, with whom Constantinople abounds, and what still remains is eaten by the scavenger dogs.

All the water for the Sultan's use, and the drinking water for all the household, is brought in barrels from two pretty streams at different places in the Bosphorus, towards the Black Sea. Another one of the Lord Chamberlain's functions is to see that a horse is kept in constant readiness, and also a carriage night and day, in case the Padishah should want to change his residence, as he often does, at a moment's notice.

Yet with all this traditional machinery of expense around him, the master of it leads the simplest life. Abdul Hamid gets up early. His toilet does not detain him long; indeed, it might detain him longer according to European codes. Dressed, he at once devotes himself to recite the prescribed prayers, after which he drinks a cup of black coffee, and instantly afterwards begins to smoke cigarettes, a pastime that he continues all day almost without intermission, for he is an ardent smoker. Breakfast ended, he arranges family affairs when these require his attention, as is most always the case with so large a family and of such varied ages and needs. This done, he quits the harem and goes into the selamlik. Here he receives the reports concerning court affairs. Towards ten o'clock his court secretary and chief dignitaries appear, bearing the day's despatches and reports. These handed in, the Sultan seats himself on a sofa with on his right these documents, and on his left a pile of Turkish newspapers and extracts from the European press, translated into Turkish for his benefit by a translation bureau specially appointed to that end. His lunch, which follows the despatch of this business, is most simple—little meat, a fair amount of vegetables.

The meal ended, he will take a walk in the park or row in a little boat upon one of the lakes it encloses, always accompanied by a chamberlain or some high dignitary. After taking two hours' exercise in the air, he returns to his sitting-rooms, where he holds an open reception, or else presides over some committee meeting. An hour or two before sunset he once more goes out to walk. His dinner is as simple as his lunch. His favourite food is *pillaf*, sweets, and a very little meat. He never touches spirituous liquors, in due obedience to the commands of the Prophet, but he drinks large quantities of sherbet and eats a great deal of ice-cream. Dinner over, he will receive company in the selamlik, or he will retire into the harem, where his daughters play and sing to him. He himself on these occasions will often seat himself at the piano, an instrument he plays fairly well. For painting, for the fine arts in general, he has no taste. His women, too, find him very cold; but he is devoted to his children, and also much attached to all the members of his family.

In appearance he is of medium height, rather short than tall, well-proportioned in his person, and carrying bravely the weight of his onerous duties, though there are also moments when an old and careworn look comes across his face, and when he almost personifies the apathy we so generally connect with the Turkish character. His beard, cut into a slight point, is black, so are his hair and eyes. The latter are tender in expression, but also penetrating, and he looks his visitors full in the face,

TURKEY.

with a scrutiny that seems to read their thoughts. What destroys the pleasant first impression made by these eyes is the constant look of uneasiness in them. The fact is, Abdul Hamid does not feel himself safe even in his own palace. He does not suspect any person in particular, but he is on his guard against every one. He knows too well that palace conspiracies are of every-day occurrence in the life of an Oriental sovereign, and he cannot forget the tragic events that led to his own elevation to the throne. Whether he need truly be thus timorous is a question. Few Padishahs have been so beloved by their subjects as he. Indeed, he is to them quite a new type of Sultan, and they do not fail to appreciate the novelty. Here is a man who does not pass his days in his harem, toying with his slaves. Here is a man who takes a real interest in the welfare of his people, who, far from following the example of his predecessors, and leaving the reins of government in the hands of some clever courtiers, insists on seeing and judging all for himself, down to the minutest particulars. Indeed, it may be affirmed that he exaggerates this practice, with the result that a deplorable delay often occurs in the execution of public business, because the Sultan lacks time to attend to everything at once.

Personally, he is most benevolent and kind-hearted, and scarcely a month passes that he does not contribute some large sum out of his private purse to alleviate suffering among his subjects, irrespective of race or religion. Quite recently he made a spontaneous gift of

250,000 piastres in aid of the preparatory schools in the isle of Crete. On one occasion he converted the greater portion of his plate and jewellery into cash for the use of the State Treasury; at another he cut down the number of his personal servants in order to devote the funds to the service of deserving charity. He spends with as little cost to his subjects as possible, and his Civil List, for a Turkish Sultan, is modest in the extreme.

His character may be summed up as having for its dominant note an extreme caution. Hence, perhaps, the source of his constant mistrust and frequent indecisions; and hence, perhaps, the reason why he discharges all business matters himself. It is well that to this extreme caution is added a real intelligence, so that he is capable of coping with all the questions of home and foreign policy, the sociological problems concerning religion, education, and what not else that pass through his hands. Fortunate, too, that he is endowed with an unusual faculty for work. In manner he is exceedingly polite, especially in his treatment of European ladies. Indeed, he understands the rare art of making himself beloved by all with whom he comes in contact. His language, which is very carefully chosen, is somewhat slow and monotonous in tone, but he can rouse himself to great fire when any theme excites his enthusiasm or his feelings. In religious matters he is no fanatic; indeed, he rather leans to freethought. Still, he always demonstrates himself as enthusiastically

Pan-Islamite; but this may be the result of well-calculated political astuteness. Hence he associates much with the Mussulman clergy, dervishes, and mollahs, and is lavish in gifts to them; as, indeed, his hand is always open to give. He likes to play the part of Mæcenas, and bestow handsome presents on all his European visitors, especially if they be men distinguished in art or letters. European princesses and the wives of ambassadors can also tell tales of his generosity in this respect.

If we would sum up the nature of his government we might with truth designate him as a liberal sovereign, bearing in mind, of course, that liberty in the Occidental sense is unknown in Turkey. But Abdul Hamid has understood how to adapt his really fundamentally liberal ideas to the local, political, and ethnological conditions of his realm. While apparently a stern despot, he is really paternal and well-intentioned. Whatever be the sins of Turkey, her present sovereign, Abdul Hamid II., is a kind, benevolent ruler, whose every inspiration is for the good and welfare of his subjects. The unrest, the discontent that certainly exists in parts of the huge, disjointed empire can, as a rule, be traced to emissaries from without, whose aim is to attack the interests of England; and to further the designs of "the divine figure from the north." Undoubtedly, the last war helped to loosen yet further the bands that hold together the jumbled population, just as it helped to give the finishing touch to its already shattered finances.

If Turkey can be saved from complete disruption—and those who should know best doubt if this seemingly inevitable evolutionary process can be arrested—it will be due in large measure to the enlightened government of her present Sultan, under whose reign it has made rapid and vigorous strides in the path of recovery and reform. What she requires now above all is that his life should be spared, and that she may enjoy the blessings of peace in order to recuperate her strength and her finances. How precariously matters stand for the Ottoman Empire no one better appreciates than Abdul Hamid himself. Hence his nervous anxiety to be left a neutral in all European complications. As far as inner revolts are concerned he may rest easy: his throne is safe; and all the stories that reach the West about family conspiracies, and a desire to depose him and restore his brother Mourad, are pure inventions, not to mention the fact that Mourad is really weak of intellect, and that the other members of the family are all devoted to Abdul Hamid.

THE EMPEROR OF RUSSIA.

THE CZAR OF RUSSIA.

THE EMPEROR OF RUSSIA.

ON the 24th of April, 1865, the Russian Imperial family was plunged into mourning, for on that day there died at Nice the Crown Prince Nicolai Alexandrowitch, after a painful illness, due to the effects of an unintentional blow inflicted by the present Czar in the course of some rough horseplay. This Czarewitch, a handsome, refined-looking man, had gained, thanks to his talents and personal charms, the love of his people, a people intensely, one might almost say fanatically, devoted to its royal house, which it looks on as semi-divine. It had been anticipated that this heir, who held enlightened modern views, would realize during his reign the hopes of progress so long caressed in Russia. And now a fatal blow, dealt by his own brother's hand, had laid him low on the very eve of his marriage, for he had been already betrothed with all form to Princess Dagmar, the brightest, prettiest, most charming of clever old Queen Louise of Denmark's three daughters. The news of his illness had brought her to Nice, and here she tended like a sister of charity the man who loved her truly, and whom she loved in return. Nicolai's brother, Alexander Alexandrowitch, was also often by that bedside, devoured by remorse, deeply distressed at the certain loss of his elder brother, whom he adored and admired. It was a few hours ere the demise that the dying man turned to his brother and promised wife and spoke his last wishes. Was it his purpose to testify his regard for his brother— to compensate his bride for, at least, the loss of a crown? Who can tell?

"I leave to you, Alexander Alexandrowitch," he said, "the heavy but glorious succession to the Russian throne; but I should like to add to it, also, a legacy more precious still, which will help you to bear its burden." So saying, he took the hand of the Princess Dagmar and placed it in that of Prince Alexander. "Marry her; it is my dying request and wish. And you, my dear bride, your destiny will be accomplished all the same; you will be Empress of Russia."

And thus it was. Eighteen months after the death of the Czarewitch, his brother and successor, Alexander Alexandrowitch, married Marie Sophie Frederique Dagmar, Princess of Denmark, who, in becoming Cézarewna and Grand Duchess of Russia, had to renounce her Protestant faith and her familiar baptismal name to figure instead as Marie Feodorowna,[*] the Russian rites admitting of no Christian name that does not appear among the nomenclature of its saints.

But Princess Dagmar was too true a woman, and had too sincerely loved her first betrothed, easily to accept

[*] Marie, daughter of Feodor.

the substitution he had imposed with his last breath. The mere title of Empress was not enough to allure her or console her. It was only after long months of mourning that she at last consented to obey his desires. That she did not forget her first love is proved by the fact that one day, unexpectedly finding herself before a portrait of the dead Czarewitch, which had been purposely and maliciously put into her path, she fainted with emotion. Nor could her husband feel hurt at this touching fidelity, for was it not a guarantee the more for the affection his wife had sworn to him, and which from that hour to this forms the happiness of their two lives? For it was no easy crown Princess Dagmar was called to wear. Was it some inkling of the difficult fate in store for her that made her, on the morning of her departure from her father's palace, draw from her finger a diamond ring and scratch on the window-pane of her little simple bedroom, "My beloved Fredensborg, farewell!"

But whatever the Princess may have thought, the world holds that she has benefited by the change, for the present Czar is a nobler and more sterling character than his brother. As a woman the Empress has every reason to be content. No breath of scandal or intrigue has every clouded her marital relations; it is impossible to find anywhere a more affectionate and devoted couple than the Emperor and Empress of Russia. Indeed, it is said laughingly at St. Petersburg that the Emperor is the only Russian who is faithful to his wife.

Alexander Alexandrowitch was born at St. Petersburg in the Winter Palace, March 10, 1845, the second son of Alexander II. by his first wife. For reasons not quite apparent he was slighted by both father and mother, so that his infancy and youth were sad. His education proceeded upon strictly military lines, as is customary for the younger sons of the Imperial house, and he himself often expressed his pleasure to think that he was not the heir. "I am the *loustic* of the family," he would say; "I have no need to learn." Destined by education to be an officer of the Guards, not dreaming of any other fate than to enjoy existence, guiltless of all scientific instruction, of even the acquaintance with foreign tongues so requisite in his exalted position, having none of the needful knowledge for governing, his position was, indeed, rendered difficult, when, at the age of twenty, he found himself suddenly, by his brother's death, heir presumptive to the Imperial crown of all the Russias. He had till then held himself much aloof from the Court. A man of uncompromising honesty, he made no effort to hide his indignation at the immorality and corruption rife there both among his relations and their surroundings. He was thoroughly out of touch with the *régime*, the tone that then prevailed, and, notwithstanding all her coldness towards him, he was further deeply shocked by the neglect to which his mother was subjected. When a few weeks after her demise (1880) her husband legitimized his union with the Princess Dolgorowky, the relations between father and son became more strained than ever.

The next year (March 13, 1881) occurred the tragedy on the Newsky Canal that murdered Czar Alexander II., and his son found himself upon the throne sooner than he had feared.

No one better than he grasped the difficulties of his position and his inadequacy to fill it, for the virtues of a private citizen, all of which he owns, are but too often in contradiction with certain qualities required of a monarch. Hence he was possessed at first with an extreme timidity, which, joined to the native reserve and mistrust of his character, was not calculated to facilitate matters, or to render him immediately popular. Indeed, with all his good qualities, Alexander III. is not and cannot be a popular idol. Already on the death of his brother, the force of circumstances had obliged him to put his hand without delay to his new duties, to interest himself in everything, to conquer his natural inclination for a merry, idle life. Putting aside false shame, he admitted his ignorance, and became once more a schoolboy to fill up the lacunæ of his early education. Above all, he set about learning the science of government, for the serious side of his nature made him at once take seriously the duties that would devolve upon him.

Brought up among young officers, who had already begun the reaction against German sympathies, the Czarewitch had embraced these views. His marriage with a Princess of Denmark, the hereditary enemy of Prussia, had further fomented these antipathies. The Czarewitch was therefore soon pointed out as a zealous partizan of the national and Slavonic cause, such as it was preached by Katkoff and his friends. These views often provoked severe conflicts between the Emperor and his heir presumptive, the one indolent and *laisser faire*, the other desirous to be respectful and conciliating, but withal easily roused to anger, and hot-headed. When the Franco-German war broke out, the Czarewitch, together with all " young Russia," took part for France, and thus, once again, he was in acute opposition to the views of his father, an ardent admirer of his uncle, the King of Prussia. It not unfrequently happened that the Czarewitch left the dinner-table as the Emperor proposed a toast to the success of the Prussian arms. In the end, however, the disorders of the Commune shook his sympathy for France and for liberal ideas. He separated from his Slavophile and Gallophile friends, saying, with a sigh,

" It is thither such ideas lead."

Yet, notwithstanding the scant sympathy between father and son, Alexander III. felt deeply the disaster that ended his parent's life. Not being a man of the mould of his forefather Nicholas, who would have beaten down Nihilism by the energy of his acts and the terror of his look and word, is it astonishing that he could not overcome the emotions aroused by the horrible deed, and that hence, during the first year of his reign, he lived in almost complete retirement at his favourite country seat of Gatschina, near St. Petersburg, with his dear faithful wife and little children as sole companions? But the people grumbled, and muttered "Coward!" when the Emperor made a rare appearance at St. Petersburg, followed and surrounded by a strong guard. It was further whispered that he wore chain armour under his uniform. Certainly, people were not permitted to approach him freely, as had been the case with his father. Nor was it evidently quite needless thus to surround himself with precautions, for various Nihilist tentatives to blow up Gatschina, to murder now the Crown Prince, now the whole Imperial family, were not calculated to reassure a nervous and mistrustful spirit, inclined towards all the hereditary melancholy of the Romanoffs.

It was only gradually, and after some while, that the Imperial family re-occupied the Winter Palace at St. Petersburg, and recommenced those brilliant *fêtes* in which the Empress shines supreme. Marie Feodorowitch loves dancing, elegance, and gaiety to an excess that often draws down on her the reproach of serious spirits. The heaviness of her dressmaker's bills, the costliness of her stuffs, the length of her trains even, provoke occasional remarks from her husband, who loves economy, and wishes his wife to set a good example in curbing the almost Oriental love of luxurious dress that prevails among the female portion of his subjects. But the Empress heeds his wishes little in this respect. Nor can she resign herself to the ravages of time and grow old with grace. Cosmetics and artificial aids to beauty are too much employed by the once simple Dagmar, who made and cut her own and her sisters' little cotton frocks. And it is to please this taste for gaiety in the wife he loves, that the Emperor tries to second her in her pleasure, though he prefers a retired life; and often, after having for form's sake made a brief appearance at some *fête* where his wife dances madly, he will retire into his cabinet with some favourite general and discuss grave themes.

Those who have not witnessed a Court *fête* in Russia cannot imagine the gorgeousness and pomp that prevails, Oriental and almost barbaric in its crudity of colour and its overlading of ornament. Great variety, too, is produced by the many national costumes, stiff with gold and silver embroidery. The ceremonial that obtains is autocratic in its rigidity of etiquette. In all official Court ceremonies the ladies have to wear an adaptation of the national costume of the Russian Boyardes, consisting of a diadem crown with precious stones, to which is attached a long soft veil of white tulle, a low-necked dress with wide-hanging sleeves, and a long train of velvet embroidered with gold, which opens in front over a petticoat of white satin worked in silver. Those ladies who hold no official rank at Court may choose the colours of their costume according to their fancy, but the maids of honour, to the number of two to three hundred, wear their train and diadem in scarlet velvet, and on their shoulder the initials of the Empress in diamonds on a blue ribbon. Each one of the Grand Duchesses has her especial colour fixed for her by rule, and which must be worn by ladies of her Court; and the etiquette is so strict on this point that even the slightest deviation in *nuance* provokes a serious reprimand. These *costumes d'honneur* are a grave expense, representing a sum of one to two thousand roubles, and are often handed down from one generation to another.

And if the ordinary Court festivals admit of such luxury, are submitted to such rigid etiquette, what is the splendour of public ceremonies?

Among these, during the present reign, the coronation of the Emperor in the mother city of Holy Russia, on the 27th May, 1883, has been the greatest; a marvellous phantasmagoria, where all the traditional treasures of the Muscovite Empire, all the wealth and brilliant colours of Asia, were displayed to do honour to a day solemn above all others. Very visible was the emotion of Alexander III., seated on his little white horse, his faithful companion in the Turkish War, as he entered triumphantly into Moscow, the people shouting frantically, and the fifteen hundred bells of the city filling the air with their brazen harmony. On arriving at the Kremlin Square seven thousand chosen voices, accompanied by a monster orchestra, intoned the grand national hymn, the Prayer for the Czar. "I truly felt, as I heard the strains," said the Emperor, "that I was wedding my people." Behind him followed the Czarina, clad in a cloak of silver, and seated in a golden coach, accompanied by the tiny Grand Duchess Xenia, whose baby hand threw kisses to the soldiers and the crowd. Careful observers noted that Marie Feodorowna's face wore a look of anxious tenderness as her eyes followed her husband, who was traversing the crowd, and truly fervent may have been her prayer for his safety as they both knelt, according to usage, in the celebrated sanctuary of our Lady of Iverskoi, which they passed on their triumphal route. The same ceremonial of alighting and kneeling to pray was repeated before the venerated *Rosto* of the Saviour, where every passer-by is expected to uncover before the image of Christ, which, according to tradition, arrested an invasion of barbarians. It is said that when Napoleon I. entered Moscow, he determined to brave the established rule, but as he passed with covered head under the sacred arch a gust of wind carried off his hat, so that he was forced to pass bare-headed before the sacred image.

Great were the hopes and fears that revolved round this important day in Russia. Intensely superstitious as are its people, they saw presages of all kinds in various incidents that occurred. Thus, the day was rainy—a bad sign; but each time the Imperial couple traversed the Kremlin Square, as they passed from one cathedral to another, the sun broke through the clouds as though to salute them on their passage, while during the great banquet that followed the coronation one of the Kremlin pigeons—the bird held sacred in Russia as an emblem of the Holy Ghost—came flying through a window of the great hall, and, after whirling about in bewilderment above the gilded crowd, alighted on the Imperial daïs, beside the two-headed eagle. "Wisdom and sweetness beside might and force," said the people.

But, although everything went off so well, the Imperial family were relieved when, at the end of the two brilliant and exciting days of the entry into Moscow and the crowning, the Emperor regained his private apartments safe and sound, and could remit to his treasurer the crown of diamonds and the ancient heavy sceptre of Holy Russia, surmounted by the famous Orloff diamond, the largest in Europe. After all these court *fêtes*, with their fairy splendour, their solemnity, came the turn of the people. Among other popular festivities was a banquet where five hundred thousand individuals each received, in presence of their sovereign, a basket containing a large meat patty, a sweet dish, a bag of bonbons, and a goblet engraved with the arms of the Czar. In the latter they were to drink the beer that flowed in rivers. It is only in Russia, where space is not lacking, that similar *fêtes* can possibly be conceived or carried out without either disorder or crowding. Eight days after, on the same immense ground, was held the great military review, where all the regiments of the Russian army were represented; and those who have seen these splendid Russian troops—with their suppleness, their discipline, their force of resistance—feel assured they would not prove wanting in the hour of battle.

"Hail to you, my children!" cried the Emperor, as his eye surveyed the scene.

"We will do all we can to content your Majesty," replied the soldiers, in chorus.

Then began the defile, which, for the splendour of accoutrement, the variety of national types and uniforms, has not its equal in Europe. Here were the Préobrajensky, the first regiment, formed by Peter the Great, and recruited among his childhood friends; the Sémémowsky, all blue-eyed; the Paulowsky, with *nez retroussés*, the favourite regiment of Paul I., decked with large golden mitres lined with red; here, too, the infantry of the line, the artillery galloping past with a noise of thunder; while last of all, in a cloud of dust, arrived the Cavaliers of the Guard on their superb steeds, and wearing their winged casques. They halted dead before the Emperor and Empress, and then divided to give place to the Blue and Gold Guards of the Empress, to the Grenadiers and Lancers, the Red Hussars of the Emperor, and many others, more than we can name, not to forget the fiery Cossacks on their mettlesome little ponies, who carried off the prime honours of the day, ending the *fête* with their marvellous equestrian games and feats.

Military discipline has improved much under Alexander III. A soldier himself, he knew where lay the strength and weakness of his army. For example, he exacts that the young officers should become the instructors of their men, not only in matters connected with the service, but in the arts of reading and writing. Thus these brilliant youths are no longer useful merely for balls, but are also of active service to their country.

We repeat, whoever has not seen Russian *fêtes*, of whatever nature, can form no idea of their sumptuousness, which recalls the marvels of the Arabian Nights, and which has, at the same time, a touching and patriarchal character. The sentiments of religion and of submission to authority are profoundly rooted in the hearts of the Russian people; their love for their God and for their Czar, who to them is the representative of God on earth, are for them almost identical. On their part the present Emperor and Empress are unassuming in their private life and habits, full of kindliness for their people, among whom they love to mingle without pomp or *entourage*. A thousand traits of their familiarity are related, and of the childlike simplicity with which the populace falls down in the dust to kiss the traces left by the Imperial carriage. They call their sovereigns Batouschka and Matouschka, which mean little father and little mother. They admire the monarch with his martial bearing, his herculean strength and muscle, his eyes that look straight and clear, the expression of regal goodwill that at moments lights up his somewhat too placid face. The charming Empress, vivacious, good, and graceful, gains all hearts by her sweet smile, exercising a fascination in which the woman triumphs over the sovereign. A Pole, whose nationality ensures his good faith, once said, "If the enemies of the Czar knew the Czarina, they would not have the courage to make her weep." In this huge empire, containing so many discontented subjects, no word is ever spoken against the Empress. She carefully keeps outside of politics; indeed, the Emperor does not confide them to her knowledge, but she shares his German antipathies and his liking for France. While remaining Danish, she has known how to become Russian besides, and to embrace Russian interests, and such public influence as she has over her husband is always exerted for good. She is a tender and anxious helpmate to him in his difficult position, who never leaves his side, accompanies him on all his journeys, shows no weakly fears of the charged mine ever under their feet, and keeps up his spirits by her own buoyancy of temperament. Like her mother, she often visits the public schools; but as her visits, unlike her mother's, are always announced beforehand, the girls are prepared to answer the questions her Majesty will put to them in French, and which are almost always the same. The ceremony ends by giving the pupils a three-days' holiday in the name of the Emperor. A great number of charitable institutions are under her protection, and wherever and whenever there are hearts that suffer they turn hopefully to Marie Feodorowna. Her *rôle* in this great empire is to console, to enliven, and to make herself loved. A brilliant woman of the world, who likes to shine and to amuse herself, the Czarina is neither light-minded nor frivolous. She is, above all, a good wife, a good mother, and a true friend. She has tried hard to conciliate the hearts of her husband's family, with almost all of whom he is on bad terms. He is too upright, too conscientious and straightforward to tolerate the frequently crooked ways and somewhat Oriental notions of honour of his relations.

We have said that the court *fêtes*, beloved and encouraged by the Empress, are brilliant in the extreme, and yet it is said that they are less splendid than under the former reign. The present Emperor is economical and discourages useless expenditure. He is said to have inherited this trait from his mother, who, though charitable to the poor, was too parsimonious for a sovereign. Alexander III. has reduced by a third all the allowances of the Imperial family, has diminished and even abolished the innumerable heavy pension and favour lists with which his house is weighted, and which, during former reigns, had attained the proportion of a huge system of abuse and exploitation by the rich and squandering upper class at the expense of the poor and hard-working taxpayer. And undoubtedly the Emperor has done well in this, though those whose means have been thus straightened are naturally loud in their laments. The chief to complain have been his brothers, who love good living and gay society. Nor must it be overlooked that the Emperor began by setting a good example, reducing his own private budget and cutting down useless expenses in his household; and almost incredible tales are told of what useless expenses may mean in a Russian and an Imperial household. Thus, in the days of Nicholas, the Empress, having a cold, once demanded a tallow-candle—to apply to her nose that homely remedy. None was to be found in all the palace; but in order that a similar lack might not recur, it was decreed that forty pounds of tallow-candles should henceforth be bought monthly. Whether bought or no does not appear, but until this reign the item figured in the Imperial household expenses. It is told of the present Czar that he often goes out alone early in the morning to inform himself of the real price of provisions in order to check the accounts laid before him. He never loses an opportunity of asking what some homely domestic item costs.

One of Alexander III.'s salient characteristics is his rigid honesty, his hatred of the malversation practised, under previous reigns, by Government employés, great and small, malpractices that in his father's time attained enormous proportions and excited public indignation. Mistrustful of those interested influences which had caused the misfortunes of his father, Alexander III. has known how to surround himself with men irreproachable on this score, but who, unfortunately, on the other hand, do not permit that any truths, any requirements of modern times, not in conformity with their own ideas or in harmony with the Emperor's views, should come to his knowledge.

Few persons have any idea how conscientiously the Emperor of Russia works, of the care with which he examines every paper submitted to him for signature. Yet this very care, this very attention to items, is cunningly utilized to their own ends by his surroundings and his ministers. These latter encourage him to absorb himself in the examination of petty Government details, while depriving him of the conduct of more important concerns. For Alexander—himself a straightforward man, incapable of double dealings, not only by natural disposition, but also by smallness of brain—never suspects when he is played upon. A sort of Chinese wall separates the monarch from all those who could transmit to him the thoughts and wishes of his people, who could instruct him as to the reforms they have a right to demand, for the internal administration of Russia is an evil that cries aloud to Heaven. Therefore, though he has the most earnest desire to be a good monarch, full of the mission to which he firmly believes he has been specially called by God, conscious of such responsibilities as he has realized, only afraid of doing that which seems to him to be wrong, little is to be hoped for Russia under the *régime* of the present Emperor, whose absolutist leanings, whose narrow-mindedness, and consequent self-sufficiency, close to him all the quarters whence he could obtain information. He could have learnt a lesson from his great-uncle, William I. of Germany, who—not a great man either—knew how to surround himself with great minds, and to allow them free action. Aware of his want of perspicacity regarding men, Alexander III. shrinks from mixing with them. He is afraid lest some word would escape his mouth which might be turned against him by indiscreet reporters. He tries to do his duty to the best of his ability, but this ability is, unhappily, much circumscribed — a fact of which he is dimly aware, but of course cannot estimate to its full extent. It is unfortunate, therefore, that he insists on directing in person the internal and external policy of the empire. Of course, not even he could do without a helper. He required a careful, intelligent co-worker, *au fait* with all a Czar has the right to ignore, aiding him by his memory and good sense, and able, if need be, to give him advice, but at the same time not aspiring to improve this advice nor to attempt to influence his master. This co-worker and chief interpreter of Alexander's thoughts in the matter of foreign policy is found in M. de Giers, a coadjutor with whom his employer is entirely satisfied.

The bearer of a German name, M. de Giers is an excellent Russian patriot, and, though the Emperor knows it not, he does exercise influence over him, if only by keeping in check the over-preponderance of the Slavonic party, whose chief is M. Pobedonostzew, proctor of the Holy Synod, and former tutor to the Emperor —a man in whom he confides. M. Pobedonostzew does not lack intelligence, but his mind is of the narrowest; he is a fanatic and a reactionary, whose ideal is that

Russia should become again what she was in the days of Peter the Great. He would draw an impassable barrier between her and Europe. Individuality, independence, he holds in detestation. According to him, all good Russians should spend their days crossing themselves before the sacred images and bowing before the Czar. It has been said of him that he is a Slav Philip II. Happily for Russia, the headstrong nature of the Czar prevents his succumbing entirely to this man's influence. Alexander likes to make up his own mind, and the very fact that M. de Pobedonostzew presents him with conclusions cut and dried weakens his power to sway his Imperial master. The Emperor does not arrive at decisions quickly; but when he does, like all limited intelligences, he holds to them with tenacity, and, even though circumstances may have changed meanwhile, no power on earth can induce him to relinquish them. Incapable of taking other than short views, it is this which makes him to a certain extent dangerous to Europe, for he might bring himself to imagine war was a necessity, and then declared it would be.

To see the Emperor to the best advantage, he must be seen in the bosom of his family. Indeed, whatever he may think of his divine mission, nature cut him out for a simple bourgeois. Both he and his wife are never happier than when they can leave all State cares behind them, throw off the yoke of etiquette, and live for their children at Gatschina, at Peterhof, or, best of all, in Denmark, in which country the Czar unbends in a manner never seen elsewhere. There is not so great a romp as he among all his nephews and nieces; he is master of all the childish revels. To these Princes and Princesses the autocrat of all the Russias is simply "Uncle Sasha," and cries of "Uncle Sasha! Uncle Sasha!" resound all over the place. A favourite pastime of his is to stand in midst the merry throng and challenge them to pull him down. But they never succeed, either separately or united. The Czar has most wonderful strength of muscle. He can bend a horse-shoe by mere force of hand. Once while in Denmark, when a conjurer was showing his skill, the Czar offered to produce a specimen of his own abilities: he took a pack of cards and tore them through with the greatest ease. At Gatschina he loves to go fishing with a harpoon by torchlight. Like Mr. Gladstone, he is fond of felling trees, but, unlike that gentleman, he equally enjoys sawing them into lengths.

The Czar has five children, three sons and two daughters. The Empress has her daughters much with her, and has not even a so-called governess for them. Her own personal attendant and her lady of honour serve also for them. In part, this springs from the Emperor's love for simplicity of life, but in part also that they try to surround themselves with as few people as possible, so that as little as may be concerning their private life should transpire to the outer world, of whom they are— and not without good reason—much afraid. The Empress superintends in person the education of the two little Grand Duchesses, Xenie and Olga, aged respectively fourteen and six. The Emperor in his leisure moments tries to do the same for his boys. Especially he loves to give them music and dancing lessons, for he thinks himself a great musician, and has a predilection for the cornet-à-piston. One day a minister, busy reading to him an important document, beheld the Czar vanish suddenly to intone in the adjoining room a rhapsody on his favourite instrument. "Excuse me," he said, returning after half an hour, "but I had so lovely an inspiration." He takes care, however, that they should also have better instruction than he can give them, remembering how his own education was neglected, and how disastrous this has been for him. His eldest son is his especial care, but the Czarewitch seems to have little aptitude for study, and rarely satisfies his masters, either by his private conduct or by his application. Nor has he in his person any of the fine bearing of the Romanoffs. He is pallid, frail, and nervous, and great anxiety is felt concerning his health. Indeed, it is whispered that he is epileptic, and, *apropos* of this, a trait is told of the Czar's vehemence of disposition, which he is not always able to hold in check. Once, when the alarming epileptic symptoms had recurred, the Emperor, resolved to know at all costs the full truth about his son's health, summoned a council of all the most celebrated doctors in the empire. None among them, however, had the courage to reveal the true state of things. Only a German professor from Dorpat spoke openly, stating as his opinion that the Grand Duke was seriously ll, and that, in short, it was a case of decided epilepsy. The Emperor when he heard these words refused to believe them, and, furious at the thought that such a terrible disease could be imputed to the son of a Czar of all the Russias, forgetting himself and his dignity, beat within an inch of his life the hapless doctor who had been too outspoken and too little a courtier.

The tale may be exaggerated, but there is no doubt that the Emperor is subject to attacks of uncontrolled fury. Even the Empress herself has to suffer under them. It was such an attack that gave rise to the story which went the round of Europe that he had killed one of his aides-de-camp. The following is the correct version. It was at the time that great Nihilist excitement prevailed, and in the Imperial household plots and sinister attempts were beheld in reality and in imagination. Now the aides-de-camp are forbidden to smoke in the Emperor's ante-chamber when on duty. It happened that after dinner one of the gentlemen, finding the time long, lighted a cigarette. Alexander came up unexpectedly at that moment, and seeing a spark and smoke in the dim light of the falling day, without stopping to consider the innocent cause of these phenomena, thinking himself the object of a Nihilist outrage, fell upon the officer, shaking him with fury, the frightened aide-de-camp meanwhile crying aloud for help. A moment, of course, sufficed to clear up the matter, and the officer soon recovered from the effects of the Emperor's angry violence. Still, the world reported him dead, and the Emperor heard of this. He therefore took occasion on their next public meeting to address his so-called victim with, "Mon cher, how do you find yourself since I have killed you?" Like his grandfather Nicholas, from whom he inherits this tendency to rage, he is often sorry afterwards, and tries to make good his errors.

A favourite pastime of the Emperor's is the theatre, and in connection with this a fact recently occurred which is yet another proof of Alexander's tenacity in having his wishes carried out. A new opera by Rubinstein, "The Merchant of Kalaschinkow," had been prohibited by the ecclesiastical censorship, although the Emperor had accorded permission for its performance. The theatrical manager complained to the Czar, who was greatly annoyed that the censorship had acted without informing him. He resolved to judge for himself, and caused the opera to be played for him alone; and, finding nothing objectionable, notwithstanding the ecclesiastical veto, commanded its public representation. It may be that this opera found special favour in the Czar's eyes because its music has, beyond all else written, by Rubinstein, a truly Slav character, for Alexander is loud in his boasts of loving and admiring only what is Russian. He highly values the national artist Bogoluboff, who is his *peintre en titre,* as well as the Hungarian Zichy, who is his personal friend, and often accompanies him on his journeys, for the Emperor has a certain love for the arts and artistic things.

Well it is for the Emperor that he is so happy in his domestic life, for from his relations—be they brothers, uncles, or cousins—he derives little pleasure. Indeed, with his eldest brothers, Wladimir and Alexis, his relations are most strained, and the Czar makes no pretence of concealing his sentiments towards them. He thoroughly disapproves of their mode of life, their conduct, and the people with whom they associate. What further particularly offended him was their failure to return to Russia on hearing of the horrible railway disaster at Borki. The catastrophe had been so terrible, and the destruction of the Emperor, the Empress, and their children so narrowly averted, that it was only natural to suppose that the Czar's brothers would hasten to his side for the purpose of congratulating him on his providential escape. The Czar considers his brothers as the first among his subjects, and that they above all must not neglect the honour and consideration to which he holds himself entitled. Indeed, the Imperial household statute exacts that each member of the family owes to the reigning monarch, as chief of the House, and as autocrat, "entire respect, submission, obedience, and subjection." They, however, preferred to remain at Paris, and none of the Czar's relatives were present at St. Petersburg to take part in the unparalleled display of loyal enthusiasm which attended the popular welcome-home of the Imperial party after the accident.

The Grand Duke Wladimir is married to a Princess of Mecklenburg, a beautiful, clever, but unscrupulous woman. She has proved the first Princess who, marrying a Russian Grand Duke, has evaded the law that obliges these ladies to embrace the Greek faith. On her arrival at the frontier she was met, as is the custom, by a pope, who sprinkled her with holy water. She recoiled in horror, asking if by this act she was made to enter the Russian Church by force, for she would not be forced, but would only cede to convictions formed after studying the Greek dogma. It seems that these convictions have never come to her, and she has remained a Protestant in defiance of the Imperial household law. This lady is popularly regarded at St. Petersburg as a secret agent of Prince Bismarck. She tries to ingratiate herself with the Empress by giving many balls. It is she who has introduced the game of roulette into St. Petersburg *salons*, for which she has been much criticized. Over her husband she exerts great influence, and employs it to inflame the ambition of Wladimir, who thinks himself the first personage of the empire. Both husband and wife are jealous of the Emperor and Empress. Wladimir had been the favourite of his mother, who thought to prophesy when one day she announced, after the death of her first-born, "It is Wladimir who will be Emperor, not Alexander." For the good of Russia, it is well that this so-called prophecy has not been fulfilled. Wladimir is intelligent, good-looking, but a man of low tastes and no moral elevation.

The Empress has a preference for the society of her sister-in-law, Elizabeth, Princess of Hesse, daughter of the late Princess Alice of England, and wife of the Grand Duke Sergius, a charming young woman, devoid of social influence, but whose amiability wins her all hearts. She is not happy in her union with the most unpopular of the Emperor's brothers—a coarse, brutal character. It is said that Alexander has often remonstrated with Sergius on the savage way he maltreats his wife, and the Grand Duke deeply resents these reproofs.

The Grand Duke Alexis, the sailor-prince of Russia, is a gay cavalier in great favour with the ladies. He was much talked about some while ago in connection with a *liaison*—some say a marriage—with Mdlle. Jukowski, daughter of the Russian poet, and maid of honour to the late Empress. A son was born of this union. After a while the affair was hushed up, and the lady, provided with a large dowry from the Imperial coffers, was married to Baron Worrmann, a retired Saxon officer. As yet Grand Duke Alexis is unmarried, but it is said he hopes to wed the Princess Hélène of Orleans. The fifth brother of the Emperor, Grand Duke Paul, is a permanent invalid, and rarely at St. Petersburg. His future marriage with his cousin, the Princess Alexandra of Greece, has been greeted with sympathy in Russia. The only sister of the Czar is the Grand Duchess Marie, Duchess of Edinburgh. She much resembles her elder brother in disposition, having his uprightness, his narrow views, his almost physical horror of a lie. Neither good-looking nor gracious, of inexpressible hauteur of manner, she has not known how to make herself popular in England, but those who know her in her small circle of intimates esteem her.

The Emperor's three uncles, Constantine, Michael, and Nicholas, have almost vanished from court circles since this reign, and have lost all influence. Constantine is ex-vice King of Poland, where he and his wife made themselves cordially detested. Under the former reign he was ever at the head of the opposition faction. He, together with his brother Nicholas, disgraced their position by the gross scandals in which they were implicated at the close of the Tukish War, when they were shown to have been the recipients of enormous bribes from fraudulent army contractors. Grand Duke Constantine's wife is a Princess of Altenburg, once celebrated for her beauty and her amorous intrigues. She now lives in absolute solitude in the lugubrious Marble Palace, where she tries by works of charity to console herself for her failures in life, her disappointments as wife and mother. For, though mother of the charming Queen of Greece, she is also mother to the notorious Grand Duke Nicholas Constantinowitch, the blackest sheep in the black Romanoff family, the hero of the adventures of Fanny Lear, an American *demi-mondaine*, for whose sake he stole his mother's jewels and robbed the Imperial chapel of its valuables. He is exiled from Russia, holding a post as chief of a regiment in Turkestan. Banishment would not seem to have improved his character. It seems that even in the arid desert the Grand Duke, no matter at what cost of suffering to his soldiers, insists on having his daily bath. One day of intense heat, when the poor men for lack of water were dying by scores, an officer represented the case to the Grand Duke, who had just taken his bath, asking if the soldiers might at least drink the water, now that his Imperial Highness had finished his ablutions. As sole reply, the Grand Duke gave a kick to the tub, and the precious liquid was lost in the sand.

Grand Duke Michael, married to a Princess of Baden, is the only one of the Czar's uncles who is above reproach. The worthy couple, however, always live in the Caucasus, where they have made themselves beloved.

A favourite Imperial residence is the castle of Spala, in Poland, where Alexander III. usually spends the month of September to enjoy the shooting. But this palace has yet another attraction, for close by is the little parish whose Roman Catholic priest, Ludovic Zmudowski, is an old and devoted friend of the Czar's, whose acquaintance he had made while hunting in these parts as Grand Duke, and for whom he conceived a real affection. Indeed, he often came here for the sole purpose of conversing with his friend—so often, truly, that the late Emperor, Alexander II., fearing the influence of a Polish priest over his son, forbade these visits. But once in power himself, Alexander III. made every effort to persuade his friend to come to St. Petersburg, and when he absolutely and repeatedly refused—not wishing to quit his humble parish for the great world—

the Emperor built himself this castle of Spala, where he can enjoy his friend's society and forget State cares and ceremonial. This priest is a good, simple-minded man, of some intelligence, energetic, and fond of action, who in his youth had seen the world. It is to this man that the Czar confides his secret cares and joys, with him that he confers without reserve. It is known that Zmudowski makes use of his influence to solicit favours for his poor, but is he also the political counsellor of the monarch? Does he hope to obtain some day concessions in favour of Poland? He loves France and detests the Germans. Does he help to augment this bias in Alexander III.?

The chief friends and companions of the Emperor, General Tcherevine and Count Daschkoff, are equally Russophile, Francophile, and Gallophobe. It cannot be denied or overlooked that Slavophile leanings accentuate themselves more and more in Russia, and are encouraged by both Emperor and Empress, though with prudent reserve on account of their positions. It is chiefly hitherto exerted against German emigration. The country is overrun with these strangers, who have penetrated into all departments, yet have never identified themselves with the people among whom they live, and whom they too openly despise because of their inferior education. Russians on their part accuse the German Socialists of having been the first in Russia to sow the seeds of discontent and revolt against authority. In reality, it is an antipathy of race which the German-loving Alexander II. could not overcome, and which threatens any day to become a cause of European carnage. Happily, an aggressive policy is not in favour with the present Czar, who is a man of peace and prudence. It is to be regretted, however, that in their zeal to russify Russia the Czar's advisers insist on forcing the Russian religion upon the people's consciences in those districts that have ever been Catholic or Protestant, such as Poland and the Baltic Provinces. The former are accustomed to oppression, to the latter it is new; and this may drive them into the arms of Germany. Curiously enough, this mistaken policy is not pursued in the newly-acquired Asiatic possessions. Here the people are allowed to retain all their privileges and the free exercise of their religions. The Government has even gone the length of restoring ruined mosques or building new ones where these were lacking. Trade is encouraged, works of irrigation are founded, railways are built, sterile tracts are rendered fertile. Hence in these lands the name of the "White Czar" is blessed among the peoples, who under him taste of security, freedom, and juster rule than under their former masters.

Another fanatical Slavophile in the immediate vicinity of the Czar was the late Count Tolstoi, who was Minister of the Interior. Also of upright nature, energetic, full of his duty towards God and the nation, going straight to the goal he fixed for himself without flinching, the great aim of his life was to stem German preponderance, to make the Greek religion triumphant, and to cause Russia to live on her own resources. To him is due indirectly the great increase of Nihilist views among the students, to whom he made himself hateful while Minister of Public Instruction. His successor, M. Dournovo, distinctly continues the policy of his predecessor. All his acts, too, are imbued with the spirit of resistance to modern ideas which Count Tolstoi personified. He is, in fact, his political executor.

Still, modern ideas cannot be wholly excluded even from Holy Russia, notwithstanding censorship of the press, tampering with private letters, espionage of all sorts and kinds. Nor does the Emperor himself wish to restrict education; he only wishes that its results should lead to given conclusions, and this is not possible. As the homely proverb has it, "You can lead a horse to the water, but you cannot make him drink." Slavophile and retrograde thinkers cannot be made to order. During the present reign primary schools have increased in number in St. Petersburg from sixteen to two hundred and fifty, and they are beginning to penetrate even to the villages.

One of the first acts of Alexander's reign was to destroy in part the work on which his father based his claim to national gratitude—*i.e.*, the liberation of the serfs. He declared that the Government would not continue to buy up the land for the peasants, as had been done since their liberation, affirming that the peasants abused this privilege to satisfy their own avidity, and that, further, it too much impoverished the proprietors. Instead, he has founded a Mortgage Bank, out of which the State furnishes the nobles, at little cost, with the means of keeping up and cultivating their lands, for since work is free it becomes daily more costly even in Russia, whose peasants emigrate in numbers to Asia. Yet another bank, also under State protection, supplies the peasants with facilities for paying their rent and buying ground. Manufacture, too, has been encouraged under this reign, and has taken great strides, and the inexhaustible mineral wealth of Russia is at last being turned to some account. Still, much remains to be done in Holy Russia, and the accident at Borki, which has opened the eyes of the Czar to the careless—not to say dishonest—administration of his railways, may make him perceive that in other departments also there is much that halts.

This railway accident, which some persons tried to convert into a Nihilist attempt, but which was undoubtedly a *bonâ fide* case of gross mismanagement, seems likely to have important results for the land. It has certainly immensely increased the popularity of the sovereigns, who, hurt themselves, behaved with admirable fortitude and self-denial in aiding those more severely injured. For once etiquette broke down, and master and servants were men and women together. There were twenty-one dead and thirty-six wounded on this occasion from an accident, the mere result of jobbery and bad workmanship on the one hand, and servile adulation of the Czar on the other, no one having the courage to tell him that on this bit of the line the train must not go at the full speed he always demands. When the shock occurred, the Empress, with a scream of despair that rang in the ears of those that heard it for many a long day, cried out in French, "*Où sont mes six?*" meaning her husband and five children, while the Grand Duchess Xenia, thinking it must be a Nihilist attack, called out, "Do not kill me, do not kill me," and ran for protection to an officer. Among the dead were many of the Czarina's favourite attendants, for whom she has never ceased to mourn. She herself received a deep wound on her arm, a fork having run into it, for the Imperial party were at table at the time.

This wound has left behind it a nervous trembling of the arm, while the accident itself proved to have given her nervous system a severer shock than at first appeared, when she bore up so bravely. A sad period of nervous prostration followed, and some feared for her the fate of her sister Thyra. This terrible malady has, however, been averted; the Empress's naturally good health and high spirits have reasserted themselves, and, whenever occasion offers, she dances as madly as ever, and continues to hold receptions and *fêtes*.

A loss to the Emperor, at Borki, was that of his pet dog Mahzutcha, a Siberian long-haired greyhound, which always slept at his bedfoot, and was his constant companion in his study. When audiences lasted longer than pleased the Czar, or Mahzutcha, she had the habit, on a sign from her master, of pulling at the coat-tails of the importunate visitor. Among the few objects not smashed to atoms in the Imperial carriage was a picture of the Saviour. The Emperor's superstitious nature at once beheld in this a sign. He had the picture reproduced in gold, together with his own and his wife's initials, and presented a copy to each person present at Borki. His superstition has been further nourished by his almost miraculous escape. He regarded it as an indication that the Almighty visibly protects him, and since that day he no longer fears Nihilist attacks, and has abandoned almost all the precautions with which he used to surround himself. And the populace, yet more ignorant and superstitious, are a hundred times surer still, seeing in the escape at Borki yet another demonstration of the truth of their favourite saying, "God loves the Czar."

Russia, and especially ignorant peasant Russia, adores its Emperor. The Moujik figures to himself his Imperial master with head surrounded by a golden nimbus, clad in flowing gown, with three fingers raised in benediction, and seated upon a throne of rubies, side by side with the Trinity. When they see the Czar and Czarina in flesh and blood it is often at first a shock to them. But all Russia does not consist of benighted Moujiks. This vast empire is also full of discontented subjects, who crave reforms and insist that they will have them. What Russia needs, however, is not a constitution, it is not ripe for that, but a different system of administration.

The Russians themselves do not know precisely what they do want, nor what they lack; but they are advancing and developing daily. The people begin to feel their power as an entity in the State, begin to comprehend that they have the right to be something else than a parcel of ignorant boors, who blindly obey and blindly worship.

From the day of Alexander III.'s accession all eyes turned hopefully to him. The late Emperor had made himself most unpopular, especially during the last year of his reign; it was hoped his son would inaugurate a new era. And certainly no Czars of late have taken so serious a view of their part, or have been filled with a sense of responsibility and moral obligation towards their God and their subjects, as the present Emperor. He knows that he was called to the throne by dynamite, that he lives and reigns under its constant menace; but he does his duty unappalled, goes about his work unperturbed, though aware that it is but too probable that his father's fate may be his also, for his ideas run counter to modern aspirations and desires. He cannot, on that account, however, modify or alter them; he believes them to be the right and true ones, and his subjects must accept them so long as he holds the reins. The most kindly and unassuming of men in private life, in public matters his mind is that of an insufferable autocrat. His ideal is Peter the Great, he would wish to restore those times.

The petty interferences which he encourages are carried even into private life. Thus no man can alter even his house front without special permission of the Czar. As he cannot be either omniscient or ubiquitous the obvious result is that important matters are often settled without his cognisance, while he is busy with puerilities. It is he, too, that encourages strict and absurd censorship of the press. He objects, for example, to expressions like "the machine moves freely." The word "freely" has to be erased, as suggestive of revolutionary ideas. Added to all this there is also something quixotic in his character, which makes him think it dishonest to take long views and to calculate probabilities. Neither will he listen to the counsels of expediency. When any particular act seems to him clearly wrong, he will not do it, be it ever so convenient. He is level-headed, conscientious, healthy of mind and body, but no genius. Had he more initiative, larger, broader views, and a little more confidence in himself—for this autocrat, strange to say, is the most diffident of men—he might prove a great ruler for Russia. But to be this many prejudices, personal and public, would have to be vanquished, many ancient traditions must be set aside, many things established for centuries overturned. Will Alexander have the courage, the will, the inspiration to carry out all that is asked, hoped of him? Will he find enlightened advisers able to aid him? That is the question. The desire to act for the good of the people is not wanting; but can such desires overcome natural shortcomings of intellect? The future alone can solve the question. Meanwhile, even such as he is, a long life must be wished for him, for it is greatly to be feared that his son will not attain the moral or intellectual level of the father.

THE EMPEROR OF AUSTRIA.

THE EMPEROR OF AUSTRIA.
(*From a Photograph by Kollar Károly.*)

THE EMPEROR OF AUSTRIA.

IN the placid provincial garrison town of Olmütz, in Moravia, not far from the dreaded fortress of Spielberg, made for ever famous in Silvio Pellico's narrative, there reigned, in the early winter of 1848, a most unusual excitement.

For it was here that the Emperor Ferdinand, all the Imperial family, the Court, and the high dignitaries of Austria had suddenly pitched their tents after their ignominious flight from Vienna, at that time in the hands of an insurgent populace, who loudly clamoured for a constitution to replace the traditionary Austrian autocratic Government.

It is true that after a stout resistance the capital was at length retaken, but it was evident to all concerned that the inhabitants had only yielded to overwhelming force, and that discontent with the tyrannical Prime Minister, Prince Metternich, and with the amiable but weak-minded Sovereign Ferdinand, was therewith by no means allayed. The assemblage of nations over which the Hapsburgs ruled, seemed to have grown tired of them.

Long and serious and secret were the discussions held on this subject in the bosom of the Imperial family. They had begun in those dreadful March days, the days that saw the dismissal and hasty departure of Prince Metternich, who had to seek refuge on hospitable English soil to escape from the hands of those who hated him throughout the length and breadth of Europe. These March days put an end for ever to the famous "system"—a gust of storm wind had carried it away. New men, young men, were required for the new situation. Since the 13th of that dreadful month it had pretty well been decided in private Imperial conclave that the eldest son of Archduke Charles Francis should succeed his uncle. But of this decision only about six people knew, and among these was neither the young Archduke himself nor Metternich, for forty years the repository of all State secrets.

In a letter addressed to him in London, Archduchess Sophia, mother of Francis Joseph, says (March 23, 1848):—

"Poor Franzi was my one consolation in our distress. In the midst of our troubles I blessed heaven for having given him to me such as he is! His courage, his firmness, his downright mode of thought and action might almost give us hopes that God will yet open up a future for him, since He has gifted him with the necessary qualities."

We feel through this letter an echo of the intimate conversations held at this time in the Vienna Hofburg.

The old Chancellor's reply to the Archduchess's letter is worthy of note. Once again he explains his policy, but at the same time condemns all political systems, and makes this strange avowal :—" I was born a socialist, in the true sense of the word; I have always looked on politics as a luxury compared with social dangers, and it is not my fault if I have received but little support in the direction which my mind follows, and which my actions have followed."

Prince Metternich, Chancellor of his Apostolic Majesty, a socialist! It was, indeed, well for him that he had passed the Austrian frontier ere proclaiming such opinions, or the police might have made it hot for him. Still, no doubt, there was a notable difference between Prince Metternich's socialism and that of Proudhon. However that may be, the old Chancellor had not been informed of the abdication ideas of the Emperor Ferdinand. Besides, it was urged, by the few persons in the secret, that the time for carrying them into effect had not yet come. It was needful still to pass through all the various phases of that terrible year before the moment seemed ripe.

One morning—it was December 2, 1848, a dismal winter's day—the unwonted movement in the streets of Olmütz appeared yet greater than before. Since seven o'clock, when it was barely daylight, carriages and coaches of all kinds had been rumbling over the paving-stones towards the Episcopal Palace, where the fugitives lodged, vehicles that contained ministers, ambassadors, Court dignitaries in gala dress. The streets were patrolled by regiments in full-dress uniform bearing in their shakos a branch of greenery, always a sign of rejoicing in the Austrian army. There could be neither ball nor banquet at this early hour. What did it all mean? asked the wondering inhabitants. Nor could the dignitaries themselves, when interrogated, reply. They could only point to a letter summoning them to appear in gala at eight o'clock precisely in the Episcopal Throne Room. Here they saw nothing but a heavy daïs, beneath which stood two armchairs embroidered with the Hapsburg arms, and at their feet a black wooden chair and a little table strewn with papers. A young man, afterwards the famous Baron Hübner, stood beside it, trying quill pens and making order among the documents.

What was this mystery? Even the nearest relations of the Emperor were in ignorance. Not a soul except the initiated even suspected the truth.

"What are we doing here?" asked one of the Archdukes of the Minister of War.

"Your Highness will learn in a moment," was the cautious reply.

And indeed, while he spoke, the great doors that led to the private apartments were thrown wide open, and there entered, with all state pomp, the Emperor, the Empress, the eldest brother and sister-in-law, the nephews and State functionaries, many in number. A close observer might have remarked that the eldest nephew, a tall lad just eighteen, looking even more elegant than usual in his uniform as colonel of dragoons, had a face of extreme pallor that morning. Ferdinand, too, looked agitated; but he had long been ailing, and late events had been too much for his slender strength.

The Sovereigns took their seat, the Archdukes and Duchesses grouped around them. Prince Schwarzenberg now advanced and put into the Emperor's hands a sealed packet. Ferdinand broke it with a trembling hand, and then read, in a low but firm and distinct voice, a brief decisive declaration, to the effect that he had taken the irrevocable decision of renouncing his crown in favour of his well-beloved nephew, his Serene Highness the Archduke Francis Joseph.

It was done. The veil of the great mystery, so carefully shielded for seven long months, had fallen. But never had secret been so well kept. Intense surprise greeted the short address.

There now followed various formalities, among them the renunciation of all rights to the throne by the Archduke Francis Charles, the young heir's father, who had the first right to succeed his childless brother, but who, even more weak and easy-going than his brother, was still less fitted to guide the reins of the Austrian State at a difficult moment of its history. Nor could anything have rendered this kindly, simple person more miserable than the idea of being forced to give up his quiet burgher existence.

All the great personages present now signed the charter that recorded the solemn deed. Then the new Emperor, tears in his eyes, knelt down at the feet of Ferdinand, as though to implore his blessing and his pardon for taking his place. Soon after, the family quitted the Throne Room, and the new-made Emperor at once mounted his horse to review the troops drawn up outside. Thus he inaugurated his career as Sovereign.

Meanwhile the late Emperor and Empress set out in a modest travelling carriage for Prague, where, beloved by all their surroundings, they lived quietly and happily until their death. Ferdinand resigned the crown at the age of fifty-five—the same at which his great ancestor Charles V. retired to the Convent of St. Just.

On the day following the ceremony of abdication, Ferdinand's successor had to receive a deputation from the Parliament which was then sitting at Kremsier, and reply to the welcoming speech of the president, the Polish Dr. Smolka, who still holds that office. It appears that the speech which he then made at Olmütz was very long. The young Emperor listened without flinching, but showed emotion in his reply. His voice trembled, he had difficulty in finding his words. However, little by little, he gained assurance, and the end of his speech was given with firmness and energy. In a moment this Sovereign of eighteen had taken definite possession of his throne; hardly on the throne he had begun to reign, and for forty years he has continued so to do.

On the same 3rd December, the accession of the Emperor Joseph was solemnly proclaimed with sound of trumpet in all the cities of the empire that were not in the hands of the Revolution. Strange, indeed, does it sound in our days of telegraphs to learn that the news took thirty-six hours to reach Vienna. The people greeted the tidings with cries of "Long live Francis Joseph I., the constitutional Emperor!" thus with one word striking the keynote of the whole situation.

Truly the task set before this newly-made Emperor of eighteen was no sinecure. The crown of Austria, one of the finest on earth, had been easy to wear until the days of March, 1848; till then a word, a look, had been a command to forty million faithful souls. Now all was different. Francis Joseph did not take a light crown upon his head. He was called on to rule a dissatisfied people, a people that could no longer be kept down either gently or forcibly; a people that claimed its human rights, its privileges to choose its governors, and to be ruled in accordance with more modern views. Well might he say, "Farewell, my youth!" as he took on his shoulders the burdens of such a government.

And this youth had been a tranquilly happy one, well suited to the eminently retiring nature of the man. Francis Joseph was born, August 18, 1830, at Laxenburg, some nine miles to the south of Vienna, in an Imperial residence which Francis I., inspired by reminiscences of Sir Walter Scott and Anne Radcliffe, had built strictly on the lines of a baronial castle of the middle ages. Conscientious imitation even went so far as to instal in a tower a figure which, by means of a spring, rattled its chains and uttered plaintive sounds. Franzi, as he was called by his family, was his grandfather's great pet. Like the young Duke of Reichstadt, he, too, played for hours in the monarch's cabinet, while the latter was busy with State affairs, which he sometimes interrupted to have a hearty romp with the little boy.

A scene out of this childhood was painted by Peter Fendi, and hangs to this day in the Imperial apartments. It was Franzi's fourth birthday, and he was happily playing in the gardens of Laxenburg, in company with grandpapa, Francis I., with the toys the day had brought. By chance his eye fell on a soldier keeping guard. The child looked at him fixedly, and stopped his play. Suddenly the little Prince asked,

"Is it not true, grandpapa, that this sentry is very poor?"

"Why do you think that, my child?"

"Because he has to go on duty."

"My child," replied the Emperor, "every one, rich or poor, has to go on his duty. Princes, too, must take their turn. But this man is poor. Go and give him this bank-note."

The Prince needed no second bidding, he ran up to the soldier on duty, and, holding out the bank-note, said joyfully, "Here, poor man, my grandfather sends you this."

The orders to sentries are stringent; the soldier shook his head to show that he could not take it. Prince Franzi put his finger in his mouth in great disappointment, and looked from his grandfather to the soldier and back again. The old Emperor enjoyed the scene.

"Run along, Franzi, and put it in his cartouch box."

But, alas! it was too high up, so the Emperor came near, and, lifting up his grandson, with the assistance of the Empress, they managed between them to drop the bank-note into the cartouch box.

"Now the soldier will be no longer poor, grandpapa!" said the child, delighted with his first deed of charity.

When Franzi was five, death deprived him of this grandfatherly petting. At six years of age his serious education began, shared later by his three brothers, the unfortunate Emperor Maximilian of Mexico, and the Archdukes Charles Louis and Louis Victor. The mother, a Bavarian Princess, of virile intelligence and noble soul, herself superintended the children's bringing up.

The principles on which the Austrian Archdukes are all educated was laid down as a family law by the wise Emperor Joseph II. His words run: "Every burgher can say that if his son turns out well he will prove useful to the State, and if he turns out badly he can do it no harm, since he will get no post or office. An Archduke, a royal heir, however, is not in that position. As he will one day hold the highest office, that of ruler of a State, it is no longer a question whether he will turn out well; but he must turn out well, because every detail of business which he does not learn sufficiently, concerning which he does not imbibe sound views, and towards whose execution his body and soul are not tempered, is baneful and hurtful to the general weal."

In the choice of tutors for the young Prince the mother had been careful rather that they should be good Catholics than well instructed in their various branches of tuition. The result was that the Emperor and his brother Maximilian regretted in after years that much of their instruction, especially in the departments of physics and history, was so inadequate that only later private study enabled them to make up the lacunæ in the latter study, which is of such importance to royalty. Everything that had artistic bearing was also too much neglected; and yet it was just for this that Prince Francis Joseph had the most pronounced taste, as his sketches made during a trip to Italy prove. He had also a great liking for the natural sciences, such as chemistry and botany, but none of these tastes were much encouraged.

In languages, however, the Prince received excellent instruction. At an early age he could speak and read fluently the eight languages which are used in the polyglot Austrian Empire, to which, of course, French and the classical languages had afterwards to be added.

These royal children were subjected to a stern discipline—too stern, perhaps—leaving little room for play and innocent recreation. It crushed the joyousness of youth out of at least one of them. Prince Franzi is described at thirteen as a silent lad, reticent almost to brusqueness, and painfully shy. He was nervous, too, and so fearful, for example, of horses, that he wept bitter tears each time he had to bestride one. For his military studies he at first showed neither aptitude nor inclination. Fortunately his military tutor was a man of rare and real ability, who had not been chosen merely for his unimpeachable orthodoxy. Colonel Hauslab elaborated a most careful plan of instruction by which the young Archduke had to serve in the same way as all other recruits in each branch of the service; his theory being that he who would command must also know all the minutest details of the services.

And the colonel was successful with his pupil, only, unfortunately, this plan required time to carry it out, and the events of 1848 intervened ere the scheme was completed. Had it been accomplished, who can tell whether the course of events might not have taken a different turn in 1859 and 1866?

When the imperial scholar had attained the age of sixteen a tutor of a different stamp was given him. He was neither priest nor soldier, and yet the wiliest plotter, the greatest strategist contemporary Europe knew, for it was Prince Metternich who was to initiate him into diplomatic business, though circumstances, the pressure of public opinion, and awakened national self-consciousness, never permitted the Emperor to put into practice the lessons received.

In 1847 the Archduke Francis Joseph made his first appearance in public as the Emperor's deputy to instal the Governor of Pest. The national Magyar movement in Hungary was then in its first fever heat of excitement, and patriots attached special value to the use of the Hungarian language in official acts, instead of German or Latin, till then employed. But no Archduke had hitherto taken the trouble to learn their speech. What was their joy, then, when Francis Joseph addressed them in purest Magyar! They sprang from their seats, they shouted "Eljen!" till they were hoarse, they drew their swords and swung them after traditional Hungarian fashion as a sign of joy. And when, some months later, Hungary was in full revolt against the Emperor, a deputy arose, and, reminding the assembly of the young Archduke who had enchanted Magyar hearts by his Magyar speech, proposed that this youth should be elected future King of Hungary.

The deputy who made this speech, which was applauded to the echo, was no other than Lajos Kossuth. And the speech found an echo in Austrian breasts during the March days of '48, with the result that, while the rest of the imperial family were often publicly insulted, the young Archduke met with respect everywhere.

Thus trained, and under such auspices, Archduke Francis Joseph ascended the throne, a sober lad, who was aware to the full of the greatness of his responsibilities. This is proved by the motto he chose for his own. It runs, "Viribus unitis," for he recognized that it needed all united forces to weld again into a whole this distracted, discontented, heterogeneous Austrian Empire. The old decaying Austria had to die, it was no longer suited to its time; but a new strong sapling must spring from the ancient trunk, and to see that this should come about was the Emperor's duty.

And he soon showed himself not only strong and disposed to rule with a high hand, but also genial and lovable. Thus the people were pleased that on his accession he assumed his two names, Francis and Joseph, reminding the nation of its two most popular monarchs, Joseph II., whose memory lives unweakened in his people's hearts, and who believed that only under another Joseph could Austria once more be happy; and Franz, the husband of Marie Theresia, the people's friend, who, for all his misfortunes and losses, had yet made Austria great. It is true that some wiseacres shook their heads over this decision, regarding it as a weak and almost despairing bid for popularity.

It was some months ere Francis Joseph could enter his capital, which had been seized and sacked. When he did arrive it was silently and almost incognito. He took up his residence at once in the castle of Schönbrunn, famous for its memories of Marie Theresia, of Marie Antoinette, of Napoleon, and the Duke of Reichstadt. When the news leaked out it spread like wildfire, and all the Viennese, that essentially pleasure-loving folk, were anxious to see the new Emperor of eighteen, whose portrait they had often beheld, but of whose person they had taken very little notice, as he rode among his brothers in the leafy Prater.

But Francis Joseph made these pleasure-lovers understand from the first that his motto was business, not enjoyment, and all his reign long he has accorded them few of those occasions for public festivities which are dear to their hearts as life's blood.

He set to work immediately, and indeed there was much to put in order, for the kingdom was all in pieces, and even sections of the army proved disloyal. Winter and summer, at five daily did the Emperor leave his couch in the first years of his reign, using the early hours to continue his studies. Then he worked, held audiences, received ministers. A short walk, a rapid ride, and a visit to the theatre were his only recreations. He threw himself with ardour into his duties, surprising his ministers by his industry and energy.

"For matters of business," said Prince Swarzenberg, "I can always gain admission to the Emperor, no matter what the hour may be."

It is difficult to realize nowadays the peculiarly difficult task that awaited Francis Joseph; and Ferdinand was right when, descending from the throne, he said, "Austria needs a young, robust monarch." It needed all the physical strength and elasticity of youth to cope with the problems presented to Austria's Emperor, and it is greatly to Francis Joseph's credit that he has, on the whole, acquitted himself so well of his most thorny task, a result largely due to his personal character. There is perhaps no European country where the problems of government are so difficult as in Austria, and in some respects they have grown even more difficult of late years. The personal responsibility of the sovereign is greater than ever. The Emperor has not only to tread the well-marked path prescribed by duty and by law for a constitutional monarch. He has to exercise, as an individual, a regulating, moderating, and dominating influence over the two co-equal sovereignties of the Cisleithan and Transleithan States, complicated in each case by the recognized or unrecognized pretensions of races struggling for "autonomy," and drifting into "Parliamentarism." Anxious and laborious duties these, since the position of the Empire in Europe and the character of its component parts cause its very existence to depend on internal unity and diplomatic skill.

A stern task, a complex problem truly; and, though no doubt he made mistakes, being but mortal, on the whole the world will agree that Francis Joseph apprehended it in all its sternness. He saw that the position of his country was probably unique in Europe, and that Parliamentarism, Constitutionalism, were terms that must be changed and modified according to the nature and idiosyncrasies of his widely differing subjects. Adaptability and self-effacement were the two great characteristics these circumstances required from him, and rigidly did Francis Joseph carry them out in his own person. The result is that at this day the true personal character of the Austrian sovereign is what no one, not even a diplomatist, professes to understand. Indeed, diplomatists frankly admit that his character perplexes them, and his own ministers do not profess to understand it. He has managed to escape the Argus eyes of even the newspaper special correspondents; no one has ever attempted seriously to analyse his character. Actual as well as nominal master of eighteen European States, the image of the man himself stands in shadow, so far hidden in the gloom as to be personally unrecognizable, and this by his own voluntary wish and will.

And yet he is no mere lay figure; those who think this are greatly mistaken. Doubtless he is not a great man of the first category, for in that case he could not have smothered his individuality, no matter how hard he tried. But neither is he a small one, for self-repression and self-effacement at the command of duty are not the gifts of petty natures. The smaller a nature the more self-satisfied, the more filled with an idea of its own importance.

Comte Paul Vasili has no doubt well grasped the situation when he writes as follows: "For the sake of his people he sacrificed all his tastes. Born to govern brilliantly, he loved the pomp of Courts, show, fine armies. He would have liked in great wars to have himself led the charges at the head of a brilliant staff. Political circumstances forced him to become a constitutional king in a Federal Empire, which defeat doubly wounded his national pride.

"Then, with an adaptability which has often been taken for indecision, he renounced personal power; not, however, without sorrow and a sharp struggle with himself. All that he had looked forward to was crumbling away. Instead of being the successor of Maria Theresia, of carrying out the traditional policy, he had to content himself with a Constitutional Monarchy, under which the ministers are responsible, to become a mere bureaucrat without initiative. He accepted the position as a duty. From five o'clock in the morning on, the Emperor signs the documents placed before him; he discusses them with his Ministers, but without animation. He reads a few newspapers, runs through a *revue de la presse*, compiled daily for his use at the office of the Cisleithan Press, which keeps him informed of the exigencies of public opinion, always paternally taken into account by him. He is also very popular at Vienna, as in the different Austrian provinces. The Emperor goes to bed early, and his sobriety is proverbial. He takes his breakfast hurriedly at a corner of his desk.

"He never oversteps the privileges which he has accepted. It is only at the chase that he becomes himself, free to exert his energy and strength, employing his strategy against an innocent quarry, following it up till conquered.

"Occasionally, as in the coronation at Pesth, his nature shows itself. The Hungarians, who are so magnificent, so regal, so proud of their *fêtes*, saw how grand a figure the Emperor Francis Joseph might cut.

"Austria is full of contradictions, and the Emperor is the victim. The countries bordering on the east, which require show, with the Poles, the Hungarians, the Slavs, the very town of Vienna, which adores *fêtes*, elegance, luxury, are not satisfied with the Emperor. They would like him to be more personal, more representative, more of an Emperor; and at the same time these small peoples, tied to tradition, to their customs, with a horror of centralization, unwilling to be governed uniformly, are irritated at the least pressure from the State. Now, the Austro-Hungarian State can only be represented by the Emperor, since the only bond of union between interests of the different provinces is centred in the dynasty of the Hapsburgs; and since 1848—especially since 1867—all direct power is refused to him from whom they expect the exercise of direct power. The Parliamentary system has never been accepted in Austro-Hungary; there is no longer room for a Cæsar. We must be logical, and give Francis Joseph credit for not having resisted the modern current; but, at the same time, we must not find fault with him for having withdrawn himself from the crowd, and for remaining the vague symbol which his people insist on his being.

"All who approach him recognize that Francis Joseph is a good man. He is charitable, but he exercises his charity as discreetly as he governs. He leaves his left hand in ignorance of what his right hand does. How can the crowd be expected to appreciate benefits whose origin is concealed when it has so little gratitude for known benefactors? . . .

"The circumstances which we have described, have detached Francis Joseph from the personal interest which he would have taken in politics had he governed absolutely. Military questions alone animate him; he follows them with the greatest solicitude. A scrupulously constitutional monarch in all things, he has, however, refused to surrender the army to the hazards of parliamentarism. Outside the army Francis Joseph's opinion is that which predominates in his kingdom. This explains the shufflings which have characterized his reign. . . .

"He is, in short, what he has described himself, if the saying attributed to him by Count Andrassy be correct: 'I am thankful that those who have been condemned to death for treason have not all been executed, for I afterwards was able to make them my prime ministers.'"

Indeed it is this impassibility that is the source and secret of Francis Joseph's strength, and explains the apparent riddle of his character. Neither as a young man nor as an old one has he ever been carried away by emotion, and he has that rare gift, that even Prince Bismarck might envy him—he knows how to wait, to wait calmly and with dignity. Some men in his position stand revealed by their history, but as has been well remarked, the history of Francis Joseph baffles ordinary comprehension by its unexpectedness. He has been the unluckiest of sovereigns, and one of the most successful; the most detested and the best obeyed. Indeed, after forty-one years of reign, it is worthy of note that defeat, against which few dynastic reputations can stand, has been powerless to affect the regard of his subjects for Francis Joseph. Their loyalty has become only the more sympathetic. A note of tenderness has been infused into it.

The fact probably is, that Francis Joseph was originally a proud and rather headstrong man, not cruel, but indifferent to suffering, and intent, like most of his predecessors, on attaining his will by force. Called to fill the throne in a difficult juncture of European history, he understood that his absolute instincts must be restrained, and that his haughtiness —the haughtiness of this semi-Spanish house, which claims to represent Charlemagne—must be controlled and take a new direction. In his case it had been to think, above all, of the great heritage entrusted to him by his ancestors, and to see that this, at all events, be not diminished. Forty years of terribly severe training have made of Francis Joseph as accomplished a diplomatist as his powers will permit him to be. These powers do not allow him to see far, or to recognize facts needing imagination to reveal them, or to appeal to masses of men with immediate success, but within these limitations they are really great. No wise person will hastily say that the Emperor of Austria is unwise;

and yet he has committed actions that would admit of that interpretation.

An authoritative person has pointed out that from the day when, as a boy of eighteen, Francis Joseph was ordered by the family council to dethrone his uncle, since otherwise all hope for the House was lost, down to the present moment, he has never succeeded in any great undertaking, and yet he is ten times as powerful, as popular, and as much respected as he was then. Beaten in battle after battle, flung out of kingdom after kingdom, tricked successfully by Frenchman, Italian, and German, his vast army follows him with hearty obedience; he has gained, not lost, in European position, and there is not a diplomatist in the world who, when Austria wants anything, has not a secret doubt whether, in the end, Austria will not be found tranquilly enjoying the secure possession of the object which seemed so unattainable. With half his dominions in insurrection in 1848, the Emperor was in 1850 their absolute and rather cruel lord. Beaten in 1860 by France; beaten in 1866 by Prussia; driven in the former year out of Lombardy, and in the latter out of Germany; obliged, in 1848, to beg alms from Russia, and in 1867 to yield to the Magyars, he sits, in 1890, as great a monarch as ever, with as many subjects, a greater army, larger revenues, and a far more secure position, the first of the great alliance on which the future of Europe hangs; but still, in comparison with his rivals, scarcely known. He has never won a great battle, but he is a great military power; he has failed repeatedly in diplomacy, and he has acquired grand provinces without drawing a sword or firing a shot. He has fired on his own capital, and is the only sovereign in Europe who dare lounge about it; he has ruthlessly oppressed half his subjects, and has won them back so thoroughly that loyalty to his person is the cement of his many kingdoms. He has shown fierce ambition at every turn, and he is regarded as the one ruler who may be trusted not to use any successes he may gain to further schemes of aggrandisement. Men who should know, and who are rarely mistaken, say that he is not an able State charioteer; but he drives, and has driven for years, eighteen horses abreast, and they all go on the course he dictates, and he stands all the while quite tranquil, and not perceptibly touching the reins.

From his accession to the present day, the history of the Emperor of Austria's life is to be sought and found in the history of Austria. He has lived and lives but for his public duties. The first thing he had to do was to pacify the revolted States. This done, the spirit of reaction once more awoke, and the constitution accorded in 1848 was revoked in 1851—a mistake that was to end in the exclusion of Austria from the Germanic Confederation; for Prussia and its adherents saw that the moment was favourable for playing that trump card which enabled them to realize, sooner than they dared hope, the programme that triumphed on the eve of Sadowa.

In August, 1853, the Emperor made his customary journey to Ischl, there to keep his birthday in domestic privacy. On this occasion, his mother, the Archduchess Sophia, gave a small ball, for Francis Joseph and his brothers much enjoyed dancing, being in this respect true children of Vienna. Among the guests then at Ischl was the Duchess Louise of Bavaria, with her two elder daughters, Helene and Elizabeth. Francis Joseph desired that they, too, should be asked to the family party. The Duchess accepted for herself and Princess Helene, but refused for Princess Elizabeth, on the plea that she was not yet out, and that, further, they had brought no dress in which she could appear. But the Emperor, who had already been charmed by a brief view of his young cousin, insisted, and would take no excuse, saying, in his simple, good-natured way, that the simplest of dresses, with a coloured rose in her hair, would suffice to make his pretty cousin Queen of the Feast. Upon this the mother yielded, the pretty cousin went to the dance, with the result that she became, not only queen of the feast, but queen of Francis Joseph's heart, and future Empress of Austria. It is related that the Emperor danced almost exclusively with her all the evening, which naturally attracted attention. Towards midnight tea was served. During this pause the Emperor and Princess approached a table on which lay a huge album containing a collection of pictures of the various national costumes to be found in the eighteen States of Austria. The Emperor turned over its pages showing them to his pretty partner.

"They are my subjects," he said. "Say one word, and you shall equally reign over them."

The Princess, who, it must be remembered, had known the Emperor already as a child, in lieu of any answer, placed her hand in the hand he held out towards her.

"Later," he said, "I will give you your betrothal bouquet."

And, indeed, during the cotillion Francis Joseph presented his future wife with a magnificent bouquet of those curious soft white Alpine flowers, the Edelweiss, which he had gathered himself in his intrepid rambles among the hills.

Next day, at ten o'clock, an Imperial carriage already stood at the door of the hotel where the Duchess of Maximilian was staying.

"Is the Princess Elizabeth up?" the Emperor asked of the man in waiting.

"Yes, sire, but she is dressing."

"No matter, I will go to the duchess." And then and there he asked for Princess Elizabeth's hand.

Half an hour after the whole Imperial family present in Ischl assembled in the little parish church, and here, to the strains of Haydn's popular national hymn, the betrothal of the Emperor of Austria with Princess Elizabeth of Bavaria was celebrated with all solemnity.

The news, of course, spread through the little watering

place like lightning, and the same evening all the hotels and villas were illuminated.

Francis Joseph has indeed chosen well in the matter of his wife, who has proved herself in all respects suited to his taste and ideas. She, like him, loves retirement and solitude, and shares his passion for riding and hunting. How devoted to the latter sport her repeated visits to England and Ireland during the hunting season has often proved. The daughter of Duke Maximilian of Bavaria, a plain bourgeois, addicted to literary pursuits, and loving retirement, she had been carefully reared, with her three sisters and only brother, in one of those romantic mountain castles with which Bavaria is dotted. This brother, the Archduke Theodore, who has since become a famous oculist, had brought, together with the father, an atmosphere of culture and love of study into the house. It was a patriarchal environment from which Princess Elizabeth went forth, one in which there was no love for meretricious pomp.

In April, 1854, Princess Elizabeth made her State entry into her future husband's dominions. She came by way of the Danube to Linz. Those who were present say it was a pretty sight to behold the lovely maiden of seventeen standing on the deck of the gaily-flagged steamer, ready to greet her Imperial lover, who stood awaiting her at the landing-stage. Francis Joseph could hardly wait till the boat was made fast. He sprang across the open space and pressed his bride to his heart in presence of all the people. That night the Princess passed with her parents in the castle of Schönbrunn. Next day she made her triumphal entry into Vienna, in a State chariot drawn by eight milk-white horses, all caparisoned with gold-embroidered trappings of heavy red velvet. She herself wore a dress of pink satin, covered with white lace, and in her hair a wreath of red and white roses, above which rose a diadem of diamonds. She was the youngest as well as the most beautiful Empress that had ever borne the sceptre of the House of Hapsburg, and this procession was one of the most magnificent spectacles ever seen in Vienna, that city of spectacular effects.

Not less striking was the marriage ceremony in the church, twenty-four hours later. The Court church of the Augustines glittered with the lights of tens of thousands of wax tapers; the treasures of Golconda, all the colours of the rainbow, seemed showered down in the multitude of precious stones and jewellery in which the Court ladies, the sword-begirt magnates, and the heavily-decorated dignitaries of the Empire sparkled. When the bride, led by her mother and mother-in-law, appeared in the church, she seemed a mass of white velvet embroidered in gold. The fair face was pale and set as marble, but nothing of pride or *hauteur* was there; only the look of a true woman in the most crucial hour of her young life. Later, when the newly-made Empress appeared in the Throne Room, leaning on the arm of her husband, to receive the homage of her lieges, the rosy colour had come back into her cheeks, but the happy, pure light still shone in her beautiful eyes. As for the Emperor, no one, it is recorded, had ever seen him look so happy, nor unbend so much as in that hour that first saw him with his young bride at his side.

Since her marriage it may be said of the Empress Elizabeth, as of fortunate natures, that she has no history. The union so romantically entered upon proved a happy one, and when in the days of their common sorrow, bowed down at the tragic end of their only son, the Emperor Francis Joseph addressed a few words to his faithful servant, Dr. von Smolka, he raised to his wife a monument that will cause her to live in history more nobly than if she had been commemorated in stone or bronze. He said:

"How much I owe in these days of bitterness to my dearly beloved wife, the Empress, and what a great support she has proved to me, I cannot describe. How can I be sufficiently grateful that such a helpmeet has been given me? Tell this to every one. The more you spread it, the more will I thank you!"

Outside court circles few people know the Empress Elizabeth. Many Viennese have not even seen her, which is a loss for them, for Elizabeth of Bavaria was very lovely, and has preserved into middle age many remains of youthful charms. She believes in Diane de Poitiers' elixir for perpetual youth—the morning dew. An intrepid horsewoman, she is often in her saddle at dawn, scouring the royal parks. Indeed, it is as a horsewoman, a bold huntress, a lover of dogs, that her Majesty is noted throughout Europe. It is all the more surprising, therefore, that this intrepid amazon was never taught to ride till she was twenty, and already a mother. For the rest, she has a virtue rare in a woman who shares a throne, of never meddling with politics. Indeed, she openly admits that she neither cares for politics nor understands them, a remark which, when made on one occasion to Jokai, the Hungarian novelist, and member of the Anti-Imperial faction, elicited from him the remark, "It is the highest politics to win the heart of a countryman, and that is what your Majesty knows well how to do." But if the Empress keeps away from politics, she loves, on the other hand, to rule her Court, and here the Emperor leaves her a free hand, allowing his wife the same independence in their home as he allows his ministers in the cabinet.

Of Court life there is, perhaps, less in Austria than in any other European capital. Both sovereigns love retirement, and only do what is strictly necessary in the way of entertaining, giving an occasional dinner and two balls, at which, however, no ladies who have not sixteen quarterings of nobility are allowed to be present. One of these balls is known as the "Court Ball," to which go the Corps Diplomatique, and all those who have the right of presentation. The other is called the "Ball at the Court," to which go only those invited by the Emperor and Empress. When the Emperor is thus dragged out of his shell he goes through his functions in a dreamy, uninterested way, very different from the eagerness with which he stalks a deer or shoots a capercailzie, only obtainable at sunrise, or the ardour with which he throws himself into dreary details of business.

The descendants of the sixteen children of Marie Theresia, and of the seventeen of Leopold II., have surrounded the Austrian Court with a crowd of Archdukes and duchesses. The Court is, therefore, a most aristocratic one, into which no outsider penetrates. The present Emperor of Austria is not obliged to say, like his forefather, Joseph II., that in order to have the society of his peers, he must go into the Capuchin crypt.

It is difficult to imagine a court and courtiers dissociated from their chief, yet such is the case at Vienna. The Emperor lives much alone, and his life is one of great simplicity. He rises early all the year round, and often he is surprised by his personal attendants sitting at his writing-table by four in the morning; and between the hour of rising and that of going to bed, usually at ten o'clock, lies a day of harder work than that of the tillers of the soil, relieved only by some reading. He has a wonderful memory, which is, of course, of great service to him in his public duties; but he achieves more by hard work and painstaking. His scrupulously-regulated life also provides him with the necessary time for all his duties, even on days when he has to speak with from one hundred to a hundred and fifty persons, as is not seldom the case. He passes from a council of war to one of the audiences which he gives twice a week to the poorest of his subjects who have anything to ask, and he is always self-possessed, attentive, and patient. As there is no apparent hurry in his movements, so there is no haste in his words or his resolutions. So-called popular movements never carry him along with them. If there be a public outcry against any official, for instance, one may be quite sure that the Emperor will not seem to notice it. Yet, if the outcry prove to be justified, he will act in accordance with it. As regards petitions preferred to him by individuals, when once a case has been fairly made out for the Emperor's mercy or bounty, the applicant, however humble, may rest assured that what he has asked will be granted. When work is done the Emperor thinks over the questions and decisions of the day. Should he, in consequence, have further light upon a subject, he does not hesitate to alter his opinion. This has laid him open to the charge of vacillation, which is scarcely just. He is rather careful and cautious, fully aware of how much depends upon his personal decision, and afraid to exercise it unwisely.

"The Emperor has once more hit the nail upon the head," is a remark that has become proverbial among those who work with and under him.

Four children have sprung from the Imperial union. The firstborn, a Princess, died at the age of two; the second, the Princess Gisela, is now married to Prince

Leopold of Bavaria. It was not until 1858 that an heir came, the "Rudi," so ardently beloved by all the peoples of the composite Austrian Empire, and upon whom they built such high hopes for the old house of Hapsburg dynasty.

Prince Rudolph early showed a great taste for literature and the fine arts, while showing also his parent's love for field sports. In the army he took little interest, preferring the more refined pleasures of travel or reading. He was also an excellent ornithologist, an active naturalist, an elegant writer, and these refined and educated tastes, added to the social charms, made him beloved by all who came in contact with him. He was, beyond all doubt, the most modern-minded of all Crown Princes, the most fit to deal with modern conditions, the most in harmony with these changed modes of thought.

Archduke Rudolph was to his father's subjects a sort of hero of romance; his tall figure, his well-cut face, his soft blue eyes, his fair moustache shading the ugly Hapsburg mouth, were familiar throughout the Empire. He had the strongest love and admiration for his father, although his sentiments were, perhaps, mixed with a little fear, for the relations between a Crown Prince and his father are controlled by a number of stiff-backed persons, and subjected to laws of etiquette against which gushing natures like Archduke Rudolph rebel. No heir apparent to a throne, however, had a kinder father than he.

From his earliest youth he was fond of writing; his literary tastes he has inherited from his mother, and was quite young when his first work was published. He has left considerable literary remains behind him, part printed, part yet in manuscript. It was in 1884 that he first conceived the idea of the monumental serial work, "Austro-Hungary in Word and Picture," to which he subsequently became one of the most active contributors, presiding in person over the sittings of the editorial staff. Only a month before his own death, lamenting the demise of a member of this staff, the Prince said, "Whose turn next, I wonder?" even hinting that it might be his own. Indeed, for some time before his suicide his ideas had dwelt much on the theme of death, which had a ghastly attraction for him. It is said, though this probably is not the whole truth, that the bitter disappointment of having no son, nor the hope of obtaining an heir, weakened his interest in life.

In 1881 Crown Prince Rudolf was married to Princess Stephanie, daughter of the King of the Belgians, a Princess known for her gaiety, her charms of mind and body; a favourite with court and people. .By her the Prince had an only daughter, the little Archduchess Elizabeth, whom Salic law debars from the throne. Why the marriage was not happy it is difficult to know, but the fact remains. Already during their engagement sinister whispers were abroad, and, after the marriage, news came from Vienna from time to time bringing to the royal parents sad confidences regarding the princely *ménage*. The Archduchess complained of being abandoned, asked for leave to return to her mother, sued for divorce. Later, this petition for divorce was endorsed also by the Prince. But their demands had no effect. The rigid Catholicism of both the Belgian and Austrian parents would not listen to such a measure of human mercy.

Reconciliations were again and again patched up in vain, when suddenly, on January 31, 1889, the whole world was startled with the intelligence that Crown Prince Rudolph of Austria lay dead at his shooting castle of Mayerling. Official announcements could not hide the truth, and it soon leaked out that the Prince had committed suicide, together with the Baroness Marie Vetsera—the girl for whose sake he implored divorce, or, failing it, for permission to renounce his heritage and live with her in strict retirement. The exact details of this double death will probably never be known, or, at least, not for many years to come. Such, then, was the end of one on whom had been built hopes so high, and which his talents had justified to the full—a tragic end, full of lessons, full of warnings.

The youngest offspring of the Imperial Austrian couple is the Archduchess Marie Valerie, ten years the junior of her brother. She also possesses literary gifts, and has published poems that betray genuine feeling. After much domestic opposition, she is now the bride of her cousin, Archduke Franz Salvator, a love-match of which her parents at first would not hear.

We have said that the biography of Francis Joseph must be sought in the history of his Empire. Only on two occasions during his reign has he departed from the rule of avoiding all public manifestations, and of keeping his person in the background. The first was in 1867, when he and the Empress were crowned King and Queen of Hungary. The Emperor, mounted on a white horse, galloped up the hill that surmounts Budapest, and cut the air with Matthias Corvin's sword to the north, south, east, and west, to mark that he had taken possession of St. Stephen's crown, that henceforth Hungary had an independent King and Parliament, and was merely a federal portion of the Austrian Empire. Curious that while this *fête* was proceeding, while all was joy and acclamation, three thousand miles away the Emperor's unhappy brother was at that moment being led to execution. Maximilian of Mexico was shot by his own subjects as Francis Joseph of Austria was greeted Apostolic King of the Magyars.

In 1879, the Austrian Imperial couple celebrated their silver wedding. On this occasion Vienna organized a most splendid procession, that rivalled the pageants arranged by Rubens in the palmy days of the Netherlands. The period chosen was that of the Emperor's great ancestor, Charles V. The whole was planned and executed upon a scale of grandeur and wealth indescribable. It proved one of the most splendid *fêtes* ever given in Vienna, which will, no doubt, never again see a public festival during Francis Joseph's reign.

That pleasure-loving capital hoped, but hoped in vain, to celebrate with equal splendour the fortieth anniversary of the Sovereign's accession, which fell on December 2, 1888. But Francis Joseph had early made it known that he requested his subjects to abstain from any manifestation of rejoicing. He was well aware, he said, of the loyalty of his people, and he thanked them from his heart for their good intentions, but if they wished to please him they would abstain from all useless expenses, from all empty addresses, from everything that had no real or permanent value, and would instead devote the sums they would thus have spent to works of charity, or to promote art, science, industry; in fact, to any object for the general weal. And so sincere was he in this respect that to avoid the smallest publicity, he retired to Miramar, the lovely castle on the Adriatic, where he spent the day in the strictest seclusion, with no company but that of his wife and his thoughts, many of which may have been sad enough. But he cannot have passed it without some gladness also, for at least he has the satisfaction of knowing that for forty years he has honestly tried to do his duty—a fact to which the love his forty million subjects bear him testifies. And that they carried out his request was proved by the daily paper, which continued for weeks to publish the lists of subscribers to the various charitable works founded and suggested afresh in memory of December 2, 1848-88.

It was a dark, a dangerous hour in Hapsburg history when Francis Joseph took the reins of Government into his imperial hands. The old Austrian Empire was cracking to its foundations. It was a corpse of a Government, but not a State, an object of contempt. And yet the worst that was then apprehended fell far short of what actually did happen. The events that followed would certainly have left an unpopular Emperor discredited and helpless. It has been a remarkable sign of Francis Joseph's power that out of every national disaster he has found elements for reconstituting national prosperity. Adversity has been a school in which he has been for ever learning with profit; and to-day, after over forty years of a reign overfull of troubles and anxieties, he finds himself clothed with more real authority than any of his predecessors possessed. He rules with a light hand, but his supremacy is unquestionable. Austrians would be indeed ungrateful if they forgot their debt to a nature which has enabled a born, bred, and crowned despot to educate himself into a model constitutional sovereign. And this result would have been impossible but for the possession by the Emperor of remarkable gifts of character and intelligence; he is a good man, animated by high moral courage. His subjects, who sincerely love him, have a well-founded conviction that circumstances are responsible for his failures, and not he—that the calamitous issues of Magenta, Solferino, and Sadowa are not to be imputed to their Emperor-king. They lamented them as much on his account as on their own. They regarded him as the principal victim, whom it was their foremost duty to guard against the temptation to reproach himself for the calamity. This personal devotion to the Emperor has been a most important agent in the extrication of his dominions from an extraordinary and exceptional succession of ordeals and afflictions. By it the shock of catastrophes has been softened, and a series of deadly pitfalls have been securely passed.

Will his successor be able to guide these realms free from the jeopardy that ever threatens them? Who can tell? Had Crown Prince Rudolph lived, no doubt his popularity would have equalled that of his father: but of the present heir little is known. At best he has not been early trained to a position entailing as heavy a burden of responsibilities, and requiring so rare a combination of qualities as any the world has to offer. Prince Francis Ferdinand is the son of Francis Joseph's brother, Charles Louis, a devoted and somewhat bigoted adherent of Mother Church. In these principles his children too have been reared. All Francis Ferdinand's tutors were Ultramontanes, members of that party which led Austria to Sadowa. But in the instability of human things who can say whether he will ever sit upon the throne that now seems to await him? Happily, Francis Joseph, notwithstanding his melancholy temperament and constitutional delicacy, remains upright as an oak, and his strong sense of duty will make him feel that this is not the moment to yield to personal inclination, and to abdicate or retire. All who wish well to Austro-Hungary, that curious complex monarchy, so needful for keeping the balance of European powers, can but hope that the day when it may be needful to speak seriously of his successor is far distant.

The Emperor Francis Joseph is perhaps the most tragic figure among the living sovereigns of the world. His romantic history, his lifelong devotion to the duties of his position, and his patient submission to its trials and its burdens, his overwhelming sorrows, and his noble endurance, have endeared him to all his subjects, and extorted the admiration as well as the compassion of the civilized world.

WILLIAM II., EMPEROR OF GERMANY.

THE EMPEROR OF GERMANY.
(After a Photograph by J. C. Schaarwächter, Photographer to the Emperor.)

WILLIAM II., EMPEROR OF GERMANY.

IN the latter days of January, 1859, Berlin was on tiptoe of expectation. The Princess Frederick William was about to give birth to a child, and for Prussia, where the Salic law still obtains, the sex of that child was a matter of vital importance. As is usual at the birth of royal scions, one hundred and one guns announce the birth of a prince, twenty-one that of a princess. In these days, therefore, whenever and wherever firing was heard in Berlin—and when is it not heard in that military capital?—people steadily began to count the discharges. On the morning of the 27th a shoemaker's boy heard cannon firing. At once he set to work to count one, two, three, up to nineteen, then the guns stopped. "What, not even a girl!" he exclaimed, in disgust, unaware that he had merely listened to artillery practice. But a little later, at four in the afternoon, the cannons boomed and thundered so that all Berlin could hear their hundred and one reports, and from the palace chapel bells resounded the chimes, "Praise the Lord, the mighty King of Hosts."

William I., then acting Regent for his deranged brother, Frederick William IV., heard the cannon also while busy in the Foreign Office. He jumped into the first cab that crossed his path, too impatient to wait for his carriage, and hurried to his son's abode. As he entered the courtyard Field-Marshal Wrangel left the house.

"Your Excellency, how is it?" demanded the eager populace of its favourite general.

"Children," he answered, "all is well; it is as fine and sturdy a recruit as we could wish."

Thus William II.—for it was he whose advent had caused this commotion—was from his birth dedicated to the army—as indeed, for the matter of that, is every Prussian prince and every Prussian citizen, for, as Mirabeau well remarked, "War is the national industry of Prussia." Prussia is not a country that has an army, but an army that has a country.

And yet Prince William of Prussia was near being excluded from a military career — perhaps even from the throne, if that be true which the Court party industriously tried to circulate at the time of the Emperor Frederick's illness, namely, that according to Hohenzollern family law no member who was infirm in mind or body might succeed to the throne. The Princess Frederick William had a difficult and dangerous confinement; an accident happened which might have cost her her life. She was to be attended by Dr. Martin, as well as by her own household doctor.

About 8 a.m. the latter wrote to Dr. Martin to say his services were required immediately, but the servant to whom the letter was entrusted, instead of taking it, put it into the post; the consequence was it never reached Dr. Martin till after 1 p.m., and when he arrived at the palace he found it was too late to do what ought to have been done hours before. For some time the Princess's life was despaired of, and when the child was born a slight injury was inflicted on the left arm, which appeared withered from below the elbow.

Time, science, and a strenuous determination on the Prince's own part to conquer this defect, have minimised the inconveniences of this imperfection, and only on close examination is it possible to perceive that the present German Emperor has not the equal use of both his arms. Little incidents like that of his dropping his helmet at the feet of the Pope alone recall that he has not equal strength in his right and left hands.

This defect, trifling though it is, has had, however, a very marked influence upon the Emperor's character, as well as on his mode of thought. To this those who know him well ascribe his pronounced dislike to all that is English, though his mother was English in heart and by birth, and his father, too, professed great admiration for the freer political institutions of Great Britain, and had become much anglicised, for English doctors and nurses had, at Queen Victoria's wish, attended the birth of this her first grandchild, and nothing can persuade the present Emperor but that clumsiness on their part was the cause of the physical weakness which embitters his life.

Neither could any moral suasion move him. Dogged obstinacy is the keynote of his character, and is its mainspring for good as well as for evil. Nor is this quality to be wondered at if we examine his ancestry. He is the offspring on the one hand of that family in whom hereditary energy is apt to turn into stubbornness, and on the other of the Hohenzollerns, in whom self-will and self-esteem are prominent features — features only redeemed from unamiability by a dash of idealism, a strenuous sense of rectitude and honour. It is this that has made the Hohenzollerns great, this that has made them feared and respected, this that has caused an obscure Pomeranian family to subjugate the whole of Germany, and to take upon its shoulders what was once the Holy Roman Empire.

The present Emperor of Germany is born on the paternal side of a family characteristically and traditionally national, a successful race, enriching and elevating itself with astonishing rapidity, though at times by methods which do not perhaps bear too close an examination, and lacking the art to endear itself to the nations around it. His grandfather had done much by sheer dint of living beyond the appointed space of man to convert himself from a despised and insignificant person into a picturesque and remarkable figure, for part of which—not to say almost all—the events of his reign and the sudden rise of his country into a dominating and imperial power, as well as the group of great statesmen and generals which he had the good fortune to gather round him, had to answer. His son Frederick William, with his genial and gracious manner, his native kindness of look and word, his real sentiment, was to a certain extent a spurious plant that did not take after its kind, and of which his own family did not know what to make. His son was again to prove true to tradition; in him atavism speedily pronounced itself. It may be said that from his birth the little William gave evidence of one of those strongly pronounced individualities which no outward circumstances seem able to alter or to mould, and which are wholly unaffected by even the mightiest outer influences —a curious crystallized unit which maintained itself intact throughout all phases of its development, in all the natural metamorphosis of the human being. This innate resistance to transmutation made itself felt quite young, and surprised the observer in this very pretty, almost girlish-looking, boy, whose delicacy was heightened to weakness through the awkward impotence of his left arm. But the slightest attempt to exert pressure from without at once provoked a firm opposition. Naturally, the etiquette that rules in princely families, and is especially rigid in Prussia, made it easy to form the outer life and behaviour of this scion into prescribed forms, and to force upon him habits, and even accomplishments that were naturally distasteful to him; as, for example, politeness of speech and bearing, knightly exercises, and the learning of foreign tongues. All these it was possible to impose on him, since neither physical nor intellectual resources were lacking, and since the need of obedience to outer discipline was quickly recognized as an inevitable necessity by the cool reflective faculties. Here he was helped by the eagerness to do his duty that is a heritage of his Prussian ancestors. But while it was a comparatively easy task to impose upon Prince William these external qualities, it was more hard to obtain a hold upon his inner nature, and to bend its evolution into a given groove. This stubborn nature resented intensely the mere discipline of thinking. Royal children suffer much from the superabundance of impressions and emotions that pour in upon them from all sides, and this is apt to produce the pernicious result of a certain desultoriness of thought and a precocious weariness of pleasure. It has been justly remarked that to conquer this disastrous lack of power of concentration is ever the most important task of the tutor of princes. This office was specially onerous in the case of so intractable a nature. Only the greatest severity and the energetic co-operation of all concurring authorities were able to conquer this mute intuitive resistance, until the hour struck when perception was awakened. Then his own will came to the rescue, after which all difficulties were overcome. But even then, while doing what was required of him, the inner nature of the

Prince remained untouched and uninfluenced, developing in its own manner, modified and directed by outer influences, but never fundamentally changed or diversified. From his mother he has inherited a portion of her pronounced love for the fine arts, her ability of pictorial execution; from his liberal bourgeois father an interest for other classes than the merely aristocratic, though in his case it has never approached the father's freedom from class prejudices and from the Hohenzollern tendency to overbearing. From his earliest tutor he has imbibed a love of discussion, yet not one of these supreme authorities could give the child, the boy, or the youth the full impress of their character. There were moments when it seemed as though this was the case, and many false hopes were based on such passing phases, much bitter disappointment was aroused when it was once more made evident that this obstinate nature remained in change unchanged. This curious human being sucked the nutriment needful for its development from everything that came into its way, but resolutely refused to assimilate aught that it instinctively rejected as useless to the growth of its peculiar organism.

We have, however, anticipated a little, and must return to March 5th, 1859, when the baptism of the new-born boy took place with great pomp in the Royal Palace of Berlin, emperors and kings, princes and archdukes, queens, princesses, archduchesses and duchesses standing sponsors to this new-born scion of the stalwart house of Hohenzollern, who received at this ceremony the names of Frederick William Victor Albert.

Of his babyhood is told this anecdote. He was nine months old when a deputation of burghers waited on his father, and the Crown Prince, to give them pleasure, presented to them his child. One of the assembly gave it his watch to play with, which the little Prince grasped tightly and could not be induced to resign. "You see," said the Crown Prince, in one of his merry moods, moods natural to his temperament, but that grew rarer as time went on, "you see, what a real Hohenzollern gets into his grasp, he never lets go of."

From the first his parents, though still so young, felt the solemn nature of the great task laid upon them of educating this child aright for the high station that promised to await him, though in those days it was no higher than that of King of Prussia. The Princess, a worthy daughter of her father—of whom, indeed, she was the favourite—had been reared in his strenuous views as to the duties of royalty, the solemn obligations with regard to their children's education, and with these she also imbued her husband, who was devoted to her, and willingly let himself be led to higher wisdom by her wise hand.

The couple in those days lived like two quiet burghers, having but a few rooms in a tower of the Castle of Babelsberg, near Potsdam, or in a wing of the Berlin Castle. Their modest establishment, their simplicity of living, their high mode of thinking, their keen intellectual interests, were the wonder, the stock theme of talk, the derision of one-half of Berlin, and the admiration of the other. Not till their little son was born was a house of their own assigned to them. After this event they went to live at the New Palace of Potsdam, rechristened during the brief reign of the Emperor Frederick Friedrichskron, in memory of his great ancestor Frederick the Great, who had built this vast, pretentious pile at the conclusion of the Seven Years' War in order to prove to his enemies that war had not exhausted his pecuniary resources, and that if need be he could go to war again. On the cupola that crowns the centre of this roccoco building are enthroned three female genii. Popular tradition assigns them as Frederick's three mortal enemies—the Empress Maria Theresa of Austria, Elizabeth of Russia, and the notorious Madame de Pompadour. Over the cornice is placed the Prussian eagle, with the audacious motto, "Nec soli cedit." To this palace, to this suburb of Berlin, distant from it some half hour by rail, and containing in its small area the only sheets of water, the only woods and scenic features the arid Berlin sand-wastes can produce, there came to live, early in 1859, the little family of Prince Frederick William of Prussia. He himself loved Potsdam, as all his ancestors had done, and had a special liking for this huge house, with its two hundred rooms, its quaint theatre, its reminiscences of the greatest of Prussia's kings, its spurious pictures of the Bolognese and Venetian school, for in this block he had himself first seen the light of day. It was here, too, that he had conceived his admiration for his great ancestor, so that one of his first acts was to see that every memory of him should remain intact. Thus, for example, the workroom of the "Old Fritz,"* as the Berliners ever called this sovereign.

Little Prince William grew up in this atmosphere of enthusiasm for his great forefather. No wonder he caught the infection also, no wonder that his highest ideal and aim is to be a second Frédérick the Great. But it is not so easy to be "Old Fritz" at the end of the nineteenth century as in the middle of the eighteenth; other elements of character are required by the changed moral conditions, the manners and modes of thought of the barrack-room have been replaced by more refined and nobler aims; there is something higher and finer in the world than mere brute force. As founder of a kingdom, Frederick the Great deserves all praise; as an example to be followed in order to maintain that kingdom, there are other chords to be touched. The Emperor Frederick's admiration for Frederick the Great was for the founder of his dynasty, his son's is for the military despot, the man who ground his heel remorselessly upon whatever came in his path. These are two very divergent matters. Still, this hero-worship was one of the few interests father and son had in common in later life, when their views and ideals had

* "Our Fritz" was the name the Prussians gave to the Emperor Frederick after the war of 1870.

grown widely apart, and it is pleasant to learn that among the last gifts exchanged between Berlin and San Remo that sad Christmas of 1887 were some relics of "Old Fritz," unearthed by his young descendant.

In the New Palace of Potsdam, therefore, amid these memories of Prussia's first glory, was passed the childhood of Prince William, and of his brothers and sisters, for the Princess Frederick William followed her mother's example, and the house filled rapidly with little people. To rear these little ones carefully, to make them strong in mind and body, was the Princess's one care and consideration. After much careful thought and discussion between the father and mother, it was resolved to aim very high, and to try by every means available to attain the goal. The native and inherited seriousness of both parents made this task comparatively easy. It was also resolved between them — to the no small scandal of the grandfather, who clung with adamantine force to old tradition—that in the case of these royal children class traditions should, above all, be broken down, that they should have as far as possible a simple burgher training, and that the civil element should equalize, if not preponderate, over the military—until then alone held in esteem in the Prussian royal house. The purpose of the parents was that their children should profit by the mistakes made in their own education, and no mistake seemed to them so great, so fatal for a ruler who should comprehend all classes of his people, as the rigid and artificial isolation in which royal people are usually reared. Subversive ideas truly, and which were to draw down upon those who promulgated them—and especially upon the mother, the more defenceless person—an amount of malevolent criticism, a wilful and baseless misconstruction of her views, an ungenerous treatment that has not had the decency to be repressed even by her sorrow and her irreparable privation. A Frenchman once seriously discussed the problem whether a German could have *esprit*. It might seriously be discussed whether the German nature is capable of chivalry. Fortunately, however, the odium of such treatment generally rebounds upon those who set it in motion, and there can be no doubt that Time, that great adjuster of wrongs, will place the Empress Frederick's character in its true light before posterity.

Whether she would, bowed down by sorrow and tempered by grief, have the combative powers left to recommence her work is perhaps doubtful, but in the early days of which we are treating she and her husband were full of youth, strength, hope, and enthusiasm, and they set to work with good will and happiness at the labour of educating their babies for the State and for humanity. The nursery and all that pertained to it was the mother's province, and she looked after it—not like a princess, but like a good burgher's wife, introducing into her household many of the customs of her native land. The Princess Frederick William and her nursery soon became a favourite theme for picture and talk. A governess was assigned to Prince William, who watched over him till his sixth year, after which his education was entirely entrusted to Dr. Hinzpeter (son of the man who had filled the same office for the Emperor Frederick), who remained with him till his majority, and under whose direction the other tutors worked. Very special care was bestowed on the body as well as the mind of the royal children, in accordance with the mother's English ideas, that they might be also physically able to meet the demands made on them by their high station. To this day there exists in the park of Friedrichskron a large space specially railed off as a playground, and here, in the early sixties, could be seen Princess William and Henry and Princess Charlotte * enjoying themselves, and being as dirty, as wild, and as merry as they pleased, in company with a group of children from the neighbourhood, selected from among all c'asses of the population. Gymnastics were especially favoured, and under the watchful eye of an old marine the boys clambered up tall scaffoldings and imitative masts planted in the arid sand. The wastes of ground around the palace had also not escaped the notice of the intelligent Princess. She amused her leisure with landscape gardening, after the pattern of her father, and entirely metamorphosed this space. She also encouraged her children to follow this healthy pastime, giving them each their little domain, in which they

* Now Princess of Saxe Meinigen.

might plant strawberries, currants, and gooseberries—and, what was better still, eat them to their hearts' content when they were ripe. The Emperor William may sometimes even now think of the little feasts he gave from his own garden produce, of the merry games played under the oaks and limes with his companions, now his subjects, when he and his brother Henry built fortresses of mud and sand and stormed them; in short, of all the quiet peace and true domestic happiness that was ever found at "Crown Princes," as the Berliners familiarly designated the family.

A few amusing anecdotes of his early childhood have been preserved, one of which we give here. Like many small children, Prince William had a great dislike to being washed, and above all to the English daily cold bath. He often contrived to escape from the servants unwashed and to slip out into the garden, when he invariably sought out the nearest sentry box, for it flattered his baby pride, and pleased his already strong taste for soldiers, to see the sentinel present arms. One morning, however, when the Prince had scamped his bath and scrubbing and found himself upon the terrace in eager expectation of the happiness of seeing the tall grenadier face and present arms, what was his dismay when the sentry quietly continued his patrol, just as if no prince were present. This was a catastrophe that had never happened before. Bathed in tears of rage and disappointment he rushed back into the palace and straight into his father's study. "Why what has happened, my boy?" tenderly asked the parent, when he saw the child's disturbed mien. Sobbing bitterly, the child told how the sentry had not presented arms as usual, although he had gone quite close up to him, so that he must have seen him, and yet the soldier did just as though he were not there. "Really," said the father, "that seems strange; just come a little nearer." Then looking at the boy all around, he quietly said, after a pause, "The sentry did his duty not to present arms to you." More astonished than ever, the Prince asked, "But why, papa?" "No soldier presents arms to an unwashed prince," said the father, quietly, and turned away to resume his work, taking no further notice of his son. Amazed, the boy stood rooted to the spot. But after a moment he roused himself and seemed to comprehend. In an instant he was back in his bedroom and begged as eagerly to be washed as before he had resisted the process. Of course the whole scene was a plot of the father's, who had counted on his little son's love for this pastime in order to cure him of his repugnance to his tub.

Among the items on the educational programme of the young princes was rowing upon one of the Potsdam lakes.

For this purpose during the summer months a detachment of sailors were told off to serve the royal pleasure boats, anchored at this spot. A light bark was placed at the special disposal of Prince William, called the *Cuckoo.* It was in the early autumn of 1866, the Prince Frederick William was in the field conducting the campaign against Austria, and the children were left to the sole care of their mother. Prince William was then a fair boy of some seven years. By maternal orders he was sent down to the lake regularly every morning at an early hour to row for a while on the water. The smallest and lightest of the sailors was selected to accompany him and teach him the technique of the art. One day the prince arrived earlier than usual. The sailor, who had just been tarring, was still in his working clothes, liberally smirched with the blackness. When the little prince saw him in this attire, and smelt the piercing odour, he roundly declared that nothing would induce him to row now or in future with such a dirty man. The sailor, a true Prussian and a countryman, forgot his respect on hearing the child's animadversions, and came out with some anything but polite or gentle observations. The prince's tutor, who had listened to the scene, then turned to the child. "Prince," he said, "you are gravely unjust to this man in reproving him for his dirty clothes. In doing his duty as a sailor he cannot, when tarring, have regard to his dress. In touching a tar-brush, spots are inevitable. Your remark was too hasty and therefore unjust; I feel sure you already are sorry that you let yourself be carried away to insult needlessly a faithful, dutiful sailor of the king's navy." On hearing this the prince at once held out his hand to the man. At this moment it happened that the Princess Frederick William drove past. Seeing her eldest hand-in-hand with this sailor, she asked what had occurred, and on hearing the incident, at once enforced yet more strongly on the boy the wrong of which he had been guilty.

So good, so just and honest, so in some senses unprincely an education ought indeed to bear good fruit.

He certainly was as a child what is called "a pickle." To this an anecdote told by Frith bears witness. This artist had been appointed by Queen Victoria to paint the marriage of the Prince of Wales. It was in 1863. The painter writes in his diary of the time, "As to Prince William of Prussia, of all the little Turks, he is one of the worst, and how I am to get a likeness of him, I don't know." The picture was ten feet long, "Uncle Albert's marriage" the child called it, and to keep him quiet Frith had portioned off one of the lower corners, about a foot square, which was lent to the young prince, to paint a picture on. He was also given brushes and paints, but told to keep strictly in his boundary. The artist was working quietly at his own part of the picture when he was roused by an exclamation of alarm from the lady in charge of the prince, who cried, "Look at his face! What has he been doing to it?" It appeared on examination that the boy had simply been wiping his brushes upon it, for it was streaked with vermilion, blue, and other pigments. "What is to be done?" cried the distressed lady. "If the Princess should see him, she would——" "Oh," interrupted Frith, "I can easily remove the paint." And so saying, he put some turpentine on a clean rag and effectively wiped off the colour; or rather was doing so, when he was stopped by violent screams from the young gentleman, accompanied by a severe cuff from his fist. The turpentine had found some little spot or scratch on his face, and was no doubt giving him great pain. He tore from the artist, after administering to him a vigorous parting kick, and took refuge under a large table, where he yelled at the top of his voice till he was tired, his governess all the while in terror lest he should be heard. Nor did he ever forgive Frith his remedial efforts, or the involuntary injury he did him; and this is characteristic of him, and perchance explains why he and Bismarck, who also never forgets or forgives an injury, have so much in common. From that day forward he took a malicious pleasure in tormenting Frith by sitting as badly as he possibly could, so much so that the painter absolutely failed in producing anything resembling a likeness to him in the picture.

Into the early youth of Prince William there fell the three mighty wars which made Prussia strong and Germany a nation—the Danish, the Austrian, and the French. They inflamed the imagination of the boy with a love of military glory, of which he only saw the pomp and tin-trumpet splendour, whereas his father had beheld its terrors and horrors too close to love them. That this father was the central hero of all this clashing, flashing, dazzling romance yet further excited the young prince, who was all alive to the military enthusiasm that surged around him, but blind to the anxious sorrow-worn looks of his mother, to his father's grave or solemn mien when war was the theme of discourse. And especially did he get carried away by the military intoxication that took possession of all Germany in 1870–71. With ardour he studied the history of his native land and of his land's arch-enemy, the geography of France and Germany, the military situation, the state of the army and navy of both countries. He shed tears of rage at the thought that he was too young to take part in these days of his country's glory, and the laurels of this campaign do not let him rest to this day, anxious to measure himself also with the hated foe, and to earn for himself military renown. When, in March, 1871, grandfather and father returned to Berlin crowned with victory, the youngest soldier in the Prussian army, namely Prince William, then but twelve, could not be held back from going in person to the railway station that he might be the first to greet the heroes. And in the national festivities that followed, little Prince William was always to the fore, there was no keeping him quiet and attentive to his studies in those days.

We can understand that this martial ardour gave food for anxious thought to the earnest parents, who looked at life through no rose-coloured spectacles, had no illusions, were not blinded by powder smoke. While still in the field, on January 27th, 1871, the then Crown Prince wrote in his diary: "To-day is my son William's thirteenth birthday. May he become a strong, loyal, faithful, and sincere man, a true German, and keep himself free from prejudices. It is enough to frighten one to think what hopes already rest on the head of this boy, and how we are responsible for the direction which we may give to his education. This education encounters so many difficulties owing to family considerations and the circumstances of the Berlin Court."

After his return, this subject of their son's education was once more the theme of grave deliberation between father and mother. They finally decided, to the no small dismay of the grandfather, who was rooted to tradition and etiquette, that their boy should go to a common public school, and receive not only the same education as his future subjects, but should sit on the same school benches. It is easy to imagine the holy hands upraised in pious horror at this decision. Why such a thing was unheard of in the annals of royal houses ever since the foundation of the world. But "Crown Princes" were firm and not easily daunted when once they recognized a measure as right and wise, and though the Crown Prince proved all his life how well he knew how to practise self-repression, and to bear himself with dignity against all the enforced, accidental, and intentional difficulties that stood in the way of his difficult secondary position, where his children were concerned he evinced the energy that was native to him. Prince William was therefore prepared for entering a gymnasium, and in 1873 passed, with some distinction, the preliminary examination at the Berlin gymnasium of Joachimsthal, being classed for the upper-third form. But here, again, "Crown Princes" did the unexpected, unconventional. They decided against letting their boy go to the Berlin institution. Nor was he even to go to the Potsdam gymnasium, proposed as a substitute. Their aim was to place him as far as possible from the Court and Court life, from the flippant, military, and Chauvinistic atmosphere of Berlin, so that the Prince should be surrounded only by an academic atmosphere, and should, if possible, become completely absorbed in his studies. To this end the gymnasium of Cassel was chosen, a town only lately incorporated into the Prussian dominion, in which, therefore, Prussian traditions did not yet obtain, where there could not as yet be an exaggerated reverence for the family of their conquerors. Moreover, the director of this institution was reputed a wise and careful tutor, and a man free from servility and time-serving.

Indeed, when this man, Dr. Vogt, was asked if he would admit the princes to his school, he replied with characteristic frankness, "I regard the wish of these parents as a command," he said, "but I require from the future pupil of my institution the strictest observance of its duties, the most entire respect for its rules and *régime*, as I require from all others, and I can admit of no distinctions." This was just what the royal parents desired. They had found a man after their own heart.

When all was settled, however, Prince William did not at once take his place on the school benches. His parents wanted him to wait till his brother Henry was far enough advanced to accompany him. It was therefore not till the autumn of 1874 that the two young princes entered the Lyceum Fridericianum of Cassel.

Before going, Prince William was confirmed. This is a solemn ceremony in the German branch of the Protestant church, the candidate having to present a written profession of faith, drawn up by himself. These documents are carefully kept in the Prussian royal family, which always celebrates religious *fêtes* with a pomp which is imposing in its simplicity. Prince William's, which he read with a firm voice, was well composed, and showed a comprehension of theological difficulties. In the course of his speech the young Prince said (underlining his words, as is his custom to this day), "I know that difficult duties await me in life," and added that his courage would be stimulated by them, and not cast down. His mode of delivery, his matter earned him the praises of the august assembly who had collected in the Friedenskirche of Potsdam to witness the ceremony, the church in which the Emperor Frederick now sleeps his eternal sleep.

Almost at once after this important ceremony the two princes left for Cassel. This little town, situated in the former duchy of Hesse, lies in a pleasant undulating district, with some pretentions to natural beauties. It was at once decided that the two princes should live in winter in the former palace of the town, but in summer at the neighbouring castle of Wilhelmshöhe, which had so lately housed as State prisoner the ex-Emperor of the French. This was done to gratify Prince William's taste for natural surroundings and every form of outdoor and field sport. Their retinue was small and modest in all its appointments, and study, real earnest study, was enforced by precept and example. And, indeed, both the lads proved themselves industrious and willing scholars.

Dr. Wiese, Prussian Inspector of Schools, who in 1875 visited Cassel, has left on record his impression of the royal pupil. He writes: "In appearance and deportment I found no difference between him and his schoolfellows, and his whole behaviour was modest and unassuming. The first lesson at which I was present in the Lower First was Thucydides. It had already surprised me to find this most difficult of all the Greek prose writers who are read in our schools in a class of which the scholars, as was the case with the Prince himself, had been but lately transferred from the Second; but my astonishment increased when I observed that the teacher, omitting the historical portions, had immediately fixed on one of the interwoven speeches, which are omitted even in the Upper First on account of their difficulty. Towards the end of the lesson I began to speak, and asked the Prince if he had already read other Greek historians. He named Xenophon. To my question whether he could indicate any difference between Thucydides and Xenophon, he answered, smiling, 'Oh, yes; I could understand Xenophon, but I can't Thucydides.' . . . He failed in none of my searching questions. . . . The Director praised his willing submission to all the rules of the school, and his easy intercourse with his schoolfellows, although he could with great tact repel any undue familiarity. His honest diligence was also praised by his teacher; perhaps none of his schoolfellows were so severely accustomed to so exact and conscientious a division and use of their time. Faithfulness to duty—the virtue of the Hohenzollerns—was an ornament of his youth. This severe learning alternated with corporeal exercises, walks, and exploring excursions. Especially on the Wednesday and Saturday half-holidays the Prince might be seen tramping the country, accompanied by a selection of his fellow-scholars. Winter was his favourite season. No weather daunted him, no matter how bad. If it was a half-holiday, Prince William might be encountered tramping over the heavy ground, covered up to his knees with the red-clay soil of Westphalia, and busy either with his surveying-rod, his botany-box, or his geological hammer. He would often come in wet to the skin, but only the more energetic and contented if he had conquered some physical difficulty. Thus while at Cassel he not only learned to swim, but to become expert in that art—no mean feat when it is borne in mind how he is handicapped by his lame arm. Skating, cricket, and croquet also found in him an ardent votary. In all things his life was submitted to rigid *régime*, and this was the case also with Sunday, kept in accordance with German Protestant traditions as a day of stern abstinence from ordinary occupations. Attendance at divine service was obligatory, and was never missed. He was, however, allowed to ride or drive in State on that day, and to receive guests at his table—usually the dignitaries of the little town. Sunday evening was the Prince's favourite portion of that day. Then a number of his schoolfellows came to his house as guests, and it was usual to read German classics together. Sometimes charades were also permitted, or *tableaux vivants*. The holding these little festivities was the only thing that distinguished the Princes from their comrades, but it was, of course, practically impossible for them to forget that they were princes of the reigning house, or for their schoolfellows to ignore it. For example, when from time to time the parents came to see their boys—unexpectedly, often, it is true, and always without ceremony—what a flutter they created! And with what almost fetish respect did the school receive the silken banner sent by the Crown Princess for the *fête* of Sedan, which Prince William in person carried triumphantly through all the streets of Cassel at the head of a *cortège* of his schoolfellows.

Although the parents were sincere in their wish to promote equality between the boys and their comrades, and the director was sincere and conscientious in treating them as pupils on the same footing as his other scholars, yet for all that, this education in common could only impress upon the princes the fact, borne in on them by a hundred and one trifles, of the distance that separated them from their fellows. Prince William in particular, as the sentry incident proves, was early penetrated with the idea of his exalted station, and at Cassel it was remarked how, while seemingly charming with his comrades, he really held them far from him. Never for once did he appear to forget that he was a prince—a being, to his own mind, apart from the common herd. And yet he no doubt honestly tried to make himself one of them, but the native haughtiness was rooted too deep, and had lasted too many generations.

Thus it is related by one of his schoolfellows that he never excluded himself from any of their general actions, even when these were of a refractory character. For example, it had been resolved at head-quarters, contrary to all tradition, that henceforth certain marks on the school cap, which distinguished the upper and lower classes, should be abandoned. Incensed at this, all the boys determined that they would appear at school next day not in the regulation cap. Prince William duly put in an appearance wearing a tall hat.

Before leaving the gymnasium he had, like all the other boys, to go through his *abiturienten* examination, that *dies iræ* of the German schoolboy which marks for him not only the close of childhood, but is the terrible day which irrevocably fixes his fate. For unless they qualify at this examination, all the learned professions are closed to them, and three years' military drill instead of one is their doom. No wonder this is an anxious fortnight for the boy who is leaving (*abiturient*). Prince William went through his week of papers and week of *vivâ voce*, together with his class-fellows, and received the qualification of "sufficient," the lowest of the three standards required, which run sufficient, good, and excellent. Among the seventeen who were up for examination he was classed as the tenth. This was in January, 1877. It was a great pleasure to him that at the distribution of three medals left by a former rector of the school for donation to the three most industrious and worthy *abiturienten* of the year, one was accorded to him. Doubtless he owed this honour a little also to his station, but that he did not think so is proved by his words when thanking the director. "You cannot think what pleasure you give me in bestowing this medal on me. For it happens that I know I have deserved it. I have honestly tried to do all that lay in my power."

The prescribed formula of quitting the gymnasium requires each scholar to state what profession he proposes to embrace. Prince William assigned as his "Statecraft and Law."

The examination ended, he hastened to Berlin, for in two days from his dismissal from school there awaited him an important function that should close an era of his life, for January 27th, 1887, was his eighteenth birthday, which constituted his majority. The event was celebrated as a festival throughout the length and breadth of Germany. By birthright the princes of the house of Hohenzollern are entitled to receive the order of the Black Eagle, the highest German decoration. On this day Prince William received the solemn investiture.

The order of the Black Eagle of Prussia was instituted by the first king of Prussia on the day of his coronation. "The eagle," said Frederick I. in the charter of foundation, "with one of its claws holds a crown of laurels, with the other a thunderbolt. Above its head we have written our device: *Suum cuique*. The crown signifies the justice of reward; the thunderbolt, the justice of punishment; the *Suum cuique*, the absolute impartiality with which we will reward each and every one according to their deserts. But that is not all. The eagle, as is well known, always flies towards the sun: it aims at nothing small or low. These qualities are a symbol, by which we are reminded, we and our knights, that we must elevate our hopes and our confidence towards the Most High God alone. The *Suum cuique* reminds us that we must not only give to man what is man's, but to the Most High what belongs to Him, and to God what comes from God. We must join together, above all else, to fulfil this duty towards God, the first duty which we enjoin on our knights."

The Emperor William I., who was, perhaps, the best informed man in Europe on matters relating to orders of knighthood, delighted in these souvenirs of an age of chivalry. He was most particular about the strict observance of the provisions of their statutes, and presided over their ceremonies with all his natural dignity. On the 27th of January, 1877, the Emperor, preceded by the Crown Prince and by the princes, followed by the Knights of the Order belonging to the princely houses of Germany, by the knights having a seat in the chapter, by Ministers, &c., made his entry into the Hall of the Knights. Helmet on head, and wearing the red velvet cloak of the Order, he seated himself on the throne and commanded the master of the ceremonies to introduce Prince William. The Prince entered, accompanied by his father and Prince Albrecht, his great-uncle, and advanced to the steps of the throne. The Emperor ordered the form of oath to be read. Each knight must swear "to lead a virtuous Christian life, agreeable to God and men of honour, and to encourage others to lead the same; to maintain at all times and places the true Christian religion; to protect the poor and forsaken, widows and orphans, and all who suffer violence and injustice; to defend the royal family and the royal prerogative; and to preserve everywhere peace, unity, and good morals."

In reply to the Emperor's question, whether he would swear to fulfil these chivalrous duties, the Prince, mounting the steps of the throne and placing his hand on the book of statutes, answered, "Yes, I swear it." He returned to his place to receive from his father and

Prince Albrecht the cloak of the Order. Then he again mounted the steps of the throne and knelt before the Emperor, who, bending forward, placed the collar on his neck, and, raising him, embraced him three times.

Before this ceremony the Prince had received the English Order of the Garter as a birthday gift from his royal grandmamma of England.

Ordinary schoolboys would now have been permitted a little rest before resuming study, but not so this prince, whom his parents worked hard in order to harden him for the fatigues of his onerous station. It was now needful to initiate him into the special branches of training requisite for a ruler, and for a Prussian Prince this training, in first rank, deals with a military education. In point of fact, Prince William, after the custom of his house, was ranked as a member of the army from his tenth year, but actually he only entered it after attaining his majority.

A week after his birthday the Emperor William presented his grandson to his military superiors.

The old Emperor, who had just celebrated the seventieth anniversary of his entrance into the army, made one of those short and precise but admirable speeches for which he was remarkable, addressing himself first to his son and afterwards to his officers.

"You know from history that the kings of Prussia, while fulfilling the other duties of government, have always devoted their principal attention to the army. The Great Elector by his heroism set an example to his troops which has not been surpassed. Frederick I. well knew, when he assumed the crown that he would have to defend that daring action; but he also knew that his tried troops would make that easy for him. Frederick William I., in this same garrison (Potsdam) which you are about to join, and which has been called the cradle of the Prussian army, laid the foundation of our military organization by the severe discipline which he instituted for both officers and soldiers. . . . His inspiration is still with us. Frederick the Great with his military genius made of these troops the kernel of that army whose battles have rendered him immortal. Frederick William II. had to deal with a new school of tactics, and the army did not leave the lists without laurels. My royal father encountered the same enemy, and a terrible disaster befell the country and the army. But then, putting aside all that was antiquated and out of date, he reorganized the army and founded it on love of country and the sentiment of honour. And he won successes which will shine in the annals of the Prussian army to the end of all time. My brother, King Frederick William IV., who was so severely tried, looked with satisfaction on the army which remained faithful to him in his troubles.

"In this state I found the army.

"If ever a government was visibly led by Providence it was that of the last few years. And it is the army which, through its pluck and constancy, has carried Prussia to that position which she now holds. The corps of Guards to which you belong, and the regiment which you join to-day, have contributed to our successes in the most brilliant manner. The medals which I wear are the public expression of my everlasting recognition of the devotion with which the army has won victory after victory. You have arrived at youth in a great period, and you have in your father an honourable example of the art of conducting war and battles. But you will find, in the service which you are entering, things apparently trifling, and which will surprise you. Note well that in the service nothing is insignificant. Each stone used to build an army must be modelled with precision if the building is to be good and sound."

Then turning to the officers—consisting of the Captain of the Sixth Company of the First Regiment of Foot Guards, to which the Prince was attached; the Commandant of the Second Battalion, the Colonel of the Regiment, the General commanding the First Division of Foot Guards, the General commanding the Corps of Guards—the Emperor said:

"I entrust my grandson to you that each of you may do what lies in your several departments of military education, towards making him a worthy successor of his ancestors."

And again, speaking to his grandson, "Now go! and do your duty as it will be taught you. May God bless you!"

The same morning the Crown Prince took him to Potsdam to introduce him to the 6th Company, to which Prince William belonged.

As a French writer has well observed in surveying the

life of the Prince up to this date—" Consider," he writes, " this succession of ceremonies, the examination on leaving college, and the solemn coming of age; the medal given to the hardworking rhetorician, and the Order placed on the Prince's neck within the space of two days; then a week later his entry into the army with the injunction to neglect no detail of the service. Consider his grandfather's speech passing in review all their glories from the remote ages down to the day when the young man is about to accept the responsibilities of the future. Let us not forget the intimacy with God in the *fête* of confirmation. What a mixture of the real and the ideal, of the past and the present!

"A prince thus brought up does not belong altogether to the civilization of the century now drawing to a close. He is certainly capable of making use of its forces, less capable of understanding its spirit. God, chivalry, his ancestors have raised him. They have strengthened in him the power of command. They have made him superior to us—a superiority which has its dangers, for there are among the depths of the masses who know neither God, nor chivalry, nor ancestors, volcanoes which are working up."

From the day of his formal entry into the army the Prince took up his abode in the Castle of Potsdam, serving precisely like any other lieutenant, for in military matters the Prussians know no favour. From babyhood he had been accustomed to rise early, so that each working day might be as long as possible. It was noted that he was ever the first at his post. His military service discharged, there was no rest for this youth. He then had to attend lectures by eminent officers of the War School, selected to instruct him in the science of war. Only Saturday evening was allowed as a holiday. Then Prince William would hasten to Berlin to spend Sunday with his parents, brothers, and sisters. On Monday morning, however, early dawn always found him punctually back at his post.

That the mental atmosphere of Prussian officers in which he now found himself was congenial to Prince William will readily be understood. Nevertheless, he did not let himself be subjugated entirely by their ideas. Their antipathy to the navy was especially distasteful to him. The German navy was just then beginning to work itself up to some position, and the army, unaccustomed hitherto to brook a rival, resented its pretensions. Prince William had a special liking for the new service, whose value and importance to the new-born kingdom he rightly recognized, and he went so far as to hold public lectures before his military comrades on the theme of a fleet, trying to prove to them its equality and its value.

In the autumn of 1877 the Prince was sent to the University of Bonn to complete his humanistic studies. Here he remained two years, following a very varied course of studies, drawn up by the Crown Prince and Minister Falk, and approved by the Emperor.

He followed the courses of philosophy, physics, and

chemistry, of the history of the Reformation, and of the nineteenth century, of modern German literature, ancient art and the history of art, of Roman jurisprudence and the history of German jurisprudence, of penal law and procedure, administrative law, international law, political economy, and financial science, He attended the lectures with Prussian punctuality.

It is not known which study he preferred, but no doubt he extracted profit from all, after the manner of his mind, ready to draw to itself that mental nutriment which it finds needful to it.

He also entered thoroughly into the life of the students, where he found much to attract him, for he loved, after the manner of German youths, those rather boisterous assemblies where singing, shouting, drinking, and laughing are the order of the day, or rather night. Nor was he at all insensible to the attractions of the fair sex—quite the contrary. While at Bonn he gave a somewhat childish evidence of his hatred for all that pertains to his national arch-enemy France, anathematizing champagne, a drink which indeed is never allowed to appear on his table, and encouraging his fellow-students to imbibe the sparkling produce of their native Rhine. The Student Corps, with their customs of a past age, their uniforms, their military habits, attracted him. He was a member of one of the most celebrated corps in the German Universities, the *Borussia*. None surpassed him in performing the rites of beer drinking.

He approves of the students' duels, in which young men cut one another's cheeks open without cause, because they learn not to fear the sight of blood. Courageous as he is, he must have regretted not carrying away some scar as a souvenir of the University. He has preserved his white cap and the black and white ribbon, the colours of the Corps and of the Hohenzollerns. He has been a regular attendant at the annual dinner at Berlin of the old members of the *Borussia*, where they sing in chorus: " *Es lebe die Borussia! Hurrah! Hoch!* " and where he gave ardent toasts finishing with the *Borussia vivat, crescat, floreat!* He went to Bonn to celebrate the sixtieth anniversary of the Corps, whose history he traced in his speech.

"The *Borussia* of Bonn," he said, " has shown throughout its history its devotion to the Prussian fatherland. As in the army the First Regiment of Guards has been selected to introduce the Hohenzollern Princes to the traditions of our army, so also the Corps of the Borusses of Bonn has been selected to receive during their studies the Princes of our royal family, as well as the sons of the principal princely houses of Germany. This honour accorded to the Corps shows that they have found and followed the right spirit, *den richtigen Geist*. The Corps wear the colours of our House of Hohenzollern, of our country of Prussia. Strangers have said that these colours are not bright enough, that they are too plain. They suit the plain history of our Prussian country, which has passed through rough times, and which by a plain effort won the position which she holds to-day. The Iron Cross, too, the grandest symbol of our great struggles, bears these plain colours. May the devotion to duty which our fathers showed under these colours be transmitted to the young members of the Corps, and may each of them do his duty with devotion and fidelity!"

These words show plainly that the German Universities are very hotbeds of German patriotism, and that the spirit nursed in them for nearly a century has spread through the nation, preparing it for unity. This spirit of patriotism, to-day more ardent than ever, preserves the accomplished work. It glorifies the battles of yesterday. It looks forward to, one might almost say desires, the battles of to-morrow.

It was while at Bonn that Prince William knit yet more closely that really fraternal friendship which existed between him and the late Crown Prince Rudolph of Austria. The Emperor Frederick had also sought and found his youthful friendship in a Crown Prince, but he had selected the Prince of Savoy, now King Humbert, and his whole heart was wrapped up in that friend's fair land.

In 1879 the Prince's university studies ended. He was then twenty-one. It now behoved him to consecrate himself to his military duties, and to make his apprenticeship in his political duties. As before, he was worked very hard, and he threw himself with ardour into all martial affairs and administrative details. It was clear that he was burning to take his place in active life, and that he did not understand, like his father, how to hold himself in an attitude of unobtrusive self-repression. And yet the old Emperor William, though he was devoted to his eldest grandson, with whom he had far more in common than with his son, would allow no person to aid or support him even in the most trivial representative duties.

No less a person than Prince Bismarck initiated him into the mysteries of the Foreign Office, and from that instruction sprang the devoted worship which the old Emperor William felt for his Chancellor. He also grew attached to his son, Count Herbert Bismarck. Prince Bismarck returned the young man's regard with sincerity. He was anxiously desirous for his welfare, and in those days, above all, was preoccupied with the question of settling him wisely in life, for he recognized that, with the Prince's peculiar nature, the choice of a wife was a matter of no small moment for him. The Chancellor was also desirous that this time no foreign influence should penetrate into the Prussian Court. He had had enough, and more than even he could deal with, in the pronounced individuality of the English Princess. Conscious of her noble origin, devoted to her fatherland, and not to be cowed or subdued, she had at times given Prince Bismarck no little trouble. Prince William's wife should be a German, so the Chancellor resolved, and with this he inculcated his royal master, who was ever ready to listen to his faithful servant's ideas. She should also be of princely, but not of sovereign, origin, of no marked character, rather a good, malleable, healthy girl, not too intelligent, and with no ideals or ideas of her own. Such girls, of course, exist by the score, and it needed no Diogenes' lantern wherewith to seek her. She was selected in the person of the Princess Augusta Victoria, daughter of the Duke of Schleswig-Holstein-Sonderburg-Augustenburg, whose titles were larger than his estates, for of these he had been deprived all his life—a life spent in urging claims to which every government lent a deaf ear, as such petty States no longer fitted into the changed political conditions of Europe. It was in 1879 that Prince William accepted an invitation to shoot on the Silesian estate where the Duke lived in strict privacy, and here he first saw his future wife. Ere his death, which occurred soon after, Duke Frederick had the satisfaction of knowing that his daughter might one day be Empress of Germany.

On June 2, 1880, the engagement of Prince William was publicly announced with great pomp in Berlin. The union was viewed with satisfaction by the people, it having been well impressed on them by speeches and through the press that this new member of the imperial house was a German in every sense of the word—sprung from German stock, German in appearance, German in manners and customs. Since the reawakening of national self-consciousness in Germany with the events of 1870, no eulogy is sweeter to German ears than to

designate a person or thing as "quite German." And
the Princess is truly the typical German young woman,
and this, no doubt, is her chief attraction to Prince
William. For he, too, strives above all else to be
German, though of course a German of the Prussian
type. He will not permit the least foreign custom,
whether English or French. That he should not love
France is easy to understand, but his dislike of foreign
matters extends also to England, whose dominion, he
maintains, was too great at his father's hearth. He was
displeased at the authority his mother held in the house,
and did not hesitate to express his displeasure with not
always the most gentle or most chivalrous frankness,
and he was determined in his person to return to the
traditions of his family and marry a simple German
lady, content to be nothing but a woman and a mother.
It was not uncommon to hear the wits of Berlin making
fun of the young Princess, who, they said, could only
make sweets and jams. The Prince declared that he
preferred in a woman the talent of making sweets to an
aptitude for discussing a Constitution, and the majority
of his countrymen, jealously tenacious of male preponderance and authority, fully agree with him. That
is why a superior upper servant is the ideal German
woman of real life and romance.

On Sunday, February 27, 1881, the marriage of the
young couple was celebrated at Berlin with great pomp
in the presence of royalties without number.

The day before, the Princess, in accordance with one

of the old Hohenzollern family customs, dear to her husband, was formally conducted into the town beside her mother-in-law in a carriage drawn by eight horses, and escorted by the Guards and Dragoons.

The marriage ceremony commenced by the coronation of the Princess. A Court councillor, escorted by an officer and two guardsmen, brought the crown from the Palace treasury, and presented it, on a velvet cushion, to the Empress Augusta, who placed it on the head of her daughter-in-law, thus raising her to the rank of a Prussian Princess. The exchange of rings was marked by an artillery salute. The Court then repaired to the gala dinner, and the evening wound up with a torchlight dance executed by their Excellencies the Ministers.

It is related, and it is to the Prince's credit, that he remained on duty at Potsdam up to the last moment. He came to Berlin with his company, which was under orders as a guard of honour, the day before the ceremony. On the very morning of his wedding day he returned to Potsdam to decorate the sergeant-major with his own hands.

The following days were taken up by *fêtes*, *levées*, addresses, the presentation of gifts from the different corporations and provinces of the Empire.

After all these *fêtes* there followed domestic tranquillity, and the public hardly ever heard the name of the Princess William mentioned, except just incidentally as that of a careful and affectionate wife.

In September of this year the Prince passed an excellent military examination, in the presence of his royal grandfather. That he succeeded so well was a matter not only of pleasure to his relations, but of surprise. It had been universally held by competent authorities that no young man had ever entered the Prussian army so little physically fitted to turn out a brilliant and smart cavalry officer. Indeed, had he been an ordinary mortal, his physical weakness would have caused him to have been exempted from the need to serve. With his usual great self-command and energy the Prince had resolved that his lame arm should not stand in his way. He was proud, when conducting his regiment of hussars before the eyes of his grandfather, sharply critical in all military matters, he earned from him a meed of just and serious praise. And he was even prouder when his reticent redoubtable grand-uncle, the famous Red Prince, muttered, almost in a tone of apology, "Upon my word, you have done well; I never would have believed it." Justly proud, too, for the praise thus obtained was the due meed for a rare self-control—a rare triumph of mind over matter.

The residence assigned to the young couple was the so-called Marble Palace of Potsdam, a pile not far distant from the home of the bridegroom's childhood. Here, on May 7, 1882, was born the present heir to the German throne.

"Papa," cried the Prince to his father, the Crown Prince, who was impatiently pacing the gardens under the Princess William's windows. "Papa, papa, a boy!" The joy of the new-made father at the sex of the child was boundless, and he insisted on riding over to Berlin to deliver the news in person to his grandfather.

Almost immediately there was disseminated throughout all Germany the well-known picture representing the old Emperor seated, holding the child on his knees, his head bent towards him; standing on the right the Crown Prince, upright, strong, calm, the very picture of a happy grandfather, and young Prince William stiffer than his father, with a bold, honest face. Underneath, the proud legend: *Vier Kaiser!* which implied so much: the glory of the past, the solidity of the present, the security of the future.

This first-born now already wears the hussar uniform, and returns the soldiers' salutes like an old officer. He has four brothers—Eitel-Frederick, born in 1883; Adalbert, born in 1884; Augustus, born in 1887; and Oscar, born in September, 1888. The Emperor William II. said one day, thinking, perchance, of future wars: "It is better to have plenty of boys, one may lose some."

The private life of the Prince, so long as he was Prince, was of the simplest kind, and this simplicity is continued to this day in private, though in public he has shown a love for pomp and show that is entirely out of keeping with the traditions of his ancestors, whose economy, approaching parsimoniousness, was proverbial. Although so short a time upon the one, he has already asked for an addition to his civil list—an unheard-of circumstance in the Hohenzollern family. This is the plan of his daily life, given by an intimate. Very early rising is the order of the day. The Empress William always breakfasts alone with her husband, and even if he has to be on active service at early dawn, she never fails to appear. Lunch is an unknown meal; as a foreign custom it is abhorred by the Emperor. He clings to the burgher midday dinner at one o'clock, and clings to it so strenuously that even Court dinners are now held at this most inconvenient hour. French cookery and French names upon the menu card are both equally forbidden. At five the family partake of tea, and after an early and frugal supper, the couple retire to rest at about the hour their grandmamma of England rises from her dinner table. In the afternoon they often walk, drive, or row together, in company with their boys, to whom the Emperor is devoted. When the Emperor is from home, the Empress devotes herself to the various charitable societies she has founded or patronises, and in the evening assembles ladies around her to help her in sewing for her poor. Like her husband, she is fond of music, especially of the music of Wagner, whose patriotic and Teutonic tendencies are obviously in harmony with the Emperor's mode of thought. She has not, however, his artistic gifts. The Emperor William has inherited some of his mother's talent, and paints very fairly. Marine subjects are his favourites, as indeed he is fond of all that bears upon the navy, sharing in this respect the enthusiasms of his brother Henry, to whom he is fondly devoted.

Indeed, this curiously composite nature possesses a great capacity for deep affection, as well as a great capacity for reverence. This latter quality came into play in his relations with his grandfather and for a long while also with Prince Bismarck. True Prussian that he is, he is of course free from the slightest dash of romanticism or idealism, and sees only the concrete aspects of an idea.

One of the marked characteristics of the Emperor is a great fluency of speech—a fatal fluency some might call it, seeing that some of his public addresses since he came to the front have not always been characterized by moderation of judgment or good taste, nor can he always repress his native headstrongness. There is a little tendency too towards hyperbole and bombastic fustian, but no doubt these are the faults of youth and inexperience, which time and circumstances will teach him to modify. The fact that he never prepares his speeches beforehand may have something to answer for in this respect.

The Emperor has given great attention to languages, and can speak Russian fluently. He is the first king of Prussia who has taken the trouble to learn that language. The very fact that the heir to the German Empire, amidst his pressing military and other duties, should of his own will, after his marriage, have added

Russian to the English, French, and Italian which he had been taught as a lad, gives some hint of the strength of purpose of the man's character. Hitherto all the talk between the allied families of the Romanoffs and Hohenzollerns has been carried on in German.

The young Emperor William has thrice already visited Russia. After his first return home he determined to make himself master of the language of his neighbours, and a Russian teacher used to go daily to Potsdam. When Prince Bismarck heard of it he was delighted. "That is right," said he, "it will be good for Germany." At his second visit to St. Petersburg the Russians were indignant against Germany on account of the Bulgarian troubles. The Tzar, however, invited the young Prussian Prince to be present at the manœuvres, and here he won the hearts of the Russians by speaking to the officers and soldiers in their own beloved tongue. The Emperor William was charmed at the success of this mission. "In a few hours," said he, "my grandson has finished up an affair which had dragged on for months!"

But administration and diplomacy were extras, the ordinary day's work was the regiment.

On September 16, 1881, after the manœuvres in Holstein, Prince William was promoted Major in the Potsdam Regiment of Hussars. He took the same rank in the First Regiment of Field Artillery. Always precise in fulfilling the smallest duty, he wished to be something more than merely (to use a favourite expression of his) a good trooper. He studied his trade scientifically in its historical development. One day, at Potsdam, he gave a lecture on the theory and practice of Roman tactics, illustrating it with examples on plans. An expert of the school of war could not have done it better.

How well he kept and still keeps order in the army, innumerable anecdotes testify. He is not an easy master to serve. He does not spare himself, and he will not see his officers do otherwise. He sets his face rigidly against gentling or luxurious habits, and once offered to resign his command rather than rescind a sentence he had passed on one of his men found guilty of high play. His standard is high and Spartan.

On Christmas Eve, 1887, the last that was to see him Prince, while distributing the usual presents to the regiment, he spoke of the sadness and anxiety of the moment, of the illness of his father, whom he called "one of our greatest generals." He asked for their prayers for the return to health of "this high Seigneur." "This is a moment to think on the ancient device which we bear on our heads: 'With God for King and country,' but above all 'With God!' . . . May God, who has always helped our army, dwell with us for the King and the country! . . . You belong to the great army, to the great family of which the King is father. You are here in your little family, the regiment. I wish, as far as possible, to replace your natural family. That is why I have prepared for your Christmas, like a father for his children. I hand you these presents while wishing you a happy New Year. May you be throughout the year faithful and good hussars, and never forget that His Majesty the Emperor holds as the three pillars of the army—courage, the sentiment of honour, and obedience. To express this sentiment let us shout together: 'Long live His Majesty the Emperor and King, our most gracious Commander-in-Chief.'"

Such speeches repeated and commented upon have gained for the Prince the reputation of being before everything a soldier.

The Emperor has lately manifested a new side of his character. There exists in Berlin a society which attempts to reconcile the poor with their lot by giving them alms and good advice. The intention is praiseworthy, but it runs the risk of being misinterpreted. Besides, the religion of the "Town Mission" takes a political turn, and wages war against Liberalism as if it were a form of irreligion.

The apostle of this work is a clergyman, who is wanting in two of the principal Christian virtues—charity towards his opponents, and modesty. One of the principal personages in the society is General Waldersee, Count Moltke's successor. He is married to an American, a daughter of General Lee, who is very zealous in the work undertaken by this little "Salvation Army." Madame Waldersee is connected with the family of the Empress through a former marriage with an Augustenburg. She enjoys the affection of the

Empress, who is very religious, and the two families are on terms of intimacy. Indeed, the General, outside military circles, is chiefly notable on account of this American wife. Lord Dufferin once remarked that the importation of American ladies as the wives of European diplomatists was one of the most subtle means by which the New World was subjugating the Old, that there is hardly a capital of Europe that does not boast an American woman as one of its chief ornaments, and that some day the Old World will have to put a heavy protective tariff on this import of American heiresses. It is certain that the Emperor William, quite unsusceptible hitherto to the intellectual influence of any woman, has been much influenced by Countess Waldersee, and above all she has attracted him to give active support to the " Mission."

One evening a meeting of notables from all parts of Germany was held at General Waldersee's, with a view to raising funds for the "Mission." The General opened the meeting. He explained the character of this enterprise, which was committed to no party, adding, however, that the "Mission" proposed to propagate the sentiment of fidelity to the King, and the spirit of patriotism. After which Prince William said: " The only way of protecting the throne and the altar against the tendencies of an anarchist and infidel party, is to reclaim the masses to Christianity and the church, and by that means to respect for authority and love of the monarchy."

This speech made a great impression. Pastor Stoecker thanked the Prince and Princess William for having "boldly worked for the kingdom of God," expressing himself in terms of considerable familiarity towards both the Almighty and the Prince.

This little incident widened yet further the breach between Prince William and his parents. They were of the party supreme in Berlin, where "the kingdom of God," as proclaimed by Stoecker, the Jew baiter, the propagator of intolerance, is regarded with suspicion. Berlin, *the town of intelligence*, the town in all the world where there are the fewest churches and the fewest professing Christians, above all resents this man's pretensions. The Berliners will bow before the throne as much as you like, but not before the altar. A man devoted to the Chancellor, hot against the progressionists, one of those who counted the days the Emperor Frederick still had to live, said: "If Prince William takes the Pastor Stoecker into his confidence, no one will bow to him in the streets of Berlin."

Since his accession his zeal for the "Mission" has not abated, but his friendship with Stoecker has been less pronounced. One of the few acts of the Emperor Frederick's brief reign was to remove this man from his post of Court chaplain; and the present Emperor has in his turn been obliged once or twice to reprove him in consequence of his publicly boasting of the support which he counted on from the Empress.

Meantime this was how the Prince prepared himself

for his *rôle* of third German Emperor. To learn civil administration he worked for a winter with the President of the Province of Brandenburg, studying local and provincial government. He took a seat in a district Diet and a provincial Diet. He made reports, and took part in the discussions. The representatives of the Province of Brandenburg, that cradle of monarchy, testified their recognition of the honour done them. In thanking them he praised their patriotism and their invincible attachment to his family through good and evil days: "Happen what may, the Brandenburgians will never separate from us, nor we from the Brandenburgians."

The Prince is quick and intelligent, and he thoroughly took in the affairs which were discussed before him. But this civil and political education occupied a very small place in his life. Doubtless both he and his family thought he had plenty of time before him. To all appearance he would be, like his father, long an heir. When the death of William, and the illness of Frederick III., brought him near the throne, he felt the necessity of completing this education. The mission of teaching politics to this Emperor of the morrow was entrusted to a distinguished politician, a ci-devant Liberal, who was to give him three lessons a week.

But before the pupil could avail himself of these lessons, he was already called on to become the arbiter of his nation's politics.

In June, 1888, died that noble father, a martyr to a

remorseless disease, having followed his own aged sire all too quickly to the tomb.

Eagerly the son picked up the reins of government, after which his fingers had long been itching, and since that date the incalculable individuality for the German Emperor, his restless activity, his *volte faces*, his impetuosity, his boundless self-confidence, his vaulting ambition, his autocratic ways, have been the theme of wonder, comment, and criticism. The early months of his reign certainly did not help to ingratiate him with a non-German public. They were characterized by a series of scandals, acts of want of consideration to Frederick's widow and Frederick's memory, which if not actually instigated by the Emperor, were more or less countenanced and fomented by him. It was evident that his sudden accession to power had excited a temperament naturally mettlesome, and that he had not yet learnt to deal in a spirit of dignified calm with the multitude of new sensations and impressions that poured in on him from all sides.

Even now, after two years of government, it seems too early to decide what nature of ruler William II. will prove to Germany, but one thing appears certain, and that is, that it is his wish to be a personal ruler, who intends to give expression to his positive will and positive views. This was remarked in his first speech from the throne, where he substituted the pronoun *I* for the traditional *we*. During his brief reign he has certainly already displayed an energy and a passion for work which has almost a fevered character, and which has made those about him alarmed lest he should be overtaxing his strength; but Count Douglas, one of his favourites and confidants, has publicly assured the world that it need have no fears on this score, for that his methodical habits enable him to get through much labour.

That he is a gifted young sovereign, the world is almost beginning to be inclined to believe, though the multiplicity of tasks attempted by him, the Gordian knots he tries to untie, the Augean stables he attempts to cleanse, and all in a brief moment, frighten the prudent. He is either a great genius or a great danger for the world, and even though he be as gifted as his admirers proclaim, he has not yet proved that he can afford to dispense with the check imposed by the prudence and longer experience of older and less impetuous men. His brusque dismissal of Prince Bismarck bewildered even his partisans, and gave his critics no little right to accuse him of ingratitude towards an old tried servant, even though he was a servant-master. The man who for thirty-six years managed the House of Hohenzollern, and created modern Germany from out the chaos in which the numberless small states existed, merited at least a more delicate treatment at the hand of the youngest and least experienced of his three masters, even if delicacy and regard for others had never been a distinguishing feature of the servant's character. Even if, as it appears, the aims and aspirations of the Emperor had become incompatible with the political methods of his Chancellor, and that consequently a separation was inevitable, this separation should have been managed with less *éclat*. But clearly the Emperor William II. does not shirk publicity for good or evil. His psychology is certainly a curious study, and Europe watches with some astonishment, and no little anxiety, the acts and deeds of the son of Frederick III. It cannot yet understand the abnormal mixture of contradictory qualities exhibited by his conduct, his insatiable activity, combined with a marked tendency to reverie, almost to mysticism, his extraordinary taste for military affairs, his autocracy, and, on the other hand, the passionate initiative he has taken in humanitarian and social reforms, of which the realization seems totally irreconcilable with the existence of an autocratic and military State.

The only point in his character that seems to stand out clearly is the determination to carry out his will and to break down all resistance, no matter of what kind. "What will he do next?" people ask, for the public has had too many surprises not to expect fresh ones.

One can but hope that they will be of a happy nature, and will not interfere with the tranquillity of the world. Certain it is that it is with William II., and with him alone, that Germany and Europe have to deal. An inexperienced hand is guiding the government of a great Empire in a moment of great crisis. This is cause enough to make the thoughtful anxious. William II. has been compared more than once to Frederick the Great, and certainly one of the first labours of that king was to dismiss all the old servants of his father. But none of these servants bore the name and character of Bismarck. If, as is possible, the young Emperor does not falsify the great hopes he has aroused in his fatherland, and emulates in peace and war his great ancestor, it is indubitable that for the present he chiefly resembles him in one thing, and that is youthful impetuosity.

The future alone will show how he will develop, how his position will affect his character, and what bearing his character will have upon the welfare of his own land and of Europe. It is certain that he has, in a well-pronounced degree, the Hohenzollern self-belief in a divinely appointed mission, and he is perhaps the only younger sovereign now sitting upon a civilized throne who sincerely believes that he sits there by the grace of God. The result of such ideas held in the late nineteenth century, time alone can show.

THE KING OF ITALY.

THE KING OF ITALY.
(*From a Photograph by Vianelli.*)

THE KING OF ITALY.

THERE have probably been few monarchs whose death called forth such spontaneous demonstrations of real loyal affection, who have been sorrowed for so sincerely by all their subjects, as Victor Emanuel, the first King of Liberated Italy. It was not merely that in him the young kingdom lost the chivalrous sovereign who had learnt to make himself and his people loved and respected throughout the whole European continent; with him perished also the visible embodiment of the making of their beloved land, of the expulsion of the justly-detested *straniero* (stranger). With his demise the romance of the nation's youth, so to speak, came to an end; with him expired the era of enthusiasm, of ebullition, of creation. It now behoved the nation to set in order the house it had so nobly reconquered as its own. It became needful to justify before the other peoples the Italian claim that she would and could act for herself (*farà da sè*). An era of prose, of hard, strenuous work, of self-abnegation, must follow on lyric enthusiasm and the flash and glitter of patriotic war. It was a task no less difficult than that conducted to so glorious an issue by Victor Emanuel which awaited his son and successor, and of its full gravity he was doubtless aware when, in those early days of January, 1878, Umberto (late Prince of Piedmont, now second King of Italy) issued his brief but heartfelt proclamation to his new subjects. He told them how he should be mindful of the grand example his father had set him of devotion to Italy, love of progress, and faith in Liberal institutions—a faith that has ever been the pride of the ancient knightly House of Savoy, from which the Italian kings spring. "My sole ambition," he concluded, "will be to deserve the love of my people." And when, some days after, the people assembled beneath the balconies of the Quirinal and hailed him King with great enthusiasm, while the news of similar demonstrations reached him from all the provinces, Umberto, deeply moved, embraced the Prince of Naples, saying, "My son, I swear to you to live in suchwise, that at my death you may be proclaimed King with similar devotion."

And it is beyond dispute that Umberto has maintained the promise made in that solemn moment. Umberto is beloved of his people, and if not popular in the same manner as his father, there is no difference in degree. He has proved himself no unworthy descendant of the proud House of Savoy, whence he has sprung.

Umberto I., second King of Italy, was born at Turin, March 14, 1844, on the anniversary of the same day that had given birth to his father, Victor Emanuel. His mother was Maria Adelaide, daughter of Archduke Ranieri, then Viceroy of Lombardy and Venice. Thus in the veins of Italy's King runs some of the hated Austrian blood—the blood of that cruel oppressor of Italian soil of whom, happily, all vestige has vanished from the fair peninsula. The Princess was a very sweet and charming woman, and an excellent wife and mother, who watched with tender care over the education of her children, being herself their teacher, ever present at their studies, their recreations, their meals. In educating them she followed the principles of the House of Savoy, which requires its sons to be robust and courageous. Ancestry-worship is a family characteristic of the Savoy family, and its children have always been nourished upon the traditions of its ancestral heroes, and taught that they ought to endeavour to resemble them to the best of their ability. Their family motto runs, "Fear and Savoy have never met."

Early in 1855, when Umberto was but eleven years old, he and his brothers and sisters were deprived of her gentle guiding hand. Queen Adelaide was carried off by an early death, leaving behind her a void that was never filled. Her children were now left to the exclusive care of their father and of strangers. Both did their duty, but the strangers were always strangers, and the father was in the very thick and hurry of the liberation of the peninsula, and could not look after his children. But they saw enough of him to become imbued with his ardour, his honourable ambition, his devotion to his native land; and the great historic events that rapidly succeeded each other in those years could not fail to leave their impress upon their young and ardent minds. While Umberto and his beloved brother Amedeo prosecuted their literary and scientific studies, they longed for the hour to strike when they too could consecrate their youthful fire and love of country to their country's cause They had early been inspired by their father with enthusiasm for Italy's liberation, and as quite lads he had initiated them into military and political life.

In 1859, while still but a boy, Umberto was to be found beside his father on those battlefields which decided the future fate of Italy. He was also sent very little later on political missions of the greatest consequence. It was he who took a leading part in the reorganization of the kingdom of the Two Sicilies, and July, 1862, saw him in Naples and Palermo, amil a population celebrating with *fêtes* and joy their reconquered liberty. A little before the outbreak of the war with Austria, the Prince of Piedmont went to Paris to sound the French Government as to its sentiments concerning the alliance, then actually concluded, between Italy and Prussia. Action soon followed upon negotiations.

The moment came in 1866, when, on one June day at dawn, the Italian army put itself in motion, and the first shots were exchanged at two extreme points at the same moment—that is, before Villafranca, between the division led by Prince Umberto and the Austrian cavalry regiment led by General Pubz, and under Peschiera at Monte Croce, where fought also Prince Amedeo, and where he received not only his baptism of fire, but also his first wound. From this time forward Umberto was always in the field with his troops when occasion required; and occasion required it right often in those stirring times. And one of his first acts—to his honour be it told—was to declare that he renounced his stipend as a general, not desiring, he said, to add a further burden to the budget of his heavily burdened country. At Custozza, Nino Bixio was only just in time to save him from inevitable danger, so fearlessly had he exposed himself to the enemy.

"I shall never forgive you for not letting me manage this affair alone," was the first impetuous answer given by the Prince, after the general had pointed out to him the risk he had run.

It was not till he was twenty-four that a bride was chosen for Umberto. Heirs-apparent are not usually allowed to remain unwedded so long, but it so happened that death had carried off the wife destined for him, a young Hapsburg Archduchess. In 1868, however, Victor Emanuel grew uneasy at this single state of his heir, whose younger brother was already provided with a wife. He one day told his Prime Minister, General Menabrea, that he absolutely must find a wife for Umberto. To this peremptory command the soldier quietly remarked that she was already found; there was wanting only the will of his Majesty and the consent of the Prince. The lady on whom the general had fixed was the Princess Margherita, daughter of the Duke of Genoa, the brave brother of Victor Emanuel, whom consumption had too early borne away from his family and fatherland. She had been carefully educated, according to her father's dying instructions, *in patria*, for he had a great faith in early impressions, and wished his children to love their country as he and his brother did. She was at the time a lovely girl of eighteen, delicately fair, with eyes of a deeper blue than usually accompanies a blonde complexion, and a smile of bewitching sweetness. Indeed, Margherita's smile has become famous. It is always ready in answer to the loyal and affectionate feelings of her people, and goes staight to the hearts of the Italians, to whom she has endeared herself in an extraordinary degree. When Victor Emanuel first heard this suggestion he was surprised. He had never thought of his niece in this light. He asked the general to tell him something about the qualities of the Princess, and what had suggested the idea to him. Menabrea then related to him a number of anecdotes illustrating the Princess's noble disposition, strength of character, and delicacy of feeling, and enlarged on the advantage of securing this charming daughter of Savoy to the Italian nation before she was carried off by the Prince of Roumania, who was about to offer her his hand. All he heard greatly pleased the King, and, striking the table with his fist, as he often did when excited, exclaimed, "Bravo! From all you have related I recognize in her the Savoy blood. Now that you have told me so many nice things about my niece I will go and assure myself of it personally."

No sooner said than done, he set out for Turin at once, and arrived unexpectedly at the palace of the Duchess of Genoa. His conversation with the Princess satisfied him that her charms had not been overrated. The marriage was therefore arranged, and was celebrated in April, 1868, at Turin, with great pomp, in presence of the whole royal family. An ugly incident, however, marred the harmony of the proceeding. The officiating priest, the Bishop of Savona, whether by accident or design—more probably the latter, as the Catholic clergy lose no opportunity of flaunting their pretended ignorance of the march of modern Italian events—referred in his address to the wound the bridegroom had received in his first action in the field. It was Amedeo who had been wounded, not Umberto, and the latter looked deeply mortified, as he had to allow this allusion and the unctuous laudation with which it was accompanied to pass unrefuted over his head.

It was during one of the balls held in honour of these nuptials that the late Emperor Frederick of Germany conceived his sentimental adoration for Queen Margherita. A piece of her dress being torn and annoying her as she danced, the Prince drew from his pocket a "housewife," extracted a pair of scissors, cut off the offending bit, pinned up the rent, and finally carried off the rag as a trophy. As is known, he loved Italy sincerely, and never lost an opportunity of going there and visiting his good friends Margherita and Umberto. To one of his own daughters the Queen of Italy stood godmother, and she bears her name.

At the time of his marriage the Prince of Piedmont can scarcely be said to have been popular. For one thing he was overshadowed by his father's great popularity and that parent's *bonhomie* and general pleasant ways, of which he did not possess a trace. Moreover, the Prince had earned for himself the reputation of a gay character, and though this is by no means held a reproach in Italy, where manners and morals are lax, still, what in his father—no model of the domestic virtues—was willingly overlooked, was criticized rather sharply in Umberto's case. He was, of course, as yet untried in public life, and had still to gain a title to the gratitude and forbearance of the nation. His manners, moreover, were not conciliatory. Being of a reserved and undemonstrative nature, he had no aptitude for exchanging the small attentions which the Italians call *moine*, and which go a long way in winning their affections. Consequently, he was popular only so far as that he was his father's son and a Savoy Prince, and that he had proved himself a true soldier in the campaign of 1866. But this was enough to call forth great rejoicings on the occasion of his marriage, and to sustain the hope that when the time came to act he would prove himself a worthy successor of the great founder of Italian independence. That hope has been justified. Umberto has shown himself a man of excellent sense, tact, and good feeling; and he has gradually and quietly grown into the heart of the nation, where he now reigns supreme.

Victor Emanuel was very fond of his heir. "I know Umberto," he said once; "he is an excellent youth; he has good sense and a good heart. He will do well." One of his Ministers relates the following anecdote. Returning from Milan, where he had an interview with the Prince, he repeated the conversation to the King in all its particulars, even to some expressions of affection which the young man had used in speaking of his father. The King listened with pleased attention. Just then a letter was handed to him, which proved to be from his son. When he had read, he turned to the Minister with visible emotion, and said, "You are right. I wish you to read this letter; you will see how Umberto writes to me. In my family no one knows how to feign, much less when they are twenty years old. You are right in what you tell me."

Subsequent events have proved how unfeigned, how profound, was Umberto's affection for his father, and it is satisfactory to know that they understood one another.

On the occasion of the Crown Prince's marriage Victor Emanuel instituted the order of the Corona d'Italia, which is accorded for merit of whatever kind. After making a triumphal tour through the chief Italian cities —excluding, of course, Rome—the bride and bridegroom settled down to live quietly at Turin. A year and a half later, at a time when Victor Emanuel's life hung on a thread, was born to them their heir and only child, also named Victor Emanuel, after his grandfather, to whom was accorded the title of Prince of Naples, from the place of his birth.

When Rome became Italian, the Prince and Princess of Piedmont also moved thither to live in the Quirinal, and it was then that the young Princess gradually so conquered her father-in-law's good graces that she acquired great influence over him, causing him to conform a little more than he was wont to do the conventionalities and usages of society. It was a difficult position the Princess was called on to fill. Countess Mirafiore, Victor Emanuel's morganatic wife, claimed to rule the house and take her place in society as wife. As a woman not only not of royal birth, but entirely of the people, this was clearly out of the question; nor could such an insult be put upon the proud old Roman nobility. These, on the other hand, demanded that their King should hold some sort of Court, and a Court without a woman to preside over it is an impossibility. Victor Emanuel himself was wont to quote the words of Henry of Navarre—"A Court without a Queen is like a springtime without flowers." But it was not till after Victor Emanuel's death that Margherita took her full place at the Court, and part of the enthusiasm felt by the Italian people for their Queen may be traced to the fact that she is the first Queen this land has known, and it is beyond question that her grace, her beauty, make her fill the post with a charm that captivates all beholders.

One of Umberto's first acts on ascending the throne earned for him well-merited praise. As is well known, Victor Emanuel was most extravagant, not so much in the gratification of his private tastes—which, except for women and horses, were simple—as because his charities, his open-handedness, knew no bounds. It was found on his death that his debts were very considerable, and it was proposed in Parliament, in the first enthusiasm after his loss, that the State should pay these. To this, however, Umberto opposed a firm negative, declaring that his father's debts were his, and that he should undertake the liquidation. And instantly he set about reducing all needless expenditure in the various palaces, selling a number of superfluous horses and restricting outlays in every mode possible; and this, helped by an able major-domo, he carried through so successfully that not only has he paid his father's debts and pensioned his father's numerous dependents, but he has always a good sum in hand on which he can draw to subscribe towards any national charity or disaster, or to encourage art and science, whenever it lies in his power. The only person given to extravagance at the present Court is perhaps the Queen, who shares the feeling of her countrywomen in having an inordinate love for dress—a matter in which she unfortunately sets her subjects a bad example, encouraging them yet further to dress beyond their means. For

Queen Margherita gives the tone in these matters to Italian society, and it is to be deplored that her influence is not exerted in the direction of greater simplicity, as well as of intellectual enlightenment. But Queen Margherita is a Catholic, and a daughter of the House of Savoy—ever noted for clerical leanings—and she cannot reconcile herself to the feud that exists between the monarchy and the church. She has at various times attempted conciliations which have drawn down on her some reproach, and have caused her to lose in some quarters a little of her high favour. A point, however, on which all are unanimous in her praise, is that of her personal morality. Whatever may have to be said about her husband, against her own conjugal fidelity no one has ever dared to breathe a word, or has been able to do so; and that is saying much for Italy, where pure reputations in men and women are not easily believed in. Not even in the most vile and fire-spitting Republican newspaper has there ever been recounted any tale that could cast a doubt on the Queen's honour—and these papers in Italy are not chary of lies. Beyond a question, Margherita of Savoy has a high conception of her duties as Queen, wife, and mother; and, above all, she, like her husband, has close at heart the glory, the good repute, of that ancient House of Savoy, to which they both belong, and which they feel (and rightly) has been ennobled yet more by the aggrandisement of Italy, by all that Italy has suffered, won, and done under its banner.

It was a great shock to both sovereigns when, a year after his accession, an attempt was made on the King's life, while making his solemn entry into Naples, by a cook called Passanante. He was driving in an open carriage with the Queen and Benedetto Cairoli, then Prime Minister. The latter, sitting opposite, and seeing the attack, managed so skilfully that the stroke glanced away from the monarch and wounded him instead. The indignation of the whole nation proved how much beloved Umberto had already made himself during his brief tenure of office; and the receptions the royal couple met with after, both in Rome and Naples, were the more remarkable as at that moment the anarchist international movement was specially rife in Italy. Indeed, this dastardly attack did much to quench it. As for the culprit, after long discussions as to his mental state he was condemned to death, but the clemency of King Umberto changed this verdict into hard labour for life, a clemency that was the more noted at the time, as almost contemporaneously, for a similar attempt, Moncasi had been executed at Madrid. Passanante has since been transferred from his prison to a lunatic asylum.

The Passanante incident had unfortunately rather a sad epilogue. The Queen, who at the time was in weak health, caused greatly by mental trouble, was so unnerved by the event that she fell into a state of nervous prostration which lasted some months, and seriously alarmed the court. She saw an evil augury in the act, and kept repeating constantly, "The poetry of the House of Savoy is ended." Happily time restored her to health, but for many years she was not strong.

As a ruler Umberto has every year given more satisfaction to his people as he has gained in insight and judgment. His father, founder of the Italian monarchy, had chosen his Ministers from out the Moderate party until two years before his death, when he gave the government into the hands of the Left. The Moderate party had for their opponents Garibaldi and Mazzini, who had immense influence over the masses. Victor Emanuel, as is well known, found himself several times at odds with Garibaldi, whose impetuous nature and unphilosophical brain could not comprehend the requirements of diplomacy. He had even seen himself obliged to arrest and imprison him after the illegal attempts of Aspromonte and Mentana. As for Mazzini, he was kept out of Italy during the whole reign of King Victor Emanuel under penalty of death, although on several occasions the King and the republican agitator exchanged letters, and sometimes even acted in concert. For these reasons Victor Emanuel, notwithstanding his great prestige, could sometimes hear himself hissed by the crowd. This has never happened to his son Umberto, who, having always ruled with the Left and the Radicals in conformity, however, always with the wishes of the Chamber, has provoked at times the quiet murmurs of the Conservatives, but has always had the acclamations of the multitude. He may boast of being the only man generally respected in Italy. In studying the acts of his life, one sees in him a king who would have the noble ambition to do doughty deeds like to his father, and who has the same loyalty towards the Constitution of his land. He is a man who, in circumstances demanding heroism, would be a hero, and be so without artifice or claptrap, simply and naturally, because his nature is truly good and heroic. In fact, his character might be summed up in the word "Courage!" Not even among his ancestors were there any more dominated by their family motto, "Avanti Savoia." When during the cholera epidemic he fearlessly visited the worst cases, the dirtiest slums, he was amazed extremely to find his conduct lauded. Again and again he repeated, almost impatiently, "I have done nothing but my duty."

In every disaster that happens in his country the King is the first on the spot, aiding not only with his purse but with his person, inspiring by his example, his intrepidity. It may almost be said of him that he has been born too late. Our century does not lend itself to heroic deeds; it asks other qualities from its sovereigns. Italy is a poor country, impoverished also by the crises it has had to pass through in order to effect its unity. It has, besides, many provinces which civilization has hardly reached, and where education is but commencing its labours. Such a land has need of rest, of quiet work, of wise and prudent administrators; has need of statesmen of superior intelligence and acumen. Now, as regards intelligence, King Umberto cannot be put at a high level. Louis Philippe used to say, "All tell me I ought to do my duty; but the difficulty does not consist in doing my duty, but in knowing what this duty is." Like his *confrère*, Umberto is most sincerely anxious to do his duty, but he is continually tormented by uncertainty. He solves a situation by following closely the sentiment given by the passing votes of the Chamber, and in accordance with the solicitations of his Ministers, who are naturally more inclined to favour the temporary interests of their own party rather than the permanent interests of the State. It is said that he is always enthusiastic about the Prime Minister in office; he was so for Cairoli, for Depretis; he is so for Crispi. The persons who approach him for the first time are struck with his language, for he bursts out with the most astonishingly free judgments on what is happening in national and international politics. But this frankness of speech, most undiplomatic and unroyal, covers the timidity of a man who is not very sure of his own judgments. De Zerbi, an Italian writer, once called Umberto, Athelstan the Unready. As a result of his thirst for heroic deeds, Italy is perhaps indebted for her hapless African policy and wars, where she has been carried into adventures beyond her strength to conduct or carry through. One of the King's indubitable merits is to know how to deal with the masses, and how always on such occasions to find the right word to say, a word that goes straight to the heart of his warm-natured Italian subjects, and which causes the noblest chords of patriotism to vibrate. And this comes about because he himself is a man of heart, a sincere patriot, and because the glories and sorrows of the Italian nation for the past forty years are also the glories and the sorrows of his family. Like his forbears, he has no political philosophy, no book-learning; but this want is compensated for by a straightness of vision, and a rare good sense. A Savoyard, a Piedmontese, he hates phraseology and empty speech, and exaggerated inflated phrases. He must often suffer, no doubt, under the wordy exuberance of his Neapolitan subjects, who love him nevertheless, and whom he loves in return.

As a boy, Umberto was extremely thin—as the princes of his house are wont to be—and as a young man he was delicate, having abused the pleasures of life. He modelled his manners on those of his father, but he had not his father's robust fibre, which allowed him to carry both pleasure and work to excess. In the course of years he has grown stouter and stronger, but he has aged prematurely. For some few years past he has been quite bald. At one time he smoked to excess; but one day, his doctors having prescribed abstention from tobacco, he completely renounced the habit. It is recounted that when the advice was given that he should give up smoking for a time, he answered, " On my kingly honour I will never smoke again." And he has kept his word. Without leading the mountaineer's life affected by his father, his greatest pleasure consists in passing whole weeks under canvas in the mountains of the valley of Aosta, stalking the chamois, eating the same hard fare as the peasants. Like Victor Emanuel, Umberto loves an open-air life and exercises that fatigue the body. He rises at early dawn, and defies all weathers with indifference. Even when dressed in civilian costume he does not hesitate to allow a heavy downpour to wet him to the skin rather than raise an umbrella, nor does he shrink from standing for hours, if need be, under the scorching rays of the sun on the occasion of some popular *fête*, mocking at those who seek shade and shelter. This carelessness to excesses of weather is one of the characteristic notes of the royal house of Italy. He can in no sense be called an aristocratic monarch; indeed, a democratic king would be the title that describes him best, were this epithet not almost a contradiction in terms.

Of the beauty of Queen Margherita all the world has heard. Without having perfect features, she has been and still is beautiful, thanks to the delicacy of her complexion, the grace of her outlines, the sweetness of her expression. Early in life she, too, was very delicate, and so thin as to be almost transparent; but in the course of years she has grown stouter, and now may be said to be too stout for beauty. Her German mother was careful to give the daughter a thorough education, superior to that enjoyed in those days by Italian women. Queen Margherita knows both German and Italian literature well, is fond of music, and sings herself with taste and feeling. She has a pronounced affection for the German school of melody, but she also appreciates the Italian. She is fond of the society of men of thought and letters, and at her intimate evening teas may be met some of the leading men of the land, who drop in to chat away an hour without ceremony. Indeed, the absence of ceremony, destructive to all reasonable intercourse, is a distinctive and charming feature of the Italian Court life.

Among those whom the Queen loved to receive was the late Minister Minghetti, a simple gentlemanly burgher, who was well versed in questions of art and letters. Another of her well-liked *habitués* is Bonghi, the statesman and man of letters; also Professor Villari, senator and historian. She has even known how to gain over to her Italy's greatest living poet, Giosuè Carducci, who began life as a rabid republican and hater of royalty. To the amazement of all his friends, Carducci one day published an ode written to the Queen, one of his most beautiful, too, in which he expressed sentiments of loyalty and admiration which no courtier could have surpassed. This act made the poet lose much ground with his republican friends, but he did not therefore diminish his *cultus* for the Queen, who often sees him and discusses with him on literary themes. Recently, on the occasion of the inauguration of a new scheme of municipal elections throughout the kingdom, Carducci happened to find himself for some days head of the

Bologna municipality. His first act was to send a telegram to the Queen in the name of this municipality. Indeed, a sentimental *cultus* for the Queen, their first Queen, is widespread among the Italians, and her name, Margherita (Daisy), is symbolized in many ways, and the daisy emblem occurs in every form of festive decoration. Her own favourite emblem is the pearl, of which she wears strings upon strings around her neck, so that by her rows of pearls the Queen can always be recognized if by no other sign. And yearly this row of pearls grows richer, for the King, who shares the Queen's half barbarian love of precious stones, adds annually a string to the precious necklet, until it now descends far below her waist, and has really lost some of its elegant and decorative character. Malicious tongues whisper that the Queen so clings to this adornment because it hides a tendency to *goitre* with which she is afflicted, in common with many Savoyards.

A very cordial friendship exists between King and Queen; and the former relies much on his wife's judgment, which is frequently clear and sound. Some pretty anecdotes are told of their domestic life. Thus the Queen was anxious that her husband should follow the example of his father, and the fashion common among elderly Piedmontese officers, and dye his hair, which has become quite white. Her pleadings were in vain. Umberto's is an honest nature, that does not love these subterfuges. Seeing petition was in vain, the Queen had recourse to stratagem. She caused a quantity of fine hair-dye to be sent from Paris and put in the King's dressing-room, together with directions for its use, making, however, no allusion to the subject. The King, too, said nothing, though he could not fail to have seen the pigments. Now the Queen has a large white poodle of which she is very fond. What was her horror, a few days later, to see her pet come running into her room with his candid locks of the deepest black hue! King Umberto had expended the dyes upon the poodle. From that day forth the subject of hair-dyeing was dropped between the royal couple. On yet another occasion the husband gave the wife one of those quiet rebuffs into which enters a sense of humour, and which are on that account less hard to bear. It appears that Umberto once asked one of the Queen's secretaries what would be an acceptable Christmas present for her Majesty. This gentleman, a truer friend than courtier, had the courage to suggest to the King that the Queen had a large number of unpaid milliners' and dressmakers' bills. The King took the hint, and begged that they should all be given to him. On Christmas morning Umberto placed all these bills, receipted, under the Queen's table-napkin. There was no other present besides. It is said that she took the hint, and has been less extravagant since. Both the King and Queen are fond of petty gossip, and on their informal receptions—held on Sunday evening, to which all may drop in who have the *entrée* to their house—it is quite strange to hear them always asking after the local news, and to see how well they are posted up in all the latest scandals. In this, too, they could set a better example, for Italian society is far too much inclined to gossip and dealing with personalities.

Rome is, of course, the usual residence of the sovereigns; but when Parliament is not sitting Monza, near Milan, is one of their favourite residences. The Queen also much affects both Naples and Venice, and of late years has developed a taste for mountain climbing, and often visits the districts around Aosta and Cadore, Titian's country. She is an excellent walker and an intrepid climber, and herein she sets a good example to her female subjects, who are usually indolent in these respects. Some considerable time, however, is always given to Monza, and this because, as the sovereigns themselves say, they can enjoy greater liberty there than anywhere else. The Lombard population is naturally considerate and not inclined to trouble the royal family by undesired importunities, to which must be added that the ladies of the Milanese aristocracy are not well inclined to the Queen, whom they reproach with making few advances to them, and with loving them but little. It really seems that on the side of the Queen there is a want of cordiality towards the Milanese ladies; something in their tone and bearing is antipathetic to her. This brings it about that at Monza she only sees her real intimates; and is not therefore obliged to hold receptions. And even when royal personages stop at Monza the visit has always something of an intimate and private character. During their stay here the royal couple frequently invite their friends either to meals or to stop a few days with them, these friends being persons chosen from all social classes — deputies, senators, high functionaries, literary men, and artists. The hospitality is regal, and yet simple. The guests are met at the station by a royal carriage, which again reconducts them on their departure, a set of rooms and a servant are placed at their disposal, and the rules of the house are put before them. The first of these rules, which must be kept, is the luncheon hour of eleven, except on Sundays, when it is twelve, on account of the High Mass, which the whole royal family, their visitors, and servants all attend in the artistically decorated private chapel of the Palace, a chapel which is, however, generously thrown open to all the villagers, who are thus enabled to gaze their sweet fill upon their sovereigns; for the Italian King and Queen do not shrink from the gaze of their faithful subjects. If no royalties are present, the King gives his arm to the Queen to lead her in to luncheon, while the Prince of Naples gives his to the lady highest in dignity. After the meal, if fine, the whole company retire into the garden beside the lake. The Queen will take up her fancy work and chat with some guests in one group; the King, standing, will entertain another set in a separate circle. Or sometimes he takes them to row upon the water. After an hour, the Queen giving the signal, the company retire to the house and their own apartments until the time for driving out shall have come. If wet, the company remain together in the same way in one of the large reception-rooms. But whether out of doors or in, the two groups around the King and around the Queen never blend. The Queen's private sitting-room betrays her various tastes and interests. Books in many languages and on varied subjects not only fill the bookcases, but strew the chairs and tables, showing they are really used; stacks of music abound; fancy-work, finished and in course of making, meets the eye at every turn—for the Queen puts to good use the few hours she can call her own—and her quick intelligence and tenacious memory allow her to make the most of her reading.

In the afternoon drives the neighbourhood of Monza is ranged, and not only its beautiful sides, but also its flatter and less attractive districts, so that the natives have every chance of beholding their sovereigns several times at least during their sojourn among them. If wet, walks in the park are proposed, but these the royal family have often to take alone under their umbrellas, their household and guests being less hardy and less indifferent to the weather. At five, in the large entrance-hall, afternoon tea is served. This meal is partaken of without ceremony. No servants appear; one of the maids-of-honour pours out the tea, the gentlemen-in-waiting hand the sandwiches and cakes. After an hour's general and animated talk, the Queen once more retires until the late dinner-hour. After this meal all the ladies remain with the Queen, working, talking, making vocal and instrumental music, while the men follow the King and the Crown Prince into an adjoining room, where they talk, smoke, and play billiards—which game, besides chess and draughts, is the only one allowed in the establishment. Games of hazard are honourably excluded. A little after midnight the Queen rises to retire, after greeting each guest individually, and so ends a day at Monza, which resembles, on the whole, the days spent elsewhere by the sovereigns, except that here they have fewer social and public functions to attend.

Of the Prince of Naples little is known as yet, except that he adores his parents, and especially his mother, and is adored by her in return. She has nurtured him in the best traditions of his house, and one anecdote in especial about this has become a favourite theme for poetry and picture throughout Italy. Having gone to visit Palermo in company with her boy, it came about that on the return journey to Naples a great storm arose, and the commander feared for the safety of his precious freight. He consulted with the officers as to whether they had not best put back. It was decided to lay the matter before the Queen and abide by her decision. She happened to have in her hand a paper. Rapidly, without further hesitation, she wrote on it the words, "Sempre avanti Savoia," passing it on to the captain.

Pretty stories are told of him—how in his childhood

he saved up his pocket-money in order to buy her trinkets. He is a shy, retiring youth, who has developed late, but of whose heart and intelligence all who know him speak highly.

Like his father, he is frank of speech, and often narrates tales of the home life. Here is one. The King, in contrast to the Queen, is quite inartistic in his tastes, and, above all, has no ear for music. Of late the Queen has found it needful to wear glasses in order to read. These glasses annoy the King, who, when he sees them going up, says at once, "Margherita, put down those glasses." "Mama did not obey," says the Prince. "Then papa said, 'Margherita, if you don't take off those glasses, I shall sing.' And mama has such a dread of papa's false notes that she obeys at once to save herself from that torment."

His tutors praise his application; his military teachers his zeal and strict fidelity to duty. In appearance he resembles his mother, and like her he has the peculiarity of being short-legged, which makes him look when seated taller than he really is. Since his late journey to various European and Eastern Courts he has developed more independence, and is also drawn more to the fore. There is every reason to hope and think that he will prove no unworthy scion of that most ancient and honourable house of Savoy from which he has sprung, and that when his time comes he too will do his duty as Italy's King.

THE KING OF SPAIN.

THE KING OF SPAIN.

NO European country has had during the last half-century a more disturbed history than Spain, that kingdom once so proud, strong, and influential in the councils of Europe, and now of so little political moment, so left behind in the march of progress. Will it and its baby monarch advance together step by step to majority? Who can tell? It is certain that the land has been in a state of fermentation for many years. It saw itself constrained to depose Queen Isabella, whose life was a scandal even in a country not over squeamish on questions of morality. It could not settle down under the well-intentioned but timid and exotic rule of the foreigner Amedeo of Italy. It became after his enforced resignation the prey of rival factions, Government succeeding Government with bewildering rapidity—Republicans, Federalists, Constitutionalists, Carlists, and Alfonsists, all struggling for mastery.

In the end the Alfonsists triumphed, and in December, 1874, Alfonso, son of Queen Isabella, in whose favour she was induced to abdicate, ascended the tottering throne; the Bourbons thus returning in his person after six years of exile.

No easy post awaited this monarch of seventeen summers, called away from his mother's Christmas festivities to rule a distracted country, torn by civil war, the prey of factions. The one great legislative event of his reign was the passing of a new Constitution, a measure which annulled nearly all the benefits for progress gained by means of the previous revolutions, and which was and remains the *bête noire* of liberal Spain. It once more placed a Spaniard's liberty in the hands of the Government and, worse still, of the priests.

Hardly was this measure passed, when there arose the important political question of the King's marriage. His choice fell on his cousin Princess Mercedes, daughter of the Duke of Montpensier. But to this choice great family opposition was made. Queen Isabella hated her brother-in-law, and feared the influence of Mercedes upon Alfonso. But the young King was firm, and the story of his passion and the obstacles he had to overcome recall those of Romeo and Juliet, the Capulets and the Montagues. Alas! this marriage, which was a true love match, and offered every prospect of a happy union and of a beneficial influence upon the King's life, was dissolved all too soon by the Queen's death five months after the ceremony, in June, 1878.

This death was a terrible blow to the King, and one from which he recovered with difficulty, and it was a bitter pill to him that almost immediately the question of his re-marriage had to be urged upon him, State reasons making it imperative. And it was urged with the more insistance that Alfonso's health, always delicate, began to show signs of that general breaking up of the system which led to his early death.

Ministers took stock of the marriageable daughters of royal Europe and their choice fell upon a princess of the House of Hapsburg, a race pleasing to Queen Isabella and the Jesuits. The first meeting of the betrothed took place at Arcachon. When Alfonso entered the room of the villa in which his *fiancée* awaited him, his eyes fell on a fine portrait of Mercedes standing on her table. Involuntarily he drew nearer, and as he gazed on the beloved features a soft voice, half-choked with emotion, murmured at his side, " My dearest wish is to resemble her in all things, for if I must succeed her, I dare not hope to replace her."

The King did not answer, but the next morning she received a note, written in warm and heartfelt words, in which he told her that she had wrought a miracle, touched a hidden chord he had believed silent for evermore, and that if she consented, their union would be as much one of love as his former one.

This young Archduchess who had thus understood how to touch her future husband's heart is the daughter of the Princess Elizabeth, who has always been considered the most charming of the Austrian Archduchesses. The princess is a woman well advanced in years, and has been twice married to Austrian Archdukes and twice widowed. A special favourite with the Emperor, she embellishes the whole family life of the Hapsburgs by her wit, her physical charms, preserved even into mature middle age, and her social talents. Her children seem to have inherited some of her originality and force of character. Thus, her eldest son insisted upon making a love marriage, espousing in 1878 a daughter of the Duke of Croy, a marriage without precedent in Austrian royal annals, and which caused not a little flutter, as the Prince insisted that the union should be treated as an equal one, and his wife regarded as Archduchess.

It is his sister who is the present Queen Regent of Spain. The Princess was but twenty-one when she left Vienna to unite herself to Alfonso, and had, therefore, lacked time to take any important place in Austrian society. Nevertheless, it was felt by the Viennese Court that an attractive figure departed with the Archduchess Christina, who harboured a good heart, open to noble sentiments under a pleasing exterior. Not that the Queen of Spain inherits her mother's beauty; she is rather charming, with great distinction and *chic* in gait and mien. The Archduchess Elizabeth is a tall commanding figure with a head of the Maria Theresa type; her daughter, on the contrary, is but of middle height, fair, and gentle. At the time of her marriage her diffident bearing and look led none to suppose that she possessed a tittle of the energy that distinguishes her mother and renders her so attractive. As a young girl at Vienna the Archduchess Christina interested herself much in the Fine Arts, and especially in music. There was no great representation at the Opera, no concert at which she did not appear, accompanied by her mother. But in public life she took no part, and was only seen on the most official occasions, when the presence of the whole royal family was indispensable. She dearly loved retirement. This and her general refinement of manner made her a great favourite with the Emperor, and he and all the family were much grieved at her departure.

The departure of the Archduchess from Vienna to join her affianced husband in Spain, where the marriage ceremony took place, was most sad. All the Archdukes and duchesses were present; they embraced her tenderly and waved her last farewells. The Emperor could not await the departure of the train: his emotion was too much for him. As for the bride herself, her eyes were red with tears, and only sadness was to be read upon her face. Had she perchance a presentiment of the hard destiny that awaited her? And that makes it doubtful whether to her can be applied the famous saying, "Tu, felix Austria, nube."

The marriage was celebrated with much pomp at the old sanctuary of Atocha, the King meeting his bride as soon as she touched Spanish soil.

For some while after her arrival at Madrid it seemed uncertain what place the Queen would take in the Spanish Court and in Spanish hearts. For her subjects she had one great defect: she was not a Spaniard—an unpardonable sin in the eyes of this proud people, who still fondly imagine that they are the first nation in the world, and remain sublimely unconscious of the fact that their *rôle* in Continental politics has been effaced, that they have been left centuries behind in culture, and that even more than Turkey, if possible, they are in the affairs of Europe a *quantité négligeable*. They still fancy themselves of the importance they once had in the days of Charles V. and Isabella the Catholic. It is difficult to decide whether this attitude, based upon crass ignorance, be more pitiable or more ludicrous.

Coming from a Court mediæval enough in tone, but yet not quite so far behind as that of Castile, Queen Christina seemed too much a woman of to-day to satisfy her courtiers devoted to the traditions of a fossil past. Another fault she had in their eyes; she was not communicative. In a land where all are expansive, Queen Christina never spoke of her inmost thoughts and feelings, enfolding herself in a dignified reserve that these expansive lighter southern natures could not understand, and hence could not pardon. They held her reticence to be conceit and hauteur; and, themselves the proudest of peoples, were deeply offended at the fact that another should possess their cherished vice.

Truly difficult for the young Queen were the first years of her married life, nor did she find much support in her husband, whose easy-going nature and frail health made him anything but a strong helpmate. For example, the Spaniards desired that their Queen should speak their stately language with purity, and Queen Christina took all possible pains to learn it. But naturally she had a German accent, that ugliest of accents in a Latin tongue. The King, instead of helping her, enhanced her difficulties. From the moment of her arrival it amused him to mislead her about the meaning of words, telling her the exact opposite of their sense, and then laughing heartily at the effect produced when she, in perfect good faith, employed them in public. He was not unkind at heart, and he was sincerely attached to her, but he was mischievous and fond of fun, and callous or unconscious of the effect his jokes often had upon their victims.

Thus the life of the young Queen at Madrid was a little sad and isolated. She had no intimates, and she was of a character too serious to prove a very acceptable member of the intimate circle round her husband. Her notions of decorum were too rigid to allow her to adapt herself easily to the gay and unconventional Spanish character. As Queen-Consort, she carefully refrained from taking a share in politics, and this the Spaniards acknowledged to her credit. She was allowed to be a good wife and tender mother, and yet the Austrian royal lady was not popular with her subjects. They had no complaints to make against her except that most hopelessly irremediable of all complaints—that her temperament and theirs were essentially different. They did not fail, however, to pay a tribute of admiration to her admirable coolness in face of the pistol of

Francisco Otorio, aimed at her and her husband with a precision that made their narrow escape from death almost a miracle. Her behaviour showed she possessed a high spirit. For the rest she was nothing to them but a superbly-dressed figure on festal occasions, and when in the country a sovereign leading a quiet and homely life.

The King meanwhile, however, had learnt to appreciate more and more her true value. On every anniversary of their wedding-day he gave her a bracelet set with single stones. The last came with this note: "My soldiers bear in golden stripes on their sleeves the number of their campaigns: I want to see on your arm the record of the years of happiness you have given me."

This was but a few days before that fatal November 25, 1885, when Alfonso at last succumbed to the consumption that had long tormented him, and Queen Christina found herself a widow with two little girls, one of whom was at once pronounced *interim* Queen of Spain until it was seen whether the child with whom the Queen was then pregnant would prove a male. It was a situation for which history had until then presented no parallel. A difficult, perilous moment, too, in the life of the young Archduchess; unpopular, out of health, regent for a girl-heir, in a land where only males are held of value, in a country racked with discontented factions, and with a more popular male pretender fostering dissensions. Could a frail, youthful woman steer clear of all these difficulties and preserve the throne for herself and her children? Few persons in Europe, remembering the fate of Prince Amedeo of Italy, thought it possible, and not many would have ventured to predict that this woman's hands would long hold the reins of power. The adherents of Don Carlos acquired fresh hopes; Don Carlos himself felt confident of his success. But, as is often the case in life, the unexpected, unforeseen occurred. Queen Christina, so self-effacing, almost the mere conventional figure of a Queen-Consort, suddenly showed herself possessed of regal qualities. The day of sorrow revealed her in a new light. Thrown by the death of her husband into a position of great and manifold difficulties, the daughter of the Hapsburgs proved herself nobly fitted for the *rôle* she was called upon to fill.

The courage and self-devotion she displayed when, in the early days of her widowhood and on the eve of her confinement, she personally visited the districts devastated by a hurricane, and with her own hands distributed relief to the sufferers, won her subjects' sympathy and gratitude.

Later on she showed yet greater nerve when a young officer forgot himself so far as to speak disrespectfully of her. The insolence was perhaps part only of the arrogant demeanour the Spanish nobles are apt to display towards their rulers when they happen to be of foreign race. Such behaviour as this had led Amedeo to abdicate. Queen Christina checked the insolence at once by ordering the offender into prison and keeping him there until he was prepared to apologize, and to vow he had meant nothing of what he had said.

An instance of her kindheartedness, united to firmness, was shown when the writer Del Silvio had to be banished on account of the publication of treasonable articles. His wife, left behind in great misery, entreated his pardon from the Queen, a request which was granted. When Del Silvio presented himself before the royal lady to thank her, she asked him, in the course of conversation, how many children he had. "Six," was the reply. "That is too many," said the Regent; "share with me." And forthwith the Queen gave orders that three of the author's daughters should be educated in one of the royal colleges at her expense.

Thus things went on until, on May 17, 1886, six months after his father's death, there was born to Queen Christina and the Spaniards a prince, the much-desired boy, who from the moment of his birth deposed his sister, and was monarch of Spain. This event greatly delighted the whole peninsula. Here, then, was a legitimate sovereign—a male, and one whose tender years made it an absolute certainty that he would keep outside intrigues, while the rectitude his mother had displayed during her brief regency made it almost as certain that she would continue on the same lines until his majority, which by the

Constitution is fixed at sixteen. All Spaniards resolved to accept the present state of things, and await the development of events. They were weary of civil wars and disorders, of the misery and poverty these bring in their train.

It was in the Palace of Pardo, there where his father died, that Alfonso XIII. saw the light of day. Who knows what strange caprice made Queen Christina choose for this event this gloomy abode? For the Palacio del Pardo, situated twelve kilometres (7½ miles) distant from Madrid, is a sombre prison-like residence, surrounded by a thick wood, in its turn enclosed by a high brick wall measuring eighty kilometres in circuit (50 miles).

In the palace itself, that May morning of the baby's birth was a busy one. All the Grandees of the peninsula were gathered together in the Queen's bed-chamber when it was known that the Queen was in labour, anxiously waiting to learn the sex of the child, and availing themselves of their traditional privileges to be present at the event. Others less privileged had assembled in an ante-room, ambassadors, statesmen, lords and ladies-in-waiting, dignitaries of all sorts and kinds. At one o'clock a door was at length thrown open and Señor Sagasta, the Prime Minister, stepped in. He carried a silver salver, on which rested a velvet cushion covered with lace, and on this airy substance reposed a small red scrap of humanity, the much-desired male, his Most Catholic

Majesty, the King of Spain "by the Grace of God and the Constitution of Monarchy," who was here for the first time presented by his Prime Minister with all form to his nobles and subjects.

The monarch did not like the ceremony at all, and his first public utterances were lusty but not melodious. The ceremony over, he was at last handed over to his head nurse, Raymunda. This woman was an Asturian, in accordance with the law that obliges all nurses of the royal family to be chosen from this wild province: perhaps because they are a specially healthy and loyal people.

This choice of a nurse had been an anxious matter. The next was the choice of a name for the infant King. His mother desired that he should be called Alfonso, after his father, but to this great opposition was made. The late King had been Alfonso XII., this child would therefore be Alfonso XIII., and the Spaniards have all the Latin superstitious dread of that number. Many other names from the royal annals were proposed instead, but nearly all of them, like Ferdinand, Philip, Charles, were associated with bad qualities, cruelty and oppression. Queen Christina was firm, and in due time his baby Majesty was christened Alfonso. The ceremony, one of great pomp, was performed by the Archbishop of Toledo, with water specially brought from the River Jordan. The Pope, one of the godfathers, had sent a magnificent christening dress to his "well beloved son," but Queen

Christina, with a woman's fondness for association, preferred that her boy should be carried to the font in the long lace robe and scarlet gold-fringed sash his father had worn at his own baptism, twenty-nine years before.

Though she had now, in a measure, conquered her unpopularity with her subjects, yet Queen Christina's task had not grown less onerous since her son's birth. What could be more difficult than to rear aright a child who in long clothes already reigned as absolute monarch over seventeen millions of subjects? If it is hard to bring up a Crown Prince wisely, to save him from the evil effects of courtier adulation, false servility, distorted views of life, how much harder to educate a King, and a Spanish King withal, hedged in by all manner of ridiculous etiquette! How earnestly the Queen Regent regards her duties, how tearfully, religiously she strives to fulfil them, her private letters to Vienna prove. Her one aim and desire is to bring up "the child," as she tenderly calls him, to be good, to be unspoilt, to be high-minded and patriotic. The policy she sketched for herself is indicated in the words she one day addressed to a captain-general, pointing to the cradle of the sleeping monarch, then a few months old: "My devotion to the interests of my child and my own virtue will be my shield and my guarantee of success in this, my adopted country, and in the sixteen long years that separate me from my boy's majority."

And verily she is earning the first-fruits of that policy in the general esteem of her son's subjects. On every occasion Queen Christina has shown herself possessed of unusual political intelligence, a sense of what is due to herself as Regent for a son who, according to the national law, is King from the moment of his birth. It is this that distinguishes Alfonso's minority from that of all other European sovereigns. His mother has lent herself with unexceptional intelligence and rare national devotion to the requirements of the situation. While the King can say that he reigns but does not govern, she governs but does not reign, and her influence is supreme in the politics of a country hotly divided into inimical parties. But all these factions seem to have lost some of their fierceness, their animosity in presence of the fair young head, the pretty winning child-ways of Alfonso XIII. and his mother, who, notwithstanding her somewhat Austrian stiffness of bearing, shows herself possessed of a gentle and tender nature. In the midst of grandeur, she cares for simple things. She grieved at being forbidden, as Queen of Spain, to nurse her children. She delights in working for the little ones. Many tiny garments in the baby King's layette were made by her hand.

Her womanly love of children, as well as acts like the following, have helped to gain her Spanish hearts. A while ago the Syndic of Madrid announced to the Queen that the name of Alfonso had been registered that day among the births for the thousandth time since the death of her husband. Deeply moved by this testimony of the sympathy of her people, Queen Christina sent the thousandth child, the son of a clerk, a complete *layette*— a silver cup, a case with knife, fork, and spoon, and a savings-box containing, besides a handsome nest-egg, a paper, on which was written with her own hand, "To the thousandth Alfonso, from a woman whom two Alfonsos have made happy."

Such deeds combined with the straightness of the Queen's political vision, the romance of her position as the widowed mother of a baby-king, are winning for Christina of Spain the love of her subjects. The peasant children already care for the lady whose proud bearing repels the aristocracy. Pretty stories abound among the rustic population that not unfrequently the Queen visits *incognita* the outlying cottages, bringing toys to the healthy children who can play, and various comforts to the sick, who especially appeal to her.

As a mother, Queen Christina is careful and conscientious. The royal children are strictly brought up and educated, under her own eyes, by Spanish and foreign governesses. The Princess of the Asturias and the Infanta Maria Theresa are bright, pretty girls of eight and six years old. They already speak French, German, and English besides their native tongue. The Infanta Maria Theresa is the cleverest, but less docile, and more delicate than her sister. The Queen does not allow them to be spoilt, though the stately etiquette of the Bourbon Court obliges the attendants and courtiers to treat them with a singular attention difficult to distinguish from servility.

Of Queen Christina's determination of character Stuart Cumberland, the famous "thought-reader," gives an account in his book, "A Thought-reader's Thoughts." He writes: "I have experimented with many women of note—empresses, queens, princesses, great authoresses, artists, singers, actresses, travellers—most of them women of known strong character, but for downright concentration of thought and determinedness of purpose I have scarcely met the equal of the Queen-Regent (Madrid). The *séance* in the Palacio Real, to which I have already briefly referred, was of more than ordinary interest, for the 'subjects' with whom I operated offered the widest psychological contrasts. Two of the most extraordinary experiments I did that day were performed with the Queen-Regent and the Comtesse de Paris. With the Queen the experiment was as follows: Her Majesty had heard that I was able by my process of thought-reading to enact an imaginary murder-scene contemplated by a person acting as my subject, and she asked me if I would give her an illustration of this character. But every one seemed to be timorous about it, and the experiment ran the risk of not being tried for lack of a suitable subject. 'What!' said her Majesty, springing to her feet, 'can no one commit a murder? I will!' and she seized an antique paper-knife shaped like a dagger, and assumed an intensely dramatic attitude. At that moment I took her Majesty by the hand, and I felt her whole frame thrill with suppressed excitement. Her eyes were fixed and bright, and her lips drawn firmly together, and I was much impressed with the tragic force she displayed. Then came the experiment. I was blindfolded, and, taking the dagger in my right hand, I moved across the *salon*, holding her Majesty with the left hand. Presently we paused opposite a lady of the household who was reclining on a sofa. Quickly bending forward, the Queen's left hand was about her throat, and the ivory knife flashed in the light; then down it came full in the breast of the victim. A faint scream of genuine alarm from the lady, a tightening of the Queen's grasp for a moment, followed by a deep breath, and all was over. Then with a rapid twist our hands parted, and the knife was sent clattering across the room; and, lifting my blindfold, I saw her Majesty standing before me, radiant with delight at the success of the experiment. The whole thing had been most dramatically thought out and artistically executed, and all that was strong and determined in Her Majesty came out in that moment."

Such, then, is the woman in whose hands lies the immediate future of Spain, which she is guiding with a skill and rectitude that contrasts favourably with the Spanish female governorship of former days. And very different is the attitude of the natives from that presented to Queen Isabella, whose reign was but another trial for that sorely tried land, which, first under Alfonso XII., and now under Queen Christina, is reviving a little from its long years of trouble and mismanagement.

The Queen certainly has no easy part to play; and chief among other difficulties is the question of the education of her son. The Clerical party will not be satisfied unless the child gets a purely Catholic education; the Liberals desire that he should have an all-round training. The one party insists that he should be surrounded by persons of all shades of thought; the other would banish from his household any person only remotely suspected of heresy, or related, however distantly, to a heretic. Another difficulty is the question of bull-fights. The Queen objects to her baby-boy witnessing these bloody spectacles. The Spaniards, on the other hand, demand that the King should grace their gala day and their national amusements by his presence. By keeping him away his mother has offended many ardent Royalists, who contend that by such measures she is strengthening the Republican party. There is still a long, long minority to be passed through, during which the Queen's difficulties can but increase.

And how about the child who will, in all human probability, guide the later course of Spain? Of the character of an infant three years old little can be known; but it would seem as if he had inherited some of his father's merry temper, for the tiny fellow is lively and talkative, though at moments an expression strangely grave and far-away comes over the little face, perchance the effect of the loneliness in which naturally he must be reared, for a King of Spain can have no playmates, since he can only associate with his equals. Even from his sisters the little monarch is to a certain extent separated. From the time of his birth, little Alfonso was provided with a separate household, civil and military, a number of officials, and a distinct suite of rooms. As to his appearance, he is not exactly a pretty child, but has a winning little countenance. It is quite curious to note the resemblance that exists between the little blonde King whose curls are as yet so sparse that he seems almost bald, and his ancestor Charles IV. Though not stout or strongly built in body or limbs, he gives the impression of fair health. His features are delicate, and rather pronounced for a child, his nose has already the Hapsburg aquiline bend, his little mouth reveals firmness, his eye is bright and full of fire.

The strict Court etiquette which permits that no one but his nurse and governess may touch the sacred person of the sovereign might some day lead to grave disaster, and may often occasion the baby needless suffering, as the following anecdote shows: A swing had been fixed in one of the King's rooms. When his baby Majesty was put into it for the first time he was frightened and began to cry. An attendant who was standing near rushed forward and lifted the child out of the swing, little thinking he would be punished for his humane kindness. He was at once dismissed. He had touched the sacred person of an anointed King. Fortunately Queen Christina, who, although she had to yield to Spanish Court etiquette, is too sensible not to recognize its frequent absurdity, found the man another post in the palace. The King's favourite toy is a rocking-horse. He has, of course, one of the most expensive and beautiful that can be made. It is covered with the real hide of an Andalusian pony, and the saddle, stirrups, and other trappings are of the same pattern as those used in Andalusia. One of the most charming of the many pictures painted of the young King is that by Professor Koppaig, which represents him seated on this horse.

If the King of Spain has a worry, it is the persistency with which, since the hour of his birth, painters, sculptors, and photographers persist in reproducing his features, representing him in every attitude conceivable and inconceivable, till the child finds sitting still a torment. Perhaps no one has been more often reproduced in a brief lifetime than Alfonso XIII.

The child's life is arranged by his mother in as simple and healthy a manner as is compatible with rigid etiquette and his exalted station. Every morning, as soon as his toilet is completed he goes to the Queen, who is always eager to greet "the child." Sometimes he is present at the morning visits paid to her by the ministers or members of the royal family, listening with indifference or with merry laughter to the discussion of difficult State problems, or to the narration of how his grandmother Isabella is misconducting herself, how the Duke of Montpensier so long as he lived would persist in visiting Spain, and so forth. Often during these conversations he will tap impatiently upon the table with his tiny fingers, for he is of a highly-strung temperament, and, like all susceptible people, is easily bored. He gave an instance of this at a high church function, at which were present all the Court, the authorities, and the nobility. His baby Majesty occupied, as is customary, the first place on the Gospel side of the altar. He sat upon the knees of his nurse, dressed in pure white, a coquettish white Spanish hat upon his fair little head. A learned bishop had been holding forth for over an hour amid the general silence, and his Majesty, the baby, had been as good and patient as possible. But as the orator meandered on and on, and there seemed no end to his flow of platitudes, the tiny King could bear it no longer. Suddenly, to the surprise and no doubt secret amusement and relief of the courtiers, he pulled off his cap, threw it on the ground, and cast a furious look at the interminable talker. History telleth not whether the bishop, on this evident sign of the royal impatience, brought his discourse to a speedy end.

His Majesty is certainly self-willed and easily angered, and at times it is only needful to ask him to do a thing in order for him to do the exact opposite. When his mother finds him in these disobedient moods she pretends to cry and leave him alone. This stratagem always succeeded, until one day before his dangerous illness. He really let her leave him, and, turning to his adored Raymunda, calmly remarked, "She did well to go, for I should not have given in."

The Queen is very strict with him, and no naughtiness goes unpunished. Thus one day he was rude to his English governess. That day he was not allowed to be present at his favourite pastime, the changing of the guard in the grand saloon.

The King has a tender and faithful friend, who even during his illness never left him. This is his black Angora cat Perrito. The child adores him, and insists on having him always by him, even taking him out for a drive. Perrito may be seen in the royal carriage, reclining on a splendid velvet cushion, embroidered for his special benefit by one of the Court ladies with the arms of Spain.

It is a curious sight, which it must need Spanish gravity to bear without a smile, to see the King hold official receptions at his palace. Here, upon the throne of Ferdinand the Catholic and Charles V., sits an Asturian peasant woman holding upon her knees the little scrap of humanity that represents to the Spaniards their ruler and arbiter. On his right stands the Queen Regent, the Infantas, a few steps lower the grandees with covered heads, lower yet on each side the ladies and gentlemen of the Court, then lower still the military, ecclesiastical, and civil dignitaries, the corps diplomatique, the Cortes, the Senate—in a word, all the high functionaries of State. And all file in order of rank and merit before this little monarch, kissing the baby hand with solemn reverence, while the baby himself is often shouting with impatience or laughing merrily but scarcely politely at some of the quaint figures that defile before him. Poor baby! these State ceremonies are a cruel trial to the patience of a lively child of three. Not seldom he falls off to sleep before these ceremonies, which Spanish etiquette prolongs more than is common, are even half ended. There is a story told that he once invited a stiff old Court dignitary to play at horses with him, much to everybody's amusement. It is a fact that when the nobles assembled to celebrate his second birthday, Alfonso amused himself by climbing up and down the steps of his throne. Shade of Ferdinand the Catholic! Do not the pranks of your descendant make you turn in your royal tomb?

The little King goes out a great deal, and of this he is very fond. His carriage is simple, and he drives without outriders or pomp, only a groom riding beside the door. Every afternoon, when the weather is fine, the royal carriage may be seen in the environs and public parks of Madrid. At five in winter and six in summer his baby Majesty returns to his palace, where he dines in state at a separate table from his mother, and with his separate suite and attendants. He has already learnt to salute his subjects in the street, and he does it in such a pretty, engaging way as to win all their hearts. He adores military music, and when he hears the people shout "Viva!" to him he claps his little hands and shouts in return.

It was a sad moment in the life of his little Majesty when it was proposed to separate him from his beloved wet-nurse, Raymunda. He would not hear of it, and cried bitterly, and the woman, who loves him devotedly, cried too. At last her peasant astuteness hit upon an expedient. She taught him to say, "Nurse must stay; I command it. I wish her to stay." Before the whole Court, to the surprise of all present, the little boy slowly and gravely one day pronounced these words, after which there was nothing for it; the nurse had to stay, for what a King of Spain desires must be done, and this was his Most Catholic Majesty's first public command. But, though the nurse stays on, Alfonso has passed out of her exclusive care into the charge of a Madame Tacon, who will superintend his education as she superintended that of his late father. Of course he does not yet do any book-learning, but he is already being trained to speak several languages—that needful regal accomplishment.

It was in January, 1890, that the little monarch was taken so dangerously ill that his life was entirely despaired of, and several times it was rumoured that he was dead. He recovered, thanks to the surpassing devotion and care of his mother, who nursed him with a devotion rare even in maternal annals. Meantime, by a strange freak of fate, there died in Italy Amedeo of Savoy, Duke of Aosta, ex-King of Spain. It seemed as though Death had resolved to take unto himself a Spanish king, and, failing the child, took the elder man. During the King's illness many pretty anecdotes circulated about him. It seems he has a passion for his toys, and in every lucid moment he asked about them, wished to know if they were safe, if he could see them. Nor were his thoughts wholly selfish. It seems he has a good memory for faces, and is an acute observer. Daily, when he goes out for his drive, he notices all the people he meets in the street. Among these a lame beggar child attracted his special sympathy; whether it was community of age that drew them together, or his pity for the infant that limped after his carriage soliciting alms—certainly she always received from him the most abundant coppers. He would make the wet-nurse get down to pick them up for her, and look back towards her long after the carriage had driven on. One day, during his illness, when free of fever and being fed, he suddenly said—

"What will the lame girl be doing now, mamma? Will she be eating like I am?"

"She will be eating more than you do now," replied the Queen, "but she will eat dry bread like the poor."

His baby Majesty was silent a while, and stopped eating his soup; then—

"Why do you not send something to the lame girl?"

The Queen did not answer, but his Majesty insisted,

"Mamma, if I were you, I would send those sweets to the lame girl—see, those," and he pointed to some on a table.

That night, when his delirium recommenced, he kept repeating, "Remember, remember the sweets for the lame child."

If this anecdote furnishes a just picture of Alfonso XIII.'s character, it must be sweet indeed, and does credit to his mother's training.

If he lives to grow up, and if he grows up a good man, a wise ruler, unspoilt, untainted by the perilous, difficult position in which he has found himself from his birth, this will be due beyond question to the rare devotion and wisdom of his mother, to whom he is the very apple of her eye. So much can be said for this baby King—he has already in his brief reign quieted many discontents, rendered less acrimonious many party feelings; his pretty childish ways, his tender infant fingers, have softened many difficulties, untied many a Gordian knot. And what Madrid swore to its widowed Queen beside the corpse of her dead husband—to be faithful and true to her in his place—the Spanish people, with few exceptions, have loyally and sincerely fulfilled.

THE REIGNING FAMILY OF PORTUGAL.

THE KING OF PORTUGAL.
(From a Photograph by A. Bobone.)

THE REIGNING FAMILY OF PORTUGAL.

IN Portuguese annals the date of December 1st, 1640, is known as that of "the glorious revolution against the Spanish usurper," a revolution which placed upon the throne of Portugal that Duke of Braganza who ascended it under the name of Dom Joao IV.

For sixty long years had the country groaned under its Spanish masters. It was a period of humiliation deep and galling, following as it did upon the catastrophe on African soil that deprived the land of its independence.

Little wonder, therefore, that when the favourable moment came to reassert themselves the people turned as with one accord to the Princes of the House of Braganza as their saviours. This noble family is one of the oldest and most powerful in Europe, of vast wealth and great merit. Probably no country can show such another house privileged at all times to take almost royal rank. The Kings of Spain had long watched these dukes with anxiety, in view of their great and unusual privileges, feeling dimly that they were too important and powerful to remain vassals for ever. It was quite natural that the Portuguese should turn to their family for deliverance from the heavy Spanish yoke.

The history of this revolution that ended the Spanish domination in Portugal is romantic. A given day and hour had been secretly appointed for action. It was a cold winter's morning when one by one the actors in the conspiracy gathered together silently outside the palace, where no suspicion of their design was harboured.

At nine precisely the assembled nobles entered the gates of the viceregal abode, felled the guards, and, carrying all opposition before them, slew the Prime Minister of the Duchess of Mantua, then Spanish Regent.

"Liberty, liberty!" shouted one of the noble conspirators from the palace balcony to the assembled people below. "Liberty! Long live Dom Joao IV! The Duke of Braganza is our legitimate king!"

And the crowd echoed the cry of "Liberty!" from thousands of throats. Like lightning the insurrectionary movement spread throughout the provinces; there was no hesitation on the part of the people, no resistance worth naming on the part of the enemy. The Spanish dominion that seemed so firmly rooted vanished as though touched by an enchanter's wand, and the downtrodden Portuguese uprose again firm and intrepid as in their palmiest days.

From that time forward December 1st is celebrated in Portugal with enthusiasm, and from that date the Braganzas have held its sovereignty.

The late King, Dom Luis I., ascended its throne in 1861, in consequence of the untimely death of his brother, Dom Pedro V. The history of this accession is a tragedy. Dom Pedro was the eldest son of that Queen Maria da Gloria who became sovereign as a mere child, and whose helplessness and charms moved the pity of all Europe. He himself was but eighteen when called on to rule, but he won his subjects' love at once by his grave demeanour and solicitude for their welfare —a love that culminated in very worship after he had shown heroic virtues and rare abnegation in moments of national danger, yellow fever succeeding cholera in decimating the land shortly after he had come into power. Wherever the epidemics raged most there was seen the youthful form of the King, and no persuasion could keep him away.

"My post," he used to say, "is where the hand of sickness weighs heaviest, and where the sickle of death mows the flower of my people. My place is close to the suffering and the sorrowful; it is for this that I am king."

The city of Lisbon, considering that the King had in those sad days proved himself its greatest citizen, unanimously voted him a medal, and the Humanitarian Society of Oporto likewise conferred on him one of the decorations it grants but to the highest of all merits. These two insignia were ever of all his orders those most prized by the King, for he had won them by his own deeds.

In 1856 the young King married the youthful Princess Stéphanie of Hohenzollern-Sigmaringen. A year later, after a few days' illness, she was laid in her grave. The nation grieved with its sovereign, whose sorrow was deep and heartfelt. Touching are the words in which he thanked them for their sympathy.

"During the four years of my reign," he wrote, "my people and I have been companions in misfortune. My conscience tells me that I never abandoned them in their trials. To-day, when I myself need comfort, they in their turn do not abandon me. I find my consolation in my religion, which bids me believe and hope, and in my people's tears as they mingle with mine."

The image of this lost wife was never effaced from Dom Pedro's memory, and his grief no doubt helped to sap his strength, which was still further taxed when, in 1861, he insisted upon making a tour through all his provinces, visiting all the unhealthy districts that he might judge of their needs with his own eyes. When he returned to Lisbon in the autumn, fatigued and enervated, he found his brothers Fernando and Augusto stricken with malignant fever. Nothing could keep him from their bedsides. The tragedy that followed is familiar to all: the elder prince died, the second was long at death's door, and survived almost by a miracle, and had not yet turned the corner of recovery when the King, low in body and mind, also caught the infection, and expired within four days. The grief of the land was sincere and poignant. It is said by those who witnessed it that never was seen such a sight as that in Lisbon the night the monarch lay dying. Rich and poor flocked into the churches and prayed earnestly to God to preserve the precious life of him who was to them father and brother. The bells tolled without ceasing. Every one was unnerved; the only calm spirit in the midst of this consternation was the King's. He rejoiced that for him the hour of liberation from the trammels of the flesh had struck.

Scarcely had he passed away than his remaining brothers, Luis and Joao, arrived in Lisbon, hastily summoned thither by the dire news of the royal sickness. Dom Luis was on board the ship *Bartolomeo Diaz*, of which he was commandant, when his brother expired, and he learnt the news first by being suddenly addressed as " your Majesty " by the official who came to bring him the intelligence. The first action he was called upon to do was to listen to his subjects' prayer that he would not take up his abode in the gloomy palace of the Necessidades, which they held was certainly accursed. He consequently chose Belem as his residence. He had not been there six weeks ere Dom Joao, who had caught the prevalent infection at once on his arrival at Lisbon, also expired, despite of every care and attention.

The people now rose up in tumult, thinking that malevolence had been at work. And it took long to calm them and to prove that the malignant spirits were none other but bad drainage, unwholesome conditions, and the bad constitution inherited from their progenitors by the Portuguese royal family.

It was amid such gloom that the late departed ruler became "King of Portugal and the Algarves, within and beyond the seas, in Africa Lord of Guinea, and of the navigation and commerce of Ethiopia, Arabia, Persia, and the Indies," as the official phrase has it.

Born in 1838, he had received the same careful education as his brothers, and early gave signs of the love of study that distinguished him. A year after his accession he married Maria Pia, second daughter of King Victor Emanuel of Italy, who at the time of her marriage was but fifteen years old. The union proved a happy one, and the course of their life was tranquil. The King, though he did not gain the worship of his people like his royal brother, was yet well beloved, and they were satisfied with his reign, during whose course Portugal has seen many internal changes—changes in the direction of modern progress that have perchance been pressed upon it even a little too rapidly for its comprehension and absorption, and which of late show threatening signs of the inevitable reaction induced by a too violent mutation of conditions. A student by nature, the health of the King in his later years precluded him from taking a very active part in public affairs; but the Government, which is representative (Cortes), like all Parliaments, marched of itself without his intervention. What he loved best were literary and artistic pursuits. He was fond, too, of the society of artists, who were sympathetic to his naturally gay temperament. Though he has written nothing original, he spent much time over literary work, and translated —and very well too—various foreign authors, his best work being translations of the "Merchant of Venice," "Othello," and "Hamlet." In personal appearance he rather resembled some jolly Dutch sea-captain. His manners were unaffected and easy, his tastes advanced and simple, and he did all he could to counteract the rigid Spanish etiquette that did not harmonize with his own liberal ideas.

He was not a great monarch, but neither was it a great people over whom he was called on to rule. He was the modest sovereign of a modest country that has had a great past, but is now no longer one of the makers of history. It has been truly remarked that the history of Portugal is as the history of a family rich in tradition, poor in facts, inspired by the memory of the past, and painfully hampered by the present endeavour to achieve more than its means will allow. The late King was one of the great majority of whom audiences are generally composed. It was by a mere accident of birth that he was called upon to figure on the stage. Under the circumstances, he played his part with great credit. He had the great advantage of falling upon peaceful times, and his temperament was suited to them. For his own part, he would have liked to have been the admiral of a great modern fleet, and he looked with envy upon the navies of other nations, never having succeeded in endowing his own land with adequate warships. But his love for all marine matters was rather that of a student, or *doctrinaire*, than that of a practical sailor. He adored the great silences, the wide horizons of the ocean, its musical murmurs, its dream-inviting undulations.

Very popular is the Queen-Dowager, who has secured the affections of a people singularly warm-hearted and attached to its royal house. In person she is tall, elegant of bearing, with a mixture of reserve, grace of manner, and *bonhomie* that recalls her hunter father. Like him, too, she is intelligent, but not loquacious, and her monosyllabic incisive remarks cause her to be feared by timid persons, who feel themselves silenced by these curt replies. She likes rather to hear others talk, and frequently addresses her surroundings with that most perplexing and silencing of observations, "Tell me something amusing."

Nor does she fail to resemble her father in other respects. Like Victor Emanuel, Queen Maria Pia is an intrepid rider, a passionate votary of shooting and all kinds of sport—a taste in which the King concurred. Unable, however, to gratify it always to its full extent, the Queen, when in *villeggiatura* at the watering-place of Caldas, amuses herself with the harmless practice of aiming with a rifle out of a high window at earthenware bottles floating in the sea, and placed there for that purpose. It is said that it is not often that she misses her unstable mark.

But for all these mannish tastes she is a Queen and a woman. She dresses with taste and elegance, her jewels are among the most costly of any ruler's, and her household is ruled with an etiquette that proves that she never forgets her rank, even if it pleases her at times to disguise it. This she does most frequently when bound upon some of those errands of mercy for which she is famed, and which have gained her the name of "Angel of Charity." Philanthropy is with her as much a passion as hunting, music, or painting. She is at the head of all Portuguese charitable establishments, which she directs in person, even to the minutest details. Always to the fore if any disaster occurs, any appeals are made to the public purse, she does not confine her charitable exertions to public calamities only. Endless are the anecdotes told of her good deeds. Many and many a time will she quit the palace at some early morning hour, unaccompanied, simply dressed in black; and none of the household dare ask whither goes her Majesty, for all know she is bound on some secret errand of mercy. Once when a civic guard, recognizing her and seeing her enter one of the lowest quarters of Lisbon, followed her to watch over her safety, she sternly forbade him to divulge what he had seen, or to unmask her anonymity. In all cases of distress brought under her notice she desires, if possible, to judge for herself, and behold with her own eyes.

It is no uncommon sight to see her on quitting the

cathedral after morning mass surrounded by a crowd of poor people, who kneel as she passes, kiss the hem of her dress, or present her some petition. These she invariably takes in her own hand and reads on her return home.

The life led by the late King and his Queen was, like that of most royal personages, highly methodical. The Queen rose early, and breakfasted on a simple cup of chocolate at seven, after which she at once set to work, directing her correspondence, reading some of the newest publications, or attending to her philanthropic institutions. At midday was the general lunch, which was partaken of in company with the King and royal household. At two o'clock when in Lisbon the Queen received at the Palace of Ajuda, when she showed herself most accessible, and was ever ready to converse with her visitors, especially on charitable or artistic themes. At four o'clock she went out driving either in the town or the lovely environs of Lisbon. Most often she visited Mafra, which may be called the Versailles of Lisbon. Here she was able to gratify some of her sportswoman tastes—shooting, rowing, or driving four-in-hand. By eight o'clock she was back in the palace for dinner, after which she frequently went to the theatre. The Queen-Dowager plays the piano and sings with taste, and her water-colour paintings are graceful. Quite recently she painted a charming fan for the Queen of Italy, representing the pier at Lisbon and the tower of Belem. She is passionately fond of flowers, especially of maidenhair ferns and lilies of the valley, of which basketfuls have always to adorn her private apartments. The King, too, loved flowers; and the grounds about the Palace of Ajuda resemble a botanical garden more than a private one. But better than flowers he loved birds, and his aviaries are stocked with native and foreign specimens, which were his pets and his delight.

This palace of Ajuda, which uprises on one of the amphitheatrical hills that dominate the panorama of the Tagus, is exquisitely placed in an incomparably beautiful situation. The palace itself is a massive edifice resembling a convent or a fortress, relieved from severity solely by its beautiful gardens.

In the early days of Queen Maria Pia's residence here she was often dull, for the dominant element at the Court consisted of elderly persons, and the tone was also very homely and *bourgeois*, offending the more refined and artistic tastes of the Savoy Princess. But by and by she moulded it to her wish. Less retiring by nature than the King, she loved society, though she did not care for big receptions. She encouraged *petits comités*, when music, informal dancing, and talk formed the entertainments of the evening. She directed these little *réunions* with the tact and skill of a good hostess and a *grande dame*. Unlike most royal receptions, those held under her auspices were not dull. After the King's health declined so seriously it was the Queen who tended him, and who proved herself the best assistant to the doctors. In a word, she is in all respects a superior woman. The recollections that abide with her in these days of her sorrow must be fragrant still.

Two sons are the fruit of this royal union. The eldest, Don Carlos, Duke of Braganza, since King of Portugal, was born in 1863. He, too, like his maternal grandfather, is a mighty hunter. Until called to the throne most of his time was spent at Villa Vicosa, the ancient residence of the Dukes of Braganza, whose vast adjoining estates permitted him to gratify to the full his love of sport.

He was educated at Oporto by Portuguese professors, and only after his education was supposed to be ended, travelled throughout Europe. His great *forte* is languages, of which he knows an infinite number. It is said of him that he is good and kind-hearted, but by no means clever, nor distinguished for any salient traits. No anecdotes about him circulate in society or among the people. He remains as yet for them rather an unknown quantity. Time alone can show what manner of ruler he will make. His *début* has been unfortunate, but the Anglo-Portuguese conflict can not be said to have been brought about by his fault. At the same time had he had great powers and energy they would no doubt have manifested themselves at that critical moment. In 1886 he married the Princess Amélie, eldest daughter of the Comte de Paris. The story of this *mariage de convenance*, which has, however, turned out one of love, is told thus. The heir to Portugal, much spoilt by his adoring parents, and with no small belief in himself and his own importance, declared that nothing would induce him to marry any one but a fairy-tale princess—that is, she must be pretty, rich, and good. Various Austrian Archduchesses were trotted out, but none fulfilled all these conditions. The Comtesse de la Ferronaye, an astute Frenchwoman, saw a chance of pleasing everybody all round. Sending for a large photograph of the Princess Amélie d'Orléans, she placed it in her drawing-room; the next time the young duke called, he fell, so goes the story, straight into the trap, and inquired reproachfully why *this* young lady had not been mentioned. A flying visit to Paris followed, and the Franco-Portuguese marriage was the result.

The reception accorded to the bride on her public entry into Lisbon was something equally touching and imposing. All the splendour of the ancient days when Portugal took high rank among nations, glorious in her brave discoverers and learned men, seemed revived for the nonce in the magnificent processions that filed through the streets, gorgeous pageants whose picturesqueness was enhanced by the beauty of the town of Lisbon itself, that masterpiece of the great Minister of Joseph I., the Marquis of Pombal, who caused it to uprise more lovely than ever from the ruins occasioned by the great earthquake of 1755 that laid it low. Like Rome, this city too is built on seven hills, and its beauty has been the theme of poets and painters. A quaint German legend tells how a certain knight of Jerusalem desired to behold in a magic mirror the most beautiful city of Europe. At his desire there uprose before his gaze, in all its beauty, Lisbon the Great, as it was called in those days. And even now, though no longer the emporium of Eastern trade, no longer the wealthy busy centre, Lisbon still retains her natural charms. Her feet are still laved by the waters of the Tagus, Cintra is still framed in foliage and moss, its granite rocks still robed in the emerald green of feathery ferns; above her head, like a regal mantle, is still spread a sky of deep limpid blue.

To Lisbon the Orleans Princess was tenderly welcomed, and it is pleasant to know that she has fulfilled the fond expectations her advent awoke in Portuguese breasts. Her young daughter-in-law is also a special favourite with the Dowager Queen. Indeed, the Portuguese royal family are very united and affectionate.

The new Queen is good-looking, taller than Maria Pia, and finer featured. Her colouring is high, like that of her brother the Duke of Orleans, the State prisoner of the French Republic. Her hair, like his, is fair and abundant, her figure is a trifle heavy. Always good-tempered and gay, passionately fond of amusement, of society, Queen Amélie has that worldly *souplesse* which Queen Maria Pia lacked. She can chatter with everybody, and always finds the right word to say. But she has not her mother-in-law's intellect, and will not be able to guide her husband with wise political counsels as she did. She has, however, great influence over him, and is always at his side; even in his study she is present embroidering or drawing while he works at affairs of State.

Before the young couple had ended their honeymoon the Duke of Braganza was called upon to serve his apprenticeship as ruler during the temporary absence of his father, who had left for reasons of health. He acquitted himself of his task in such a manner that the Portuguese were well satisfied, and trust that now Dom Carlos is called upon to succeed his sire his government will be one of peace and sound administration. An heir is also already provided for. The rejoicings throughout the land at the birth of this first child were great, the late King giving in its honour a series of State banquets, on which occasion there figured on the table that far-famed service of plate, well known to amateurs, which is of such rare workmanship and of such costly material that it is seldom removed from the strong rooms in which it is safeguarded.

It was in November, 1889, that Dom Luis succumbed at last to the malady that had long consumed him. A strange fatality seems to will that the House of Braganza should die always two at a time; while the King was dying so was his brother Augustus, and the one expired but a few days before the other. Queen Maria Pia was with both at the last. Scarcely had the King died than she called her eldest born to the bedside of the defunct.

"I desire," she said, "that you should be a King like your father, just and loyal, and I bless you."

So saying she kissed him on the right cheek.

The new King Carlos adores his mother, and regards her always as his sovereign and his best State councillor. When, eight days after the funeral of Dom Luis, Dom Carlos received the diplomatic body, Maria Pia and Queen Amélie assisted at the ceremony. It was the custom during Dom Luis' lifetime that the Queen was seated between the King and the Crown Prince, who hence sat on the left. This day also King Carlos, as a good son, desired to sit on the left, and leave to his mother the post of honour. It was Maria Pia who, taking him by the hand, placed him on the right, and he duly obeyed.

The formal coronation of the new King on December 28th of last year was a magnificent pageant, though for the King and Queen the pleasure of the ceremony must have been considerably marred by the fact that both were suffering from a severe attack of the influenza epidemic that has raged throughout Europe.

The enthusiasm which prevailed among the people must, however, have made ample amends for any inconvenience suffered by the King and Queen in carrying out their resolve not to postpone the ceremony. The gorgeous procession from the palace to the Houses of Parliament, which formed the first act of the magnificent pageant, was watched by vast crowds, while inside the chamber was gathered an assembly composed of the representatives of the principal foreign Powers, and of all the chief personages of the realm. Holding the sceptre in one hand, and resting the other on the Bible, surmounted by a crucifix, the King swore to uphold the Catholic religion, and to maintain the Constitution. Immediately the heralds proclaimed the formal accession of their "high and puissant Sovereign," and hailed "his most faithful Majesty" as King of Portugal. The Coronation oath having been thus taken before the representatives of his people, Dom Carlos proceeded to hear the customary *Te Deum*, and to receive the congratulations of his loyal city of Lisbon.

In the meantime, strange and awful fatality that seems to hover over the House of Braganza, death had once more been active, striking down quite suddenly the lately exiled Empress of Brazil, aunt to the young sovereign.

Such this royal family of Portugal, of whom the Queen-Dowager is certainly the most picturesque and prominent member; good, kind, homely persons, who, as far as their personal characters are concerned, will never disturb the peace of Europe, but who, all of them, strive to do their duty in that exalted station of life to which they have been called.

GEORGE I., KING OF THE HELLENES.

THE KING OF GREECE.
(From a Photograph by the London Stereoscopic Company.)

GEORGE I., KING OF THE HELLENES.

OCTOBER 30, 1888, was a day celebrated with rejoicing throughout the length and breadth of the little kingdom of Greece, for on that day George I. celebrated the twenty-fifth anniversary of his accession to the Hellenic throne. It is strange to note that this occurrence took place exactly a fortnight before his father, the King of Denmark, completed the same number of years of reign, this being probably the first time in history that a son is an older sovereign than his father. But King George did not inherit his throne, as is the usual custom—he obtained it by election; and that he has succeeded in retaining it for a quarter of a century is doubtless due to the fact that he inherits much of his mother's cleverness and adaptability to circumstances, and also that he has taken to heart the fact that the *rôle* of a modern monarch is that the occupant of a throne *ad interim*. Only as he regards his mission and duties in that light can the ruler of any civilized country in this late nineteenth century hope to keep possession of his crown and his influence over his subjects.

When Prince George of Schleswig-Holstein-Sonderburg-Glücksburg played with his brothers and sisters in the park of Jugenheim, and shared the frugal home of his royal parents, he no doubt little imagined that a throne would ever be his. But the family of Christian, King of Denmark, have been most lucky from a worldly point of view. It was in 1862 that the Greeks, after deposing their Bavarian King Otto, who had grown hateful to them because of his extravagances and follies, looked all round Europe in search of a prince able and willing to sit on their throne. This throne, it must be admitted, offered few temptations. The newly-founded kingdom of Greece, whose liberation from Turkish bondage had roused such lyric enthusiasm throughout all Europe, failed to fulfil at first the ardent hopes of its poets and lovers, hopes mainly influenced, there is little doubt, by the traditions of old Greek glory and classic fame. But the modern Greeks were no longer the lofty-minded Athenians, the rigid Lacedemonians—they had become a mongrel race, dead to their best instincts; and when once the land was freed from the Ottoman yoke, its admirers had to note with pain that the chiefs who had liberated the country by their arms were little better than pirates and bandits; that Greece was a prey to factions — republican, monarchic, aristocratic—of conflicting interests, and was beset with adventurers. The Bavarian Prince, who had come a minor into the land, could make no headway against all these disorders. Nor was he himself a highly capable head. It was, therefore, not astonishing that his people, always more or less in a state of revolt, should have deposed him.

But whom to select instead ? that was the question ; for Otto was childless. Besides, the Greeks had had enough of the romantic Bavarian royal family; excellent kings to figure in *opéra bouffe* or to satisfy the merely spectacular demands formerly made on sovereigns, but incapable of threading the mazes of modern perplexities. England was naturally looked to as one of the guarantee states, and the second son of Queen Victoria (Prince Alfred) was chosen by popular consent. But Queen Victoria declined with thanks the doubtful position for her sailor prince. To whom to offer it instead ? It was a puzzle, truly, for the post refused by the English prince appeared but a sorry gift to offer to another of equal rank. It was needful rather to look among the small fry for one who might be willing to risk the doubtful position upon the principle that he had all to gain and nothing to lose. This was how the choice came to fall upon the second son of the "Protocol Prince," the heir-apparent of the crown of Denmark ; and he not only accepted the offer, but has had the skill to keep his place for five-and-twenty years.

It was in June, 1863, that a deputation of Greeks waited upon the King of Denmark, asking to be allowed to offer the crown of their land to his great nephew. The old King notified his official acceptance of the offer by telling Prince George to mount the steps of the throne whereon he was seated, saluting him as his peer, and as King of the Hellenes.

Prince George was not yet eighteen when he was thus chosen to rule the land of which he did not even know the language. Notwithstanding these two grave drawbacks, the National Assembly, remembering the disastrous regency during the reign of Otto, who also ascended the throne a minor, declared that he should be regarded as major from the day of his arrival in Greece. On the 30th of October, 1863, the newly-made king landed at the Piræus. "My strength lies in the love of my people," was the device he chose for himself. In his first proclamation he promised to concentrate all his efforts towards making Greece "a model for the eastern European kingdoms." And he has been true to his word; efforts have not been lacking, and the progress made towards civilization in this quarter of a century is immense.

The task was no easy one. The people showed their turbulent temperament from the first. Thus King George's arrival was celebrated by his subjects in the chief cities of his kingdom by street fights between his opponents and adherents, which neither the police nor the military could pacify. The country was entirely disorganized, the treasury drained. Fortunately for King George he did not arrive quite empty handed. England, at the instigation of Mr. Gladstone, had presented him with the Ionian Isles, an annexation long desired by the Greeks, and in which they beheld not only the accomplishment of a cherished wish, but a pledge for the future. And in this they have not been deceived. After a quarter of a century's reign, the domains of George I. have almost doubled in extent, and Greece no longer occupies the last place among the states of Europe. It is now larger than Holland and Belgium united.

It is curious here to note the contrast between the reigns of the father and the son, called to be kings within a few days of one another. Christian's jubilee found him in possession of a third less territory than when he came into power; George's found him with almost as much again. Fickle fortune has all through this space of years been favourable to the son and unfavourable to the father. The former has succeeded in consolidating his power, the latter has been involved in ceaseless Parliamentary conflicts that have paralyzed the development of the country and harmed his popularity. While the father's predilections were always with the Conservatives, King George ascending the throne sought aid from the Radicals to help him to make order amid the confusion left by Otto of Bavaria.

He soon showed of what stuff he was made. Arrived in the land a stranger and a mere stripling, he had brought with him no friends nor attendants save one, a certain Count Sponeck, who was to him an intimate adviser. Of this man the Greeks were at once jealous. What could he know, they said, of the customs and the needs of Greece? And they thought to see in his counsels a tendency inimical to their aspirations. Hardly had the King noticed this than he gave way to it. Young, friendless, inexperienced, alone, he nevertheless sent back to Denmark his one old home friend.

The act gained for him the gratitude and respect of his people.

And it was but an indication of the course the King has since rigidly followed. He has kept scrupulously within the limits of the fundamental pact made with the nation, of which the Greeks are supremely jealous. King George possesses and practises all the virtues of a constitutional sovereign, strictly subordinating his actions to the will of the National Assembly. This Assembly, it is worth noting, did not exactly exist when the King ascended the throne. The Greeks were at that moment busy manufacturing a constitution. Young and ardent deputies were charged with the task. France and the Parliamentary monarchy of July were studied as models; historical sequence was more thought of than the momentary needs of Greece. The discussion dragged and dragged, and no end seemed in view. At last the young King took matters into his own hands. He sent a royal mandate begging the commissioners to bring their deliberations to an end. This act of energy produced a good effect both upon the embryo Parliament and the Greeks. And in very deed the constitution was voted within a month after—

a constitution based upon the most liberal models to be found on either side of the Atlantic. Indeed, it has surpassed them all in Radicalism, having no second chamber.

To this brand-new Constitution the King as well as his subjects had to serve their apprenticeship. It was no easy task, especially to the sovereign; and many difficult moments had to be overcome, when both throne and constitution seemed in danger.

The revolt of Crete, anxious to escape from Ottoman rule and to be reunited to its Hellenic brethren, added to the royal difficulties, King George espousing with ardour the national cause. European diplomacy intervened with its tenderness for Turkish susceptibilities, and hindered the success of the Cretan cause; but the incident had made the Greeks feel themselves again a nation, had given them renewed self-confidence, and also a yet greater regard for their monarch.

A happy incident diverted their thoughts for a while from their Cretan disappointment. In November, 1867, King George brought home as his bride the Grand Duchess Olga of Russia, daughter of the Grand Duke Constantine. That their Protestant King should have espoused a daughter of the true Church, and moreover by his marriage have allied himself to the powerful Russians, the enemy of the Greek hereditary enemy, the Turk, was a source of universal satisfaction. And this joy was enhanced when, the following July, salvos of artillery announced the birth of a prince, thus securing the dynastic succession. Here, for the first time, after centuries of trials and disorders, was a prince born to the Greeks who would one day be their king, and who was a Greek by birth, religion, and education. Six brothers and sisters have followed in the train of Prince Constantine; there seems no fear, therefore, of the Greek throne being bereft of heirs. And the marriage of this eldest prince is a further subject of satisfaction to the Greeks, for by allying himself to the sister of the Emperor of Germany he has drawn Greece within the orbit of the Triple Alliance, which it trusts will prove of moral and material guarantee for its future.

An ugly moment for the young Greek kingdom, and its position in the eyes of civilized Europe, arose in 1869, when the brigandage it had till then failed to suppress came into flagrant view. A band of thieves had captured on the plains of Marathon two English tourists, and a member of the English and of the Italian legation. Profiting by the high social standing of their prisoners, the brigands asked not only a heavy ransom, but amnesty for their offence. When this was very properly refused, to the horror of Europe, and almost within sight of the Greek gendarmes, the brigands murdered their captives. A cry of indignation rang through the whole continent. It was a thunderbolt also for the Greeks—it was their honour that was at stake. What, after thirty years of liberty, were they still unable to guarantee safety to any tourists who happened to visit their classic land? The country was thoroughly aroused at last to this national disgrace of brigandage, and really energetic measures were taken in consequence, with the result that the era of these robber chieftains is now ended, and people can travel as safely in Greece as in other parts of Southern Europe; for this general indignation enabled the Chamber to vote not only Draconian measures against brigands, but to obtain extended concessions for the construction of telegraphs, roads, and other needful adjuncts to civilization. Indirectly, too, this murder induced Europe to permit Greece to make at last those territorial acquisitions which make it less easy than formerly for malefactors to reach the Turkish frontier, and thus find themselves outside the reign of Greek law.

In this matter of finally suppressing the brigandage, which under the Turkish dominion had been organized as a protest against tyranny, King George showed himself most active.

Activity, in very fact, is the keynote to the King's character. He is a great worker. Even in winter he is to be found in his study at an early hour. Indeed, early rising would seem to be a royal virtue. Monarchs perhaps, best grasp the value of those undisturbed morning hours. In summer, twice a week, independently of his ministers, the King receives all the persons who, passing through Athens, have asked for the favour of an audience. These visitors generally find him standing beside a little table piled with papers and documents, in a room which is the last of the three ground-floor rooms of the palace which are set aside for his private cabinets. These rooms are richly decorated with pictures, bronzes, marbles, and costly objects of art. But besides these there are also hung on the walls portraits of all the great Hellenes who have helped to make modern Greece. This is a delicate compliment on the part of the King to his native visitors, and one they never fail to appreciate; for the King himself is essentially a modern man, though he possesses all due love and respect for his nation's great and glorious past. But modern literature, modern art, the marvellous scientific discoveries of our century, have a rare attraction for him, as also has modern history. He has a most extensive knowledge of international politics.

Those who come in contact with King George testify to his frank, amiable manners. He puts his visitors at their ease, and permits them to talk unrestrainedly. He loves discussion and straightforward speech. He does not forbid contradiction. Hence it is possible for his visitors to hold true converse with him, a matter not common in interviews with royal persons, who like their dicta to be accepted as though infallible. In this wise the King learns much, and knows what is occurring, what is thought in the large world outside the narrow little circle in which royalty moves.

He also likes to inspect Government works with his own eyes, going to visit harbours, barracks, roads, and buildings unexpectedly and on foot, accompanied by but one or two gentlemen.

His programme for his reign is, of the interior, progress; for the exterior, liberation for the Greek peoples still under a strange yoke. The latter part of his task has of course to be carried out with tact and delicacy, so as not to wound international susceptibilities and jealousies. But the King has been astute and skilful as he has been patriotic. At the Congress of Berlin he understood so well how to make the claims of the Hellenes respected that much of Epirus and Thessaly was restored to its true owners, and at the end of twenty-five years he can proudly point out to his subjects how he has augmented their land by a third, without shedding their blood to obtain this result.

Indeed, the management of external politics is the King's strong point, and, thanks to his personal wisdom and his excellent family connections, he is generally most successful in all he undertakes in this line. Internal politics he meddles with less, leaving these to the Chamber, as is indeed right and proper he should do, seeing he is a constitutional sovereign. His subjects appreciate and respect him, but he cannot be exactly called popular. The Greeks never forget that he is not one of them—that he was, so to speak, forced upon them.

The same applies to the Queen, though she has the merit her husband lacks, that she is of their own faith. An intelligent and superior-minded woman, she has been a true helper to her husband. Her exemplary conduct as wife and mother has indeed won for her the esteem of even those of her subjects who are opposed to the whole system of royalty and all that is connected with it. "*Ine kali nikokirà,*" they say, as they see her drive past in the streets, which means, "She is a good housewife." Her appearance has a great charm; she is not pretty, but remarkably graceful, has a brilliant white complexion, and looks far younger than her years. A slight aspect of melancholy but enhances her personal attractions.

Under her patronage are most of the charitable institutions, many of these being of her own foundation, notable among them a model hospital. During the Russo-Turkish War she established a course of ambulance lessons for women, and attended them herself, in order that she too might learn how to tend the wounded. Indeed, she was among the most assiduous of the learners. Her open-handedness is almost proverbial. In this also she is supported by the King. Both are ever ready to give to charities, and solemnise every public occasion with gifts to the poor.

And yet they are not rich. The King's civil list is but 550,000fr. a year. But he understands so well how to manipulate it that he manages on this narrow sum to fulfil with becoming dignity the requirements of his station. His house is well-appointed, he has good horses, his table is sumptuous, and does not suggest the Spartan black broth.

Like his father, he is fond of outdoor exercise and of

sport. He is a good shot and whip, an indefatigable swimmer, and a devotee of angling. In the Gulf of Chalcis he has a little palace, whither he often retires to fish. His hunting-seat is Satoi, an hour's distance from Athens. But it is at Corfu, where he has his summer residence, that he is able to live entirely according to his tastes—a lovely domain in an enchanting spot. Here he and the Queen are able to live that free existence devoid of etiquette which pleases them both. The King turns farmer, and the Queen becomes a musician and a painter. It is flower-painting that is her forte, and she may be met in the gardens at Corfu copying from Nature many of the lovely plants that bloom in that enchanted isle. She arranges her floral pictures with much skill, and these graceful bouquets, signed "Olga," would easily find a market were their author obliged to work for her daily bread.

Happy hours of relaxation are those for the King and Queen. Their official life at Athens is a very busy one, and of necessity very worldly. In winter the palace doors are constantly thrown open for receptions, dinners, balls, and skating festivals—for the King has caused a skating-rink to be erected in a long gallery, where the inhabitants of a land in which snow seldom falls can enjoy in mock fashion the pleasures that ice affords. The theatre plays no part in fashionable Athenian life, for Greece, strange to say, produces no actors. New Year's Day and March 25th—the date commemorative of the proclamation of Hellenic independence—are high festivals at Court and among the people. Easter and Christmas, too, are great occasions. The King and Queen have each their own private chapels in the palace, but at Christmas they make an exception, and go together with their children to the cathedral to attend the service. During Passion week, too, the King goes to the Greek church, and, surrounded with great pomp by all his Court in full gala costume, listens to the sermon on the Passion. Also the night preceding Easter Day it is customary for the sovereign to pass long hours in the cathedral. As soon as day dawns the cannons boom to celebrate the Resurrection, and the archbishop presents a symbolic red egg to the monarch, who duly crosses himself, Greek fashion, and reverently kisses the hand of the prelate.

King George goes through all these ceremonies with an amiable grace, which allows his people to forget that they are for him but empty ceremonies, for he has remained a Lutheran at heart as well as by profession.

Certainly King George of Greece, notwithstanding the circumscribed sphere in which he reigns, is far from the least among European sovereigns, thanks to his efficient personal qualities. Modest though it may be, yet among the galaxy of crowned heads he has a certain influence on account of his alliances and by the bearing he has known how to give to his Greeks, whose importance grows steadily day by day. Notwithstanding the difficulties of many kinds which the young kingdom has encountered, and which it still must traverse before its internal organization attains to the height of modern requirements; notwithstanding the disorders and difficulties of which the East is the theatre, the land may with good reason be satisfied with the results of the balance it can draw at the close of the first period of King George's reign. It finds Greece aggrandized and its throne established.

And what has been accomplished up to the present is of good augury for the future. With extended commerce, an increasing national industry, much waste land reclaimed, a canal cut through the Isthmus of Corinth which opens new modes of internal communication, railways, roads and telegraphs intersecting land till then cut off from all intercourse, Greece is now one of the first among the secondary Powers of Europe.

And the merit of this is in chief part due to its Danish prince, King George.

And that which perforce he has had to leave undone the Greeks hope that his son will accomplish. Prince Constantine, Duke of Sparta, the Crown Prince, is a really popular personage in Athens and all Greece. "He is a Greek," they say, and they are apt to add, "He will manage it," which means, being interpreted, he will get us Greece, and, if possible, also Constantinople. Time alone can show whether these hopes be capable of realization, but they indicate the nature of Greek national ideals.

Taken as a whole, perhaps, however, there is no European land and scarcely a capital where the royal family plays a less conspicuous part than in Greece and Athens.

THE KING OF HOLLAND.

THE KING OF HOLLAND.
(From a Photograph by Wollrabe.)

THE KING OF HOLLAND.

THERE is perhaps no more comic incident in all history—indeed it savours rather of *opéra bouffe* than of serious story—than that which occurred on May 1, 1889, in the little kingdom of Holland. For some months previously its ruler had lain dying, bulletins as to his sinking condition were daily issued to all Europe, the most eminent physicians had pronounced him beyond hope, his necrology lay ready for print in every newspaper office of the world, and all details as to the succession were arranged. This succession was to fall on the little Princess Wilhelmina, the only surviving child of the King, in whose favour the Dutch Constitution had been revised two years previously. But since the small Grand Duchy of Luxemburg is under the Salic law, this onerous possession could not pass into the little girl's hands, but falls instead to Duke Adolf of Nassau, the nearest male agnate of the House of Orange and Nassau, a relationship that dates back to the thirteenth century. Seeing the desperate state of the King, the new Dutch regents thought it became them to call upon this Duke to enter upon his future estates provisionally as Regent, but with the assurance, as all thought, of being in a few hours, at most days, its sovereign. Duke Adolf, himself but a few months the junior of the dying monarch, hastened to obey the summons. He certainly did not display too much tact in his act of taking possession, and he spoke with an assurance, destined to prove too assured, of his future government. May Day was fixed for the formal ceremony of installation. On the eve of that day, to every one's astonishment, the King of Holland upraised himself from what all held his death-bed, and with a clearness of thought which none expected from a brain authoritatively pronounced as paralysed stated that so long as he breathed the reins of power should not pass out of his hands, and that Duke Adolf of Nassau might return whence he had come.

The event caused no little amusement throughout Europe and much mortification to the Duke, who had to return crestfallen to his villa on the Rhine, his dream of being a reigning sovereign once more demolished. The Prussians had deprived him of his hereditary little State of Nassau, and now a veritable resurrection from the dead deprived him of a realm of which he already, so ran his public declaration to his hoped-for subjects, felt himself a citizen in heart and soul. He permitted some very ill-judged criticisms of the event to appear in papers friendly to him, remarks that evinced all too clearly his keen annoyance at the sorry figure he had cut. Meantime the King of Holland no doubt laughed in his sleeve at the discomfiture of his disappointed successor.

The whole affair inevitably reminds us of the scene in which Prince Hal all too hastily puts on his head his father's crown, deeming him dead.

"Is he so hasty that he doth suppose my sleep my death?" asks the sick monarch, and when he taunts the Prince with the famous saying, "Thy wish was father to that thought," the would-be heir can find, like Adolf of Nassau, no better answer than "I never thought to hear you speak again."

Certainly no one but Charles V. ever cared to attend his own obsequies or survive his own death. Perhaps this episode of his death being too soon discounted is the first time the King of Holland has won the sympathies of Europe, for he was not a popular figure, and did not deserve to be. He was of the old type of sovereigns, now fast dying out, who did not take a serious view of their office, but regarded their exalted station as an aid towards obtaining the maximum of pleasure and amusement out of life. At the same time, while desirous of having all personal freedom possible, the King, it is fair to add, did not deny it to his subjects. He was a strictly constitutional ruler, liberal in his ideas, and desirous to do all he could for the welfare of his subjects, provided their desires did not clash with his own, which happily they never did.

While probably no single Dutchman would have chosen the handsome King, William III., for his son-in-law, or have cared to throw him into contact with his womenkind, as a ruler he was not exactly undesirable. As Edmonds de Amicis has well said: "The country is *au fond* Republican, and its monarchy is a sort of presidency without the least monarchical pomp. The King of Holland is looked upon almost more as a *stadtholder* than as a King. There is in him that which a Spanish Republican said of the Duke of Aosta, 'the least quantity of King possible.'"

William's qualities were such as specially to appeal to a people who are by nature staunch Republicans, and who look on a King, *quâ* King, as a State figurehead barely worth the expense of an annual coat of paint. The King detested all forms and ceremonies, spoke his mind to all the world, was "hail fellow well met" with every class of the community, rather preferred low to good company, and had further the great and rare virtue of being parsimonious with the money of the State while very prodigal with his own. According to an article of the Dutch Constitution of 1848, "the King orders his home as best he likes." This was interpreted in unexpected guise by William III., who, while running about Europe with *chères amies*, reduced his civil list from a million florins to six hundred and fifty thousand. Certainly at that price the Dutch did not pay dearly for their sovereign, who has been not inaptly termed *un jocrisse de l'amour*, and who will take his place in the amorous regal history of this century between Victor Emanuel and Charles XV. of Sweden.

Women have been the arbiters of William's life, for good or evil, from his cradle. His mother was the first of these determining influences, and since then, young or old, Prince of Orange or King of Holland, he has never been quite free from the tutelage, charm, or obsession of the petticoat, and often and often he has made himself ridiculous, as the nickname of *jocrisse* proves.

William III., King of the Netherlands, Prince of Orange and Nassau, and Grand Duke of Luxemburg, was born February 19, 1817, the son of King William II. and his wife, Queen Anne, daughter of Czar Paul of Russia. This Princess was the subject of various matrimonial projects. Intended first for one of the spoilt children of Europe, a Prince of Saxe-Coburg, she was, after Tilsit, destined for Napoleon I. This plan fell through, and instead the Duke of Berry was substituted. This, too, failing, thanks to Talleyrand, the Grand Duchess had to content herself with the heir to the Dutch throne, which she ascended with him twenty-four years after their marriage. Of this union William III. was the eldest male issue, and since two living generations separated him from the throne he did not apply himself with great ardour to learning the art of governing. Nor did he excel in study generally, for great intelligence was never his strong point. For only one thing did he show a pronounced taste, and that was music, into which he threw himself with real ardour, even taking singing-lessons from Malibran. And this love for music remained with him all his life, and from his own purse he founded a Conservatoire for Holland,

and gave during the course of his reign really notable musical *fêtes* at his palace.

At twenty-two it was thought needful to marry him, and choice fell upon the Princess Sophia of Wurtemberg, one year his junior. That this marriage proved ill-suited is a matter universally known. It is perhaps a little less obvious why it should have been so unhappy, and the reason must be sought for entirely in the coarse nature of the King. It is true that Queen Sophia was not beautiful, but she was attractive and singularly charming, and her intelligence was rare. Unlike her spouse she took a keen interest in politics, had a fine taste for literature, and was desirous to make the Hague a centre of intellectual influences.

Incompatibility of tastes and manners made themselves felt at once, and the Prince more and more frequented low society, and while still cultivating his taste for music cultivated it with an increased attachment for the songstresses who produced it. Gradually his *affaires galantes* became the talk of Europe, and one of them has become embodied in Alexandre Dumas *fils* famous romance of "L'Affaire Clémenceau." The King who abandons his kingdom to visit Iza *incognito* at Paris for the space of a day and a night, and then returns to his kingdom to reign, is no other than the King of the Netherlands. Nor was this by any means his only notorious connection. There were others famous and familiar, not only to the Boulevards, but to all the continent. And when Louis Napoleon made himself Emperor and surrounded himself with a court of shady morality, the star of the *cocotse* was in the ascendant. William of Holland came to be regarded as the "bad boy" of a set not too scrupulous as to morality, and was said almost to rival his brother sovereign of Belgium in his knowledge of the sinful ways of London and Paris.

The ill-assorted union had dragged on for ten years, when in 1849 William succeeded to his father's throne, where stern duties awaited him. He despatched them all with a certain conscientiousness, but his change of station made no difference in his domestic relations. Indeed, it made things rather worse than better for the poor wife. Every courtier—as is the wont of courtiers —naturally desired to stand well with the ruler. There were formed factions for the King and factions for the Queen—the partizans of the latter in the minority, it is true, but much the most reputable members of the Court. Discord among these rival parties waged sharp and keen for some years. At last their ardour cooled, and while the Queen kept the respect and esteem of all the Court, questions of interest gradually brought over all in appearance to her husband's side. It was a sad life that was led by Queen Sophia. Well for her that she found so much in literature to comfort her.

In 1877, regretted by her people, if not by her liege lord, she was released by death. But scarcely was she dead than there occurred a strange phenomenon. Whether in consequence of his wife's death, or whether by coincidence merely, William of Holland suddenly awoke to the wisdom of the advice as to men "taking in sail" at a certain age. All in a moment he became a model monarch and man. He further contemplated the wisdom of re-marrying, for the two sons Queen Sophia had borne him could scarcely be counted on as heirs. The eldest, the Prince of Orange, Prince Citron as he was called on the Boulevards, had but too faithfully trodden in his father's gallant footsteps, and had at twenty-five worn out his constitution; the youngest was rickety in the highest degree. The royal choice fell upon Princess Emma of Waldeck-Pyrmont, and loud and long was the European pity expressed for this young girl of twenty about to make a May and December marriage. But contrary to all expectation the marriage turned out well, and Queen Emma appears to have been happy with the sexagenarian spouse, over whom she obtained great influence. They were wedded in 1879, and soon after the event the Prince of Orange died in voluntary exile at Paris after a miserable career of public and private scandal. He was followed five years after by his brother, who had been a lifelong invalid. As consolation for these losses there had been born to the couple in the meantime a little princess, Wilhelmina, who is the apple of her aged father's eye, and upon whose tender head will descend the crown of the Netherlands.

Of the character of such a mere child nothing can as yet be said. Queen Emma strives by her education to make the little Princess strong and self-reliant, to fashion her, as she calls it, into a King. All that is known of the Princess's tastes is that she has a perfect passion for outdoor amusements of all kinds. She loves driving, and skilfully handles a team of six ponies which she drives in a little carriage two abreast.

A pretty merry little child, who will no doubt win the hearts of her stolid and steady-going Dutch subjects, as her mother has done before her. Nor has she any enemies to dread, unless perchance the Germans, whom it might please some day to remove her from her little ocean-rescued kingdom in order to obtain a larger sea-board for themselves. Her sex would then prove to her disadvantage, for the worshippers of blood and iron would make little scruple of sweeping away a throne possessed by a woman. But that day happily has not yet dawned. The whirligig of time and the events that follow in its train may work changes in the ponderous German Empire caused by a revolt of even that patient people against the crushing burdens of militaryism. In any case, Holland still stands safe on her watery foundation, and in material progress she has certainly advanced under the forty years' reign of William III., a reign that has witnessed a revival of Dutch trade and fostered two great engineering enterprises, the draining of the Zuyder Zee and the desiccation of the Sea of Haarlem.

On the 23rd of November the long illness from which the King of Holland had been suffering came to a peaceful end at the Castle of Loo, and by his death the male line of the house of Nassau-Orange has become extinct. The Duchy of Luxembourg has passed into the hands of the deposed Duke of Nassau, and the little Princess Wilhelmina has become Queen of the Netherlands which, until her majority in 1898, will be ruled for her by her mother, Queen Emma, as Regent. This change of government is not likely to have any influence over the peaceful course of events in that small kingdom.

THE KING OF THE BELGIANS.

THE KING OF THE BELGIANS.
(*From a Photograph by the London Stereoscopic Company.*)

THE KING OF THE BELGIANS.

IF we except the Battenbergs, who are not even of legitimate princely birth, none of the many petty German princely families have been so lucky as the Coburgs. In what European country do we not find them, either seated upon its throne or associated with it by marriage? They have known how to push themselves everywhere, these princes, whose sole fortune was their good looks and their intelligence. A canny lot they were too, for in order that no avenue of fortune might be closed to them, they split up their family into a Protestant and Catholic section, and were thus able to meet all requirements as husbands or wives for Protestant or Catholic sovereigns. The founder of the family luck, that has been theirs for half a century, was Leopold, first King of the Belgians, the youngest of the clan, who married in 1816 the heiress to the British crown. Her death after a few months of marriage deprived him of the brilliant position that would have been his, but England continued to take an interest in his fortunes, and he became further bound up with her by ties of blood when his niece, the present Queen

Victoria, ascended the throne. In the meanwhile, however, he himself had become a king. For in 1830 had occurred the revolution that severed the Belgian provinces from the Netherlands, and out of the candidates put forward for the throne was selected Prince Leopold of Saxe Coburg, whose cause England had strongly favoured. For a third of a century he filled the post with great sagacity, making himself respected by his subjects and co-sovereigns. "If you don't want me," he used to say to the former, "I will take myself off. But don't fight about it. It's not worth while." As second wife he had espoused Princess Louise of Orleans, daughter of Louis Philippe, and it is the eldest son of that union who now sits upon the Belgian throne.

Whoever studies attentively the physiognomy of Leopold II., present King of the Belgians, cannot fail to be struck with the rigid look of his countenance which rather repels advances. And this physiognomy does not belie the King. He is not, and cannot be, a favourite with men; he lacks the personal gifts to attract them, and he lacks besides his father's astute wisdom to manipulate them, and this not so much because he is wanting in intelligence—indeed he is most intelligent— as that imagination and the softer qualities are little developed in his nature. A perfect gentleman in his manners, a most fluent and charming talker, he yet strikes all who come into intimate contact with him as a man who has no soul, no inner depths, and who, devoid of enthusiasms himself, is incapable of arousing them in others. Happily for the monarch, enthusiasms would be rather out of place among the phlegmatic Belgians, and since the kingdom is a constitutional one, nothing is required from the sovereign except to fulfil his duties, and this Leopold II. does to the best of his lights.*

It was on April 9, 1835, that Leopold II. was born at Brussels. Both he and his brother, the Count of Flanders, as well as their sister, the Princess Charlotte, the ill-fated Empress of Mexico, were brought up in the simplest way possible. The boys used to run about Laeken in little blouses with leather belts just like *bourgeois* boys, and they were taught to behave to every one with the greatest civility. They even lifted their caps to the gardener of the Palace.

Under the guidance of his father, and that father's favourite adviser, the German Doctor, Baron Stockmar, the same wise personage who managed to pull the wires also of the English Court, the young heir received a careful education. The programme mapped out was indeed an extensive and a stern one, the instruction imparted both solid and diversified, embracing all administrative, financial and military departments—in short, everything that should fit the future king for his post. And indeed on every one of these subjects he has tenacious ideas, which he tries to enforce as far as is

* In his relations with foreigners, notably with Gordon and Stanley, he has shown more heart and enthusiasm than in matters of home policy.

possible within constitutional limits. Is he a Liberal? Is he a Conservative? This question is difficult to answer, yet it is one that naturally is of great moment in Belgium, where party feelings run high. The first Leopold often said to Baron Stockmar: "With us the Catholic party is the only one that offers a resting place, the Liberal party is a sand-bank," and nominal Liberal though he was, he supported the Catholic party, working it for his own ends. Leopold II. has been less exclusive, or perhaps less cunning. His is a feebler character, that has vacillated between the two great parties in his State, now inclining to the Catholics, now to the Liberals, wishing to conciliate the susceptibilities of both, and succeeding only but too often in gaining their contempt. Of late years this contempt has increased to such an extent that often he is scarcely saluted when he walks or drives in the streets of his capital, and his appearance is greeted by cries of

"Au balcon, au balcon,
Le roi de carton."

Whether in so acting and thinking his subjects are quite just to him is a question of internal Belgian policy which it is not our province here to discuss. The Belgians are a restive people, and it is doubtful whether a more despotic and self-willed King would really be to their taste. Nor does a little kingdom like Belgium give scope for the display of great statesmanship. The *début* of Leopold II. in public life was certainly favourably received. The discourses spoken by him while yet Duke of Brabant in the Senate, of which he was an hereditary member, attested maturity of judgment and patriotic ardour. He took a very real and active part in the Sessions work, and the speeches delivered by him between 1854 and 1865 would form a goodly tome if collected into volume form. What he sought above all else for his country was progress, "progress," as he expressed it, "in arts, in letters, in industry, in commerce." He stimulated the one, he encouraged the other. As Crown Prince he showed great interest in the labour question, and, above all, in the question of securing to workmen dry wholesome dwellings. He also undertook a journey to the East—Egypt, Syria, Asia Minor, and Greece—and was the direct means of establishing regular steamship communication between Antwerp and the Levant, a project which he felt assured would be of benefit to Belgian commerce, as indeed it proved.

A year after his accession to the throne (1865) a plot was formed against the independence of Belgium, the roots of which were to be sought in the Tuileries, where reigned great jealousy of the growing might of Prussia, and a mad desire to have *revanche* for Sadowa. It was a difficult moment for the King, happily overcome by great tact on his part, and by the sympathetic assistance of England. But Napoleon III. was not easily daunted, and twice again he attempted to elude treaties and violate the neutrality rights of Belgium.

The last time was in 1869, when he sought to secure for himself the Luxemburg railway, that great strategic line. Aided by Prussia and England the Belgian government energetically resisted the French Emperor's aggressions, and forced him to abandon his projects. At this moment Leopold II. showed himself anything but feeble. Though plunged at the time in deep grief, his only son, the Duke of Brabant, having died but few weeks before, he yet kept the reins of the State so firmly in his hands that needless friction between the sovereigns was avoided, while at the same time he was careful to see that all should be ready in case of any emergency.

After this there followed the war of 1870-1, with the results, so little foreseen, of the re-establishment of the German Empire and the dethronement of Napoleon. Belgium issued with honour out of a difficult trial, fulfilling exactly all the duties her neutrality imposed on her, while affirming her existence and intention to maintain the same. It was at this epoch that Leopold II.'s popularity attained its height, because of the impartiality and prudence he had shown. While remaining a truly constitutional sovereign, he had known how, in moment of interior and exterior crisis, to calm the tempest by loyalty and firmness.

Since that time, however, the King has occupied himself more actively with military questions. Belgium, essentially an industrial country, does not care to be weighted with the expensive and exhausting burdens of a large standing army, but the King is of opinion, seeing the state of armed peace in which all Europe at present lives, that Belgium too must be ready to take its part whenever the general conflagration shall break out, and that it should introduce the German system of universal military service. "If we would keep our independent position," he says again and again, "we must be ready. There are constant dangers on the horizon. In the interest of our nationality it is needful that the Belgians should take more interest in Belgian politics."

The country thinks the army is large and efficient enough for all possible requirements; the King does not agree with this opinion, and the result is that of late much tension and friction has arisen between the sovereign and his people. Whether the monarch be right or wrong, there can be no question of his sincerity. He is not by nature bellicose or fond of the army. In contrast to his father, who had something of the German military manners, a circumstance that made him feared by his *entourage*, and not always popular with his subjects, Leopold II. is essentially a *bourgeois* and peace-loving in his tastes. His father could never forget that he had been brought up in a rude school, and had to go to war at an early age. Leopold II.'s reign inaugurated a more calm, more *bourgeois* royal existence, and the Belgians, to whom this is more congenial, do not desire to see it disturbed. Time will show how the imbroglio disentangles itself.

It was in 1853, before his accession to the throne,

that Leopold married the Archduchess Marie Henriette of Austro-Hungary. Four children sprang from their union: the Duke of Brabant, whom they were to lose all too soon, and three princesses. The eldest married Prince Philip of Coburg; the second is the Princess Stephanie, widow of the hapless Crown Prince Rudolf of Austria; the third, the Princess Clementine, is still unwedded. Report assigns her to the Prince of Naples, King Humbert's only child. Both before and after their accession to the throne, the family of Leopold II. lived with great simplicity. The girls were brought up without the least pretension, and even went to a school, the Sacre Cœur of Jette, situated at half an hour's distance from the royal castle of Laeken, where they joined in all the studies and recreations of the other pupils. The King above all loves a quiet life, and devotion to scientific work. At the commencement of his reign he was rarely to be seen in the streets dressed in uniform. He is a most indefatigable walker, and with his long legs strides across the ground, tiring out almost all his companions. It is a characteristic trait that he never wears gloves. It is true, he owns a beautiful hand, of very aristocratic cut, and in this above all he proves that he is descended from the Orleans family, who were noted for their exquisitely-shaped hands.

From every point of view the King's life is one of great simplicity. He sleeps in a camp bed, and has a horror of anything that could enervate. He rises early, generally at six. After a light repast he goes into his study, where he carefully examines all the papers and documents concerning State business that have accumulated there since the previous day. To this work he gives the most minute attention, reading everything himself and annotating with his own hand. Before according a favour, a distinction, he often does not rest satisfied with what is presented to him officially, but makes private inquiries as to the person's worth. He never signs anythink à la légere, which reminds us of an anecdote little known, but whose authenticity we can guarantee. It was some years ago, at a Court ball. The King was making the tour of the rooms when he saw a functionary who that same morning had received his promotion. "I congratulate you, M. le Directeur," said his Majesty.

"How, Sire, you knew that I had been named Director?"

"Learn, Monsieur," replied the King, " that I never sign a nomination without reading the name of the person to whom I accord a favour."

And so speaking he turned his back upon his abashed auditor.

Still it must not be inferred from this anecdote that Leopold is caustic and overbearing. He knows men, he has studied and united with them much, he knows how to be indulgent and to forgive easily any little defects, weaknesses, or incoherences of human nature. Thus he gladly and readily pardons the condemned whenever possible, or commutes their sentences. Of capital punishment he is a resolute adversary. "Never," he said, before his accession, "shall a drop of blood flow during my reign." And verily in Belgium, if capital punishment is not abolished *de jure*, it is *de facto*.

To the pleasures of the table the King is also insensible. He eats little, and prefers frugal to sumptuous meals. He hardly ever touches wine; water is his favourite beverage. Amusements, too, are not loved by him. As for the theatre, he almost hates it, and never puts his foot inside one when he can absolutely avoid it. Nevertheless he contributes, out of his private purse, an annual sum of a hundred thousand francs towards its maintenance. The same dislike extends to the opera. In this he differs widely from the Queen, who passionately loves music, and is seen in the royal box almost every evening. Riding is the King's chief pastime. He rides once or twice a day, generally going to the Bois, winter and summer. He reads enormously, and keeps himself posted up with all that goes on. And this love of being *au courant*, he actually extends to a quite pronounced liking for gossip, for hearing the chit-chat, the little scandals of the town. He knows his Brussels as well as one of its most ancient burghers. For faces he has a surprising memory. In the street, at public ceremonies, he immediately recognizes and remembers not only the physiognomy, but the name and the circumstances when he last met the person.

One day his Majesty was on the pier at Ostend walking about quite quietly among the crowd of his subjects like a simple citizen. He sees a Brussels burgher and accosts him: "*Eh, bien*, and how are your orchids?" "My orchids, Sire?" "*Mais oui*, those which you exhibited two years ago."

The flower amateur had himself forgotten that he had thus exhibited, other matters having meantime absorbed his attention.

Leopold II. possesses that art, so precious for a King, of finding ever the proper word to say at the right moment to every one, no matter who it may be. For example, when he visits a picture gallery he knows how to encourage the young beginners, often buying their first works. Whatever the *milieu* in which he finds himself, he knows how to put himself at the standpoint of the people with whom he speaks. Thus when he visited the famous establishment Cockerill, in company with the Shah of Persia, he approached a group of workmen and, pressing their hands, said, "Never forget my good fellows, that we must all work. We are all workmen in our respective spheres."

England is especially dear to the King, and he takes a deep concern in all that affects it, whether great or small. He speaks the language with rare purity, and is never happier than when he can talk in that tongue. That he often visits England *incognito* is well known.

Another of the royal hobbies, and one which threatens to absorb him entirely, is the Congo State, which he may be said to have founded. The idea was one that he had long cherished. Even before his accession he was struck with the fact that Belgium since its severance from

Holland was deprived of all those trade outlets that are so profitable. Was it not possible for his young kingdom to attempt something upon the vast coast of Africa? Influenced by the recitals of Stanley and his own private studies on the theme, the King finally took the initiative in a work which will very likely secure to him an eminent place in history. He constituted himself the promoter of a crusade whose purpose is to civilize that great mysterious continent of Africa. In 1876 a preliminary conference was held in Brussels in which the King laid before the representatives of the European Powers the project he had elaborated. In 1885 was founded the Independent State of the Congo under the sovereignty of his Belgian Majesty, with a central government at Brussels and an executive government upon the spot. With the affairs of this State the King is constantly and actively occupied; it is his hobby, his passion, for whose sake he has not hesitated to spend vast sums out of his private purse, and though he is immensely rich, it is said that his speculations on the Congo have embarrassed him not a little financially. He is firmly convinced that his plan will prosper, and that one day his kingdom will find that he has dowered it with a source of great wealth. It is more than probable that he is right. But meanwhile there is rife among the people, a certain discontent with these schemes of the sovereign, of whose success they do not feel as certain as he. They reproach him with neglecting the affairs of Belgium for those of the Congo. In this they are unjust. Leopold is endowed with great powers of work, and has physical strength sufficient to occupy himself with two things at a time. A proof of the injustice of the accusation is to be found in his never tiring advocacy of the principle of universal military service. Further, he just now devotes much attention to the question of planting the sand dunes, and has himself repeatedly visited the spot to superintend in person the progress of the work.

It has been often and rightly remarked that, had Leopold II. been born in the burgher class, or no matter in whatever other condition, he would have made himself talked about, and would have become a remarkable man. As a monarch he has, for some cause not quite clear, missed that popularity which other monarchs seem to gain so easily and often without desert.

The Belgian people have much more sympathy with their Queen, who is also a woman of rare intelligence. Although but a year younger than the King, she has preserved into maturity the grace and quick wit of youth. Her appearance at first sight gives the impression of *hauteur*, but closer observation reveals that this apparent coldness covers a warm heart and also one that has suffered keenly. The mother has never recovered the grief of losing her only son. Her chief occupations are works of charity. She loves to comfort those in distress, and it is said that her goodness and patience with her poor demented sister-in-law, the Empress Charlotte, is most touching to witness. She is the only person who has some little influence over the distracted lady.

As a wife, Queen Marie Henriette is not happy. She knows full well, what all the world knows also, that her husband seeks his pleasures away from her. She tries to find consolation and distraction in the arts. Horsemanship and horses are also a great delight of hers. She frequently goes into the stables and inspects her favourite steeds, even grooming them herself at times. At all hours of the day she may be met either on horseback, followed by a groom, or driving two ponies in an elegant little phaeton.

But this love of horses does not hinder her from being an artist. She is an excellent musician, playing well upon the piano and the harp. She often composes. Few know that she has even written an opera called "Wanda, ou la puissance de l'Amour," which was once represented at the Court. She also paints, and is well versed in artistic matters. A great reader too, but her literature is of the lightest kind, consisting of most of the new French, English, and German novels that appear. She too prefers a life of great simplicity, and detests all luxury. Her dress is of a plainness many a burgher lady could imitate with advantage.

Under these circumstances it is easy to imagine that the Belgian Court is not a gay or brilliant one. The sovereigns live like quiet private citizens. Excepting two Court balls a year, a garden party at Laeken, and a few official dinners, there are never any *fêtes* at the

Palace. Early in the reign, and above all under Leopold I., things were very different. But since their irreparable loss fell upon the sovereigns, in the death of the Duke of Brabant, both King and Queen have grown grave and sad. This fatal event contributed not a little towards the establishment of a severer mode of life, banishing from the royal residence all that could give it animation. There bleeds in the hearts of the Belgian royal couple a wound that will never be staunched.

More popular than King or Queen are the Duke and Duchess of Flanders, the King's brother and sister-in-law. It is at their abode that the *elite* of society meets; they give magnificent *fêtes* and pleasant little social *réunions*, and both are extremely amiable and gracious in manner. Unfortunately the Count is almost stone deaf and very delicate. On this account it is firmly believed that in the event of his brother's demise he would resign all pretension to the crown, which would then pass to his eldest son, Prince Baudoin. This young man, who was born in 1869, is highly popular among his future subjects. Carefully educated and trained, he is said to be a youth not devoid of ability. His open physiognomy, his democratic education, the ardour he displays in favouring the Flemish tongue, all contribute towards securing for him that inscrutable halo of public favour which so well becomes young princes whose future is still enveloped in mystery.

THE ROYAL FAMILY OF DENMARK.

THE KING OF DENMARK.
(From a Photograph by the London Stereoscopic Company.)

THE ROYAL FAMILY OF DENMARK.

WHEN, in 1863, Frederick VII. of Denmark died without heirs, the throne of the "Goths and Vends" was assigned, with the consent of Europe and in accordance with the Treaty of London of 1852, to Duke Frederick Christian of Schleswig-Holstein-Sonderburg-Glücksburg. The "Protocol Prince," as he was derisively nicknamed, had married, in 1842, Princess Louis of Hesse-Cassel, whose mother had been a Danish Princess, sister of Christian VIII., the predecessor of King Frederick. It was therefore through his wife that the present King became entitled to the legitimate possession of the throne.

A troublous time it was for Denmark when Christian IX. took its crown on his head, and he himself helped to make it yet more troublous, for on his accession he first hesitated whether he should recognize the Constitution accorded to the people by his predecessor. This at once caused grave discontent, and when, further, he refused to sanction a property bill for Schleswig-Holstein, the exasperation of his subjects threatened him with a revolution; for the Danes to this day remain a turbulent people, and some "tumultuous processions," as they say at Copenhagen, soon showed the newly-made King the temperament of the nation. He yielded and signed. But it was against the grain. Christian does not love constitutional forms, and would never of his own free will have been a constitutional sovereign.

The King of Denmark's own views have, however, counted for little during his reign. He has been largely the victim of adverse circumstances. The first storm-cloud dispersed, he had, after eight months of rule, to meet a second and yet blacker one, for in 1864 broke out the war waged by Prussia and Austria against the helpless little kingdom, that was to be the commencement of Prussia's aggrandizement and Austria's Germanic eclipse.

The ostensible cause for fighting was the Schleswig-Holstein question; but little is known precisely as to what that question was. It is even more complicated than the Balkan one, which is saying a great deal; and it has caused as many rivers of blood and ink to flow. Lord Palmerston was in the habit of saying in the last years of his life—"There have never been but two men who really comprehended the question about the duchies: Prince Albert, who is dead, and I, who have forgotten it."

Roughly speaking, the whole was a drama in three acts: Act I. The German confederation, aided by Austria and Prussia, proposed to conquer the duchies.

The Germanic confederation was ousted, and Austria and Prussia undertook the war alone. Act II. The duchies conquered, the allies announced that they made over their possessions to the Duke of Augustenburg,* but the pretender soon found himself treated like the German confederation. Act III. and last. Austria and Prussia fight among themselves for the spoils; and Sadowa ensuing, Austria, ousted from Germany, left the famous duchies in the hands of Prussia, where they remain to this day, although Prussia bound herself by treaty to restore to Denmark Northern Schleswig, which was nearly all old Danish crown land, if the population desired it. A quarter of a century has since passed, and the question has not even been put, nor will it ever be.

Hence before he had been upon the throne eight months King Christian had lost a third of his dominions, and was forced to sign a solemn treaty, ceding to his foes that which they had taken by main force. Thus Christian of Denmark was the first in Europe to pay tribute to the nascent German Empire. Since that day, and not without just cause, King Christian has renounced an international policy; but for all that no peace was to be his.

Ever since his accession the King may be said to have been in chronic feud with his Parliament, and Ministerial crises seem perennial in the little kingdom. The fact is that the Danes are not an easy people to

* Father of the present Empress of Germany.

govern, and democratic ideas have considerable vogue in their dominion. Christian, on the other hand, is not a man of modern views. It would be difficult to find upon a European throne a person more upright, excellent, and loyal, or a more perfect gentleman in manners and education, but he was brought up in a petty Court, and attained a crown too late in life to enlarge his mental horizon. The King detests democratic ideas, and it is his pride to keep them in check.

Fortunately for himself personally he has had of late years in Herr J. P. S. Estrup a Prime Minister who conducts matters with a high hand and without fear of the anger he excites, or the pistol shots to which he is exposed. This species of Danish Bismarck, who since 1875 has held office, is a consumptive little man, who, in a small frame, however, possesses a great portion of energy—an energy that is, indeed, almost Bismarckian, though morally as well as physically this man is a pigmy when compared with his Teutonic model. The conflict in Denmark is also a miniature reproduction of that waged in the Prussian Diet before Sadowa, in which Bismarck supported his King. At Copenhagen, too, Crown and Parliament carry on a constant duel, in which up to the present the Crown has remained victor. But who can tell whether this will last? Indeed, in these progressive days, one may almost safely predict that it will not.

All these internal dissensions have contributed to make King Christian anything but a popular monarch, though at the same time his people, recognizing his personal qualities, in the lapse of years have come to have for the man a sincere affection and sympathy. As a man he is universally beloved and esteemed; and when, in November, 1888, King Christian celebrated the twenty-fifth anniversary of his accession, it was regarded and treated as a *fête* for domestic rather than political sympathy. And truly for Christian IX. may be reversed the saying of La Bruyère: "Il ne manque rien à un Roi que la douceur de la vie privée." The ease of public life has been lacking to the King of Denmark; all private happiness possible to man he has enjoyed to the full. A much-tried sovereign, he has been and is the happiest of husbands and fathers; blameless and irreproachable in every respect. It was not derisively that the populace of Copenhagen sang beneath the Royal windows on a raw November evening of 1888 a popular ditty of which the refrain runs: "It is a fine family, that of King Christian."

To begin with, the King has been singularly fortunate in his consort. His wife is certainly a queen among women. Fifteen months his senior, Queen Louise has remained young in visage and form, although her hair is now sprinkled with grey. Well stricken in years (72), she looks at least fifteen years younger than she is. Nor has she only the charm of looks, but that also of intellect. Queen Louise has an exceptionally bright and quick intelligence, unusual powers of judgment, a highly gifted nature, and a heart of gold. Her graciousness of manner, her kindly looks win the hearts of all who come in contact with her. Her education, her mental gifts would have justified her in taking an active part in public affairs; and perchance she would have saved her husband much annoyance. But she has preferred to keep herself in the background, and has claimed instead to rule with all liberty in the royal home. And right wisely has she exerted her sway. That the Danish Royal Family is so united, that the Danish Court is the stock instance of the power of domestic virtue in politics, that few royal houses have made for their children alliances so brilliant, thrown out so many shoots all over Europe, is all due to the Queen's goodness, energy, and wisdom.

There are certainly few ladies, even in private life, who at the Queen's age lead such a busy, active life as she does. An early riser, her days are fully occupied from morning to night, and she rarely allows herself an idle moment. And besides all her household and representative duties, the Queen keeps up an extensive correspondence, for the three married daughters and the absent son, King George of Greece, each expect to be kept *au courant* of all sorts of details concerning their much-loved Danish home, and no one can give them so well as " mamma."

The Queen is further devoted to painting and music, and does all in her power to encourage these arts, in both of which she is no mean proficient. She is perhaps most devoted to painting, admitting herself that, much as she loves music and enjoys playing—indeed, she is an untiring performer—she would always leave that to go and paint, while no one can persuade her to stop painting to go to the piano. More than one poor little village church in Denmark possesses an altar-piece specially painted for it by her Majesty, of which the inhabitants are duly proud, as will readily be understood. Of music the Queen has a most thorough knowledge. She is an appreciative and intelligent listener, for fortunately her deafness does not interfere with her enjoyment of musical sounds.* No concert in Copenhagen seems complete without the Queen's presence, and she seldom misses any. All foreign artists who come to Denmark, though they often complain that the Danish audience is a cold one, are delighted at the reception they meet with from the sovereign. One of her Majesty's greatest pleasures is to get a large bundle of new music, principally duets, and to try them over, for she has a wonderful gift for playing at sight.

In the days when the royal couple were only two poor princelings their life was a most simple one, and many tales are told of how the Princesses, now Empresses and Queens apparent, made and did up their dresses, and how the parents would drive out in one carriage with all their six children squeezed into it.

* The Princess of Wales unfortunately inherits her mother's deafness, but, like her mother, makes up for weakness in the ears by exceptional quickness of eye.

Their life was divided between Copenhagen, Jugenheim (near Darmstadt), and Frankfurt-on-Maine. At the two latter places Duke Christian—not then even nominated presumptive successor to the Danish Crown—eked out his slender income by giving drawing-lessons. No wonder, therefore, that his three little girls gave no credence to a gypsy who in those days foretold for them glorious destinies, promising to one a double crown of queen and empress, to another rule over a large empire, and to a third a queenly title without a kingdom.

But though devoid of luxury and splendour, there was still no happier, more patriarchal home in the length and breadth of Denmark. This is proved alone by the eagerness shown by all the absent children to come home—sure as they are, too, of always having a most hearty welcome from high and low, rich and poor. The King and Queen have no less than thirty-three grandchildren, all of whom, from the most grown-up to the youngest baby, are equally fond of both grandparents, and always enchanted to come to Denmark, where they enjoy a life of unlimited freedom. All the various English, Russian, Greek, and Danish cousins are the best of friends.

Bernstorff is the name of the favourite royal summer residence, situated about a couple of miles from Copenhagen, on the outskirts of that most beautiful deer-park Dyshans, of which all Danes are justly proud. The Queen is particularly fond of staying there, but when all the children and grandchildren are assembled together, as they have so frequently been during the last few years, then Bernstorff is too small to house them all, for it is not large. In consequence the Court moves yet further into the country to the castle of Fredensborg, not far from Elsinore—that spot replete with memories of the ill-fated Prince Hamlet of Denmark.

No reminiscences of any importance are connected with the castle, but the gardens were once celebrated all over Europe—that was in the days when stiffly-shaped trees and clipped hedges could make an impression. Now, in the autumn months, when the beautiful Danish beech-woods are rendered doubly attractive by their changing tints and many-hued foliage, news from Fredensborg is eagerly looked for by all loyal subjects in England, Russia, and Greece, who follow with interest the movements of their respective royalties whilst away on their travels.

Many are the anecdotes told of those happy merry days at Fredensborg, where even the Emperor and Empress of Russia are able for a while to forget their cares and anxieties, and really enjoy a peaceful life free from hidden dangers. Very frequent, too, are the little expeditions to Copenhagen, when loyal Danes are delighted to see the Empress of Russia together with the Princess of Wales, and probably the King of Greece, going about quietly doing their own shopping, or catch a glimpse of the Emperor driving about in a cab with his three English nieces. He is a great walker, this

Emperor, and, like his father-in-law, a keen sportsman; so that there are constant shooting-parties held at Fredensborg. King Christian is an admirable horseman, and rarely passes a day without riding; and walking, too, is a favourite recreation. In the winter months it is quite common to meet the King in the streets of Copenhagen with no attendant save two collie dogs, one of which, the faithful Rover, was given to him when a puppy by Queen Victoria.

No one can be fonder of a romp with the little ones than the King, and stories are told of how at Fredensborg his Majesty has been seen seated in a very diminutive pony-carriage, trusting himself to the care of a very youthful coachman. Another time he was himself the willing horse for a still younger driver. It is wonderful how at his age he has kept his freshness and elasticity. After dinner it is he who invites his grandchildren to perform gymnastics, and sets them the example. He has a great opinion of the value of physical exercises of all kinds.

When the family are assembled together the Queen always takes advantage of having her daughters with her to perform music in common. It is not rare for them to play eight hands on two pianos—the Queen and Duchess of Cumberland at one, the Empress of Russia and the Princess of Wales at the other. She has great moral influence over these daughters, but is also careful not to bias them in any way in the discharge of the particular duties required by their respective exalted stations.

As a rule their majesties spend Christmas at Fredensborg, and early in January the Court moves into Copenhagen. From then till the King's birthday (April 8th) is the so-called season in the Danish capital. When in town the royal couple go constantly to the theatre. In fact, hardly an evening passes when the King does not look in for an hour or so. There is but one really first-class theatre in Copenhagen, the Royal; but whenever there is anything worth seeing at any of the other houses, the Court always goes.

The hours are early. The opera begins at seven o'clock, and most concerts at half-past seven. The Court dinner is at half-past five, and it used to be as early as five o'clock. The hour for luncheon is one o'clock, and this meal is always quite unceremonious, no ladies or gentlemen being in waiting, only the now much reduced family party, consisting of the King and Queen, and the King's two brothers, the Princes Wilhelm and Hans of Glücksburg.

The windows of the luncheon room look out on to the open square, or rather octagon-shaped " Plads," on which the four palaces of Amalienburg stand; and every day during the severe weather of last winter the King and Queen invariably collected all that remained on the table after lunch was over, and, making up a large newspaper parcel, passed it through the window to the poor workhouse men who were always there sweeping up the perpetual snow.

Very often, just as lunch is over, some of the Crown

Prince's children come over to pay a hurried visit to their grandparents before going back to lessons or to their daily walk or drive.

The dinner, of course, is an affair of more stiffness and etiquette, as the maids of honour (of whom the Queen has three, and who live in the palace), the master of ceremonies, the King's adjutants, and the officers on duty of the guard, all dine at the same table as their majesties. After dinner, if there is no theatre that evening, they all retire to their respective rooms, and reassemble at nine o'clock for tea, when the rest of the evening is spent in card-playing. The King, as a rule, has a rubber of whist, and the rest of the party play a round game.

Prince Waldemar, the "Sailor Prince," and the youngest of the family, lives in the so-called Yellow Palace, the same in which his parents lived before they were King and Queen, and where all their children, with this last exception, were born.

Prince Waldemar is united to Princess Marie of Orleans, daughter of the Duc de Chartres. It is worth mentioning that this couple were married quite simply, without any ceremony, by the Maire of the Parisian arrondissement where the Princess lived. They have two sons, the eldest of whom, little Prince George, not yet two years old, is the Queen's favourite companion in her daily drives.

The remaining five children of the royal couple are Frederick Christian, Crown Prince, born in 1843, and married to Princess Louise of Sweden, only daughter of the late King Charles XV.; Alexandra, who was married to the Prince of Wales some months ere her father ascended his throne; William George, King of the Hellenes, married to the charming Grand Duchess Olga of Russia; Dagmar, now reigning Empress of Russia; and Thyra, married to the Duke of Cumberland, King of Hanover *in spe*. The latter Princess, after giving birth to five children, was for some years the victim of a nervous malady that affected her reason. Happily the crisis has passed, and the Castle of Gmünden, where the princely couple reside, has resumed its wonted animation.

Crown Prince Frederick, who is already forty-five years of age, has seven children. He is a model father of a family, and an excellent type of heir-apparent—studious, eloquent, amiable, rich, open-handed, and yet not extravagant. His wife, eight years his junior, is remarkable for her quick-wittedness and intelligence. On her first advent at the quiet Danish Court she shocked it a little by her mode of dressing, and her freedom of manners, but she has now toned down, and fitted herself into the simple burgher old-world *milieu*.

The residence of the Crown Prince is opposite the King's, and the two remaining palaces occupy the other side of the "Plads." One of these, which was formerly the residence of the Queen Dowager, is now given up to the Ministry for Foreign Affairs, while the fourth, connected by a covered colonnade with the King's palace, is principally used for any festivities at Court, for since the burning of Christiansborg Castle in 1884, where there were such magnificent halls and reception-rooms, they have been rather at a loss for sufficient room to receive all the invited guests on any great occasions. On the ground-floor of this fourth palace the Queen's sister, Princess Augusta of Hesse, has her winter apartments.

The Danish Civil List is not rich, especially since the loss of the duchies. All included, it scarcely amounts to two million francs. Nevertheless the Royal couple are most liberal. The Queen in especial takes a lively and personal interest in all charitable institutions existing in the realm, and above all in asylums or hospitals for children, as she is essentially a children's friend. Kind and thoughtful to a degree, always ready with generous and judicious help whenever it is needed, never forgetting a good armful of toys when she goes to visit the little patients, the children naturally feel they have a loving friend and helper in their Queen.

Such, then, is this Danish royal family, and if the Danes—or at least a majority among them—are not satisfied with their King as ruler, they are enchanted with him as burgher, as father-in-law, and father. As for their Queen, they simply worship her. Strangers who come to Copenhagen, and who have the privilege of entry at Court, can indeed say with all loyal Danes— who are justly proud not only of their King and Queen, but of the many powerful connections gained for the country by the various marriages made by their children—that the Danish royal family is indeed an exceptional one.

THE KING OF SWEDEN.

THE KING OF SWEDEN.
(From a Photograph by Gösta Florman.)

THE KING OF SWEDEN.

IN the lovely town of Pau, romantically situated in the French Pyrenees, stands, close by the church of St. Jacques, a small grey one-storeyed unpretentious house. Over its door runs an inscription, and from it the passer-by may learn how Charles Jean Bernadotte, who was born in this house in 1763, became in after years King Charles XIV. (John) of Sweden. A truly romantic history that of the Bernadottes, who, thanks to an historical accident, were raised from simple obscure burghers of Pau to be rulers of the finest kingdom in northern Europe. But if mere chance raised them to this proud position, it was not mere chance that enabled them to retain it. In the general hurly-burly that followed the fall of Napoleon, the Bernadottes were among the few newly-made dynasties who were able to retain their thrones, and this because the King, like his after-time successors, had proved to his people that though he might be a *parvenu* among sovereigns, he was a sovereign among men—a person of superior mind and merit, who had quickly learnt to comprehend the character and requirements of his subjects, and whose one desire was to satisfy the same. King Charles John, the first Bernadotte sovereign, was succeeded by his son Oscar I., and he in his turn by his son Charles XV.; and all their reigns, from 1818 down to the present date, were years of peace and prosperity for Sweden.

It was in 1872 that the fourth regent of the burgher family of Pau ascended the Scandinavian throne. King Oscar II. (Frederick), the reigning monarch, is the third son of King Oscar I. and his consort, Princess Josephine of Leuchtenberg, a daughter of Eugène Beauharnais, the step-son of Napoleon the Great. When Prince Oscar Frederick was born his father was Crown Prince, and his grandfather, King Charles John, still reigned with undiminished vigour, notwithstanding his great age. There seemed, therefore, little prospect that this younger son would ever ascend the throne. It was consequently not thought needful to educate him with this goal in view, and he was permitted to follow his own inclinations, which attracted him powerfully to a sailor's life. At the age of eleven he entered the Swedish navy. Here he worked just like any common midshipman, and passed all the grades before he was promoted to be lieutenant. The thoroughness that characterizes his mind was noticed already then. He insisted on studying *au fond* all that bore on his profession directly or indirectly; and the notes made by him of his voyages at the time attest his powers of observation. His first sea voyage took him to

England and the Mediterranean on board the frigate *Eugénie*, which at that time (1846) was commanded by Captain von Krusenstjerod, an officer to whom the young subordinate became deeply attached, and on whose death he wrote a powerful poem, full of deep feeling. The Prince was twenty when he returned from this cruise, his mind enlarged, his stock of knowledge enriched. He then, at his father's wish, attended the University of Upsala, where he distinguished himself in mathematics, while never neglecting or abandoning his naval pursuits; so that in due course he rose to the rank of Admiral. His excellent abilities, his personal amiability, made him beloved of his equals and inferiors in the navy, a love he returned, as is proved in his poem, "Memories of the Swedish Fleet" —a fleet in which, as he says in his dedication, he passed the happiest and most careless years of his youth; on the sea were dreamed his brightest youthful dreams, were knit his dearest friendships. This poem, which was a competition work written at the instigation of the Swedish Academy of Science, carried off the prize. It had been sent in anonymously. Indeed, to this day the King signs all his writings either simply "Oscar Frederick," or "Oscar."

After leaving the University and passing the needful military studies, Prince Oscar once more resumed his naval life, visiting in the course of his travels many lands and Courts. In 1852 the sudden death of his brother Gustav, a prince endowed with rare musical ability, for the first time made the world regard him as a possible Swedish ruler, for up to that date his brother Charles's marriage had proved childless. This event made it desirable that Prince Oscar should marry, and his father sent him forth to the Continent, to visit the Courts of Europe, and seek for himself the wife that should please his fancy, for at the Swedish Court mere marriages of reason and politics were not *de rigueur*. What distinguished the Swedish Bernadottes, and distinguishes all their descendants, is their truly noble and loving family life, whence spring grand and beautiful human beings, ennobled by this, the only truly potent factor of education. It was at the little Court of Wied that Prince Oscar first saw the woman who has been to him a true helpmate and loving consort. His meeting with her is told in his poem "Monrepos," the name of the Prince of Wied's family castle. In 1857 he led to his far northern home his "angel bright and good," the Princess Sophia of Nassau.

A quiet, happy, retired life was that led by the young couple, the mother occupied with the care of the baby boy who the following year came to charm their hearts, and that of the delighted grandfather; the father busy with his scientific studies, with projects for the development of his country's navy, with art, music, and literature. It was then he wrote his drama ("Castle Kronberg"), since often acted both in Sweden and abroad, originally written in French. He also at this time devoted much care to the study of military art, giving an impetus to the founding of the Swedish Military Literary Union, in which society he himself delivered a number of most admirable lectures on themes bearing upon army matters. Voyages and voyagers naturally claimed his vivid interest as an ex-sailor. He especially encouraged all Arctic explorations; wherefore a land discovered by Swedish explorers has been named after him—Prince Oscar's Land. Many academical dissertations held by the Prince also date from the time ere he was called to rule. Most notable among these, and afterwards collected into a volume, are the "Musical Festival Speeches," delivered at various intervals from 1864 to 1871. In these the King shows himself not only the excellent musician he is, but also an admirable critic. He does not treat music as an abstract art, detached from all other human endeavours; he considers it rather as part of the grand whole of our intellectual life, bound up with the sister sciences, and reflecting with them in intimate union the whole spiritual character of the people among which it takes birth. Both as regards form and language, these addresses are far above the average. Indeed, their language often rises to poetic eloquence; as in the first, in which the speaker sets forth his musical creed, of which the main dogma is that Nature is inseparable from harmony. "When God spoke that mighty word, 'Let there be light,' He created at the same time with the outer world, the world of harmony, the world of sound." In "winged language" he then goes on to tell of the cosmopolitan character of music—cosmopolitan, and yet national—for each people gives it its own peculiar stamp. A poetical translation of Goethe's "Torquato Tasso" into Swedish earned for its author the honour of election as a corresponding member of the Frankfort Academy of Sciences. It was preceded by an exquisitely graceful dedication to his wife, telling how what Leonora had been to Tasso, she had been to him—the love, the inspirer, the crowning happiness of his existence. Indeed, this royal poet is specially felicitous in translation, as he proved also in a version of Herder's "Cid," and as he may yet prove some later day, when the piles of manuscripts, original and translated, that have accumulated unprinted since he ascended the throne are allowed to see the light of day. Hitherto his royal duties have hindered him from finding the needful time for press revision, and so also has a certain timidity, a fear lest they should earn praise merely on account of their writer's rank, rather than for their intrinsic merits.

Not long, however, could Prince Oscar thus live the life of a simple burgher who has no duties to the masses. In 1859 his father died, and his brother ascended the throne. As the now King was still childless, it fell to Prince Oscar to fill the *rôle* of Crown Prince and undertake all the onerous offices of that post, a post from which he never was relieved until his brother's sudden and unexpected death in

1872 placed the crown upon his own brow. His poetic gifts hence had to rest awhile, but only for awhile. In intervals of business, in spare moments, Oscar Frederick is always ready to use his pen. The list of his published works alone is a long as well as a worthy record. After Gustavus III., he is certainly the most literary monarch Sweden ever possessed. While acting as Crown Prince, it was history that chiefly attracted his attention, and he then wrote his memoir of Charles XII. of Sweden, which he first delivered publicly in the form of a speech. Notwithstanding Voltaire's immortal work on the same theme, the King of Sweden's memoir holds its own for grace of style and narrative form, and is besides far more accurate as regards fact than that of his French predecessor on the same domain. The poems of the same date are all inspired by the royal author's keen love of Nature. His sailor life had awakened his powers of observation, his familiarity with Nature in all her moods; and this he has known well how to reflect in his verse. His very real and simple piety, too, finds an outlet in his poems. "Easter Hymn" can be worthily placed beside any of the best evangelical church songs. A German translation of these poems was, by the King's express desire, dedicated to the then Crown Prince Frederick William (Frederick III.), as "the patron of work, of peace, and humanity."

Perchance one of the most charming poems the royal author ever penned is that he calls, "In my Home."

It refers to his favourite castle in the Sound of Helsingborg (Sofiero); so called in compliment to his wife. And the verses tell of a stroll through the domain under the guidance of its lord. It is a cycle of five poems, describing what may be seen from the various windows. "A few square panes of glass," he sings, "but how many pictures it affords me!" He then describes the view, he recalls the old strange Sagas of Sweden's past; he knits that past so skilfully in union with the present that the cycle forms a perfect series of pictures of Sweden's story.

"In my home," writes the worthy host, "many a window remains unclosed. I love to feel the summer's breezes, I love to feel the sky my roof. From far the vaporous sea wind fans my brow. Here is the room in which I dwell myself. Enter it, guest, from out the breezy balcony."

After leading his guest from room to room, the royal poet arrives at last at those dwelt in by the hostess. "These," he sings, "are *her* favourite rooms; here flowers are bathed in sunshine. There is no sweeter freehold than this that she has chosen for herself. An awning covers the verandah, whence resting, our eyes look over the ocean spread beyond. And round about is room for children's sports; to learn to play, also to slumber, ever near the mother, for such is our custom. Above is my small treasure-house of books that has the view I speak of, and room is here besides for many a faithful friend, a dear acquaintance. Then tell me, could I desire a larger house, more brilliant rooms? My bed stands peacefully under a peaceful roof, my days are filled with art, science, and poesy; and day by day I drink rich draughts of nectar from the balmy forest airs, from ocean's wave."

Indeed, Prince Oscar's ambition did not rise above the laurel of poetic fame. When the kingly crown descended on his head, he accepted the burden with resignation. He sighed sadly at exchanging his quiet burgher existence for the uneasy honours of a throne. He accepted the post as his duty, and conscientiously has he fulfilled what he then undertook.

It was in 1872 that the Duke of Oester-Götland (as Oscar Frederick was called till then) ascended the dual throne of Sweden and Norway. In his first address to his Riksdag he sketched the programme of the policy to which he has ever remained faithful.

"Like my noble predecessors," he said, "I too have decided to choose a device. I am deeply penetrated with the sense that the royal crown which has fallen to me as heir is not lent to me for mere outer splendour, rather I know and admit that my responsible royal mission, of which the crown is a symbol, has been laid upon me to promote *the welfare of the brother nations*. May these words be my motto, ' Brödrafolkens Väl'! May they give expression to my ardent love for the two nations united by my great predecessor, whose happiness is my highest earthly goal! May they indicate the nature to which, with God's help, my actions, as Sweden and Norway's King, will give ex-pression!"

The device King Oscar chose for himself showed that he had realized of what nature would be his regal difficulties. Most earnestly, most conscientiously, has he striven to promote the welfare of the dual Scandinavian domain, but it has been no easy task, nor can it be said to have been crowned with entire success. The fault, however, is not the King's, it lies inherent in the character of the position, which presents an insoluble difficulty. Two nations have here been artificially put together into harness whose past history and present aims are as the poles asunder. The one has a long and varied history behind it, full of warnings and lessons— a history that tells of doughty deeds as well as of deep humiliations; the other counts its re-birth as a people but by few decades. Add to this a difference of language, an intense mutual jealousy, a fundamental leaning on the one side to Conservatism, on the other to Radicalism, and we have some faint idea of the problem with which King Oscar has to deal. No wonder he has less leisure to indite poetry.

The inimical spirit made itself felt from the first moment. Thus one of the first acts of the Riksdag on his accession was to cut down his moderate Civil List of 900,000 rixdollars by 100,000, and it is well known that the King was crowned at his own expense. Since then his one task and aim has ever been to prevent the dominant Radical party from going too far, at the same time keeping within the bounds of his very limited prerogative. The strained relations that have ever existed between Sweden and Norway since their forcible union has led to some bitter polemics. The extreme Norwegian Radicals desire a republic, and their leaders —and in particular the poet Björnson—have assailed the King of Sweden most virulently and most unjustifiably. Björnson at last went so far as to challenge the King to give him the satisfaction due from one gentleman to another for an alleged libel, the King having been reported to have said that there was not one of the Ten Commandments which Björnson had not broken. The poet was obliged to leave Norway for a time in consequence of the scandal he had upraised, but has since returned, mightier than ever, and with increased power as a demagogue. The author Ibsen, too, is among those who make opposition to the monarchy, and he too went into voluntary banishment.

So far, therefore, Oscar's desire to be a union King has not been realized, and that was what he wished above all. It is, indeed, a difficult task to rule with three Chambers, of which Sweden has two and Norway one, the latter country having by decree abolished the nobility, and with it the second House. That under these circumstances the King has never lost his personal popularity is almost marvellous, and yet so it is. He is esteemed by all, excepting, perchance, a few of the demagogues, who are so blinded by party as to confuse the man with the cause. That Oscar II.'s reign has been important and efficacious for Scandinavia it would be hard to deny, even for a purblind republican partisan. He has raised the country commercially and industrially; has encouraged art and science. By every means in his power he tries to get at the real requirements of his people. He travels much in the provinces, he interviews both public and private personages, he insists as far as in him lies on having the truth concerning all matters. He even often appears unexpectedly in the police-courts to hear the trial himself, and frequently he exercises his royal prerogative of pardoning if the offences be small. Since 1823 no Swedish king had availed himself of this right, and that such actions, and many others of a like peaceful nature, endear him to his subjects, can easily be understood.

It is beyond a question that this King takes his duties strenuously. Among the "Thoughts and Leaflets from my Journals," which he has issued from time to time, can be read this utterance: "A king must ever know how to subordinate all the inclinations of his character —even the most legitimate—to the exigencies of political wisdom and to the real, well-comprehended advantages of his Fatherland." Oscar Frederick's active, sincere piety makes it easier for him to accomplish these acts of self-sacrifice—often in his case very great, for his character, like that of all individual thinkers, is well pronounced, and his inclinations marked.

A valuable support has he found in his wife, who has made the welfare of the less fortunate of her husband's subjects her great care—the crippled, maimed, sick, and weary. Above all, everything bearing on the happiness of children elicits her interest. She holds by the maxim that the world's history is made in the nursery, and first for her own and now for the nation's young ones, she has a tender care. She has her reward in her four stately sons, who are the pride of the country, beloved and respected of all. Her own health of late years has been far from strong, and it is this that gives to her face so pathetic an expression; but she is happy, nevertheless, in her quiet, retiring way; and her counsels are sought and valued by her consort.

The four sons who hopefully surround the Swedish throne are respectively the Crown Prince, the Duke of Götland, the Duke of Westergotland, and the Duke of Nerike. The eldest, Prince Gustav, has inherited much of his father's ability, and has distinguished himself both as a traveller and as a soldier. Those who know him intimately praise his cool judgment and his penetrating powers of reasoning. He is slow to take decisions, studying a matter from all sides; but a conclusion once arrived at, he is inflexible in its execution. He married, in 1881, the granddaughter of he late Emperor William I., Princess Victoria of Baden, a marriage that gave universal satisfaction. Indeed, it became, quite unintentionally, an act of historical restitution, for it happens that the Princess is the great-granddaughter of the banished Swedish King Gustav IV. (Adolf). Thus the great-grandson of Bernadotte led back to Scandinavia the great-granddaughter of the monarch whom his forefather had chased from the throne. Two bonnie little boys have come to bless their union—children to whom their mother devotes herself with fond pride.

The second son (Prince Oscar, once Duke of Götland, now, since his marriage, simple Prince Bernadotte) was a while ago the object of much European interest on account of his romantic attachment to Mdlle. Ebba Munck, his mother's favourite maid-of-honour. For a long time King Oscar would not hear of the match. He remembered how he himself, born far distant from the throne, had been called upon to assume it, and the lady, though charming and unobjectionable in all respects, was not of royal birth. The situation of the Bernadottes as *parvenus* among the European royalties was difficult enough, and such a marriage might render it more difficult for Prince Oscar were he ever called on to rule. In vain the Prince begged to be allowed to renounce his birthright, pointing to his three stalwart brothers; in vain the Queen pleaded for the lovers. Prince Oscar travelled to see if he could forget his affection. Mdlle. Munck was removed from the Court. All proved useless. It then happened that the Queen was seized with one of her serious attacks of illness—so serious this time that her recovery was despaired of. An operation was needful. Before submitting to it the Queen made the King promise that should her life be saved, he would consent to the marriage of the lovers. Reluctantly he promised. The operation was performed, and was successful; the Queen recovered. She then sent for her favourite maid-of-honour to have her once more about her. It was Christmas evening, all the family were assembled in the invalid's room, and Mdlle. Munck, who has a lovely voice, was singing with feeling a poem of the King's, in which he pleads for the rights due to love. The charming singer emphasized her words, whether by accident or design. The King listened enrapt. Did he notice that all eyes were fixed on him in petition, and especially those of his wife? Be it so or no, the song ended, he remained for awhile in deep thought, then rose up suddenly from where he sat, and approaching Prince Oscar, took his hand and laid it silently into that of Ebba Munck. He can have little reason to repent his resolution, the young couple are truly happy. Since their marriage—celebrated quite quietly at the English seaside town of Bournemouth—they have led a modest retired life in their castle by the sea (Karlscrona). A quiet, but not an idle life. The Prince is busy all day with the pursuits of a private gentleman and the occupation of a sailor prince. The other day he emulated another northern prince, Peter the Great of Russia, in valiantly rescuing a number of drowning fellow-creatures from a watery grave. He saw from his windows that a sailing-boat containing four men was upset in a furious gale; ran down at once, and, together with a fisherman of the neighbourhood, rowed through the wild waves and succeeded in rescuing three of the shipwrecked men.

He takes a keen interest in all charitable works, and is at the head of various benevolent societies, spending for them not only his time, but his money. Like his brothers, he is remarkably handsome, of a dark type of beauty, such as is common to all the Bernadottes.

Prince Charles, who is the military Prince, is as yet unmarried. He has travelled much in the East, and has written a vivid account of his adventures, which modesty has hitherto prevented him from publishing.

The youngest scion of the house, Prince Eugène, is devoted to the fine arts, and is at present studying in Paris with a view to fitting himself to be a painter. His work so far shows a leaning towards the prevalent realism, but it is too early to decide whither his undoubted talents may lead him.

Until 1889 yet another noble soul enriched the Swedish royal family circle—namely, Princess Eugénie, the King's sister, a pious, self-sacrificing woman, whose sickly health did not hinder her from devoting herself to music and poetry, in both of which branches she achieved some charming successes, though often at the cost of bodily strength. Her charity too was unslacking, her benefits to the poor never-ending. A touching trait told of her characterizes her better than volumes of description. A poorhouse was needed near the castle on the isle of Götland, where she always spent her summers, but there were no funds to erect it with. Without making any parade of the matter, she secretly sold her diamonds and gave the money that resulted to this end. A year after, when she came again to visit the spot, the workhouse stood ready. The welcome she received from the poor people, for whom she had thus provided a home, was enthusiastic. All greeted her with smiles and cries of joy. Only one old man among the crowd wept bitterly. The Princess asked the cause, and was told that he was a hardened sinner, who had only begun to work since he came to this house, and who there had learnt to turn to God. Until this day none had ever seen him weep. His tears flowed for the first time at sight of her whom he called the "saviour of his soul." When the Princess heard this, she said, " In these tears I see my diamonds again."

It would certainly not be easy to find a more worthy family in private or royal life than this of Sweden. As for the King, he is almost an ideal personage, with his talents, his immaculate private life, his pleasant and winning personality. In public the Court life is stately, but even then he is not unapproachable. Once a week he holds open audiences, and all who like to come are received. He talks to these visitors, not with mere ceremony, but strives to enter into the true requirements of those who seek him. When at his country seat, he particularly encourages the visits of naval men. Whenever he can he wears his admiral's dress, because he loves the sea, and he likes nothing better than a long yarn with some old sea comrade. Happy in the love of his family, of his friends, Oscar of Sweden's life might truly be counted a happy one.

THE ROYAL COUPLE OF ROUMANIA.

THE QUEEN OF ROUMANIA.

THE ROYAL COUPLE OF ROUMANIA.

ONE of the youngest among the new kingdoms that have arisen in Europe during the last half century is the kingdom of Roumania. As in all these newly-established realms, some difficulty arose in finding a ruler willing to undertake the somewhat thorny task of shaping a constitution and organizing a nation. After various rebuffs, M. Bratiano, the Roumanian delegate, was in despair as to whither he should address himself in his search for a royal ruler. It happened that he narrated his perplexities one day at the Tuileries, while conferring with Napoleon III. The monarch for a moment thought of his cousin, Prince Napoleon; but, after consideration, decided that Prince Plon-Plon would feel too much out of place at Bucharest. Then it appears that a lady of the Imperial Court, one who had known the Emperor since his boyhood, ventured to ask whether the Catholic Sigmaringen branch of the Hohenzollern family had ever been thought of. With this family the Emperor had passed many hours of early youth, when he lived with his mother in the castle of Arenberg in Switzerland. The suggestion struck Napoleon as singularly happy, and he encouraged M. Bratiano to set out for Dusseldorf, where dwelt the mediatized Prince Antony, head of the house. This Prince—whose relations with his cousins, the ruling House of Prussia, were somewhat strained owing to his pronounced Liberal opinions—was able to give his sons handsome allowances, so that they could live in a style not common to Prussian princelings or lieutenants. This fortune the father had acquired by stock exchange speculations in association with the notorious speculator Strousberg, the European railway king, whose hazardous business ventures were the talk of the Continent in the sixties and seventies. The eldest son of Prince Antony was the Prince to whom later was offered the throne of Spain, and whose candidature formed the pretext for the outbreak of hostilities between France and Prussia.

Thus—curious irony of history—it was reserved for one brother to dethrone his former playmate; while the other—thanks to this same playmate—was raised to royal dignity. For Charles, now King of Roumania, is the second son of Prince Antony. He, unlike his father, was a favourite at the Berlin Court, and at the time M. Bratiano came to him with his offer he was at Coblenz, serving as captain in the First Regiment of Dragoon Guards, where he was known as an officer of conspicuous merit and a shining example of good conduct in public and private life. It was his twenty-seventh birthday when M. Bratiano presented himself before him with his important offer.

All the Roumanian Minister's eloquence was employed to paint to the Prince in glowing colours the brilliant destiny that awaited him upon the banks of the Danube. He even ventured to promise—a promise fulfilled—that the princely diadem should be speedily converted into a royal crown. Prince Charles was tempted and dazzled, but before deciding he wished to consult Prince Bismarck.

This is the Iron Prince's own account of the matter:

"People impute to me," he said one day to a friendly diplomat, "many things of which I am perfectly innocent, and it is only by reading the newspapers that I learn that I am the cause of this or that event. It is true that, on the other hand, I get credit for merits which I do not possess. For instance, it was considered a clever stroke on my part having placed Prince Charles of Hohenzollern on the throne of Roumania before the opening of the Austro-Prussian campaign. And yet I had very little to do with it. The Prince came to see me one day, and, to my great astonishment, told me that the Roumanian Boyars had offered him their sovereignty. As he asked my advice, I said, 'That is good promotion for a Prussian lieutenant, and there is no reason why you should not give it a trial. Although Roumania is a difficult country to govern on account of its semi-Asiatic customs, don't forget that you are a Hohenzollern. If you see that you can do no good there come back, but don't allow yourself to be treated like a Couza.'

"The Prince then said that he had no time to obtain permission to resign his commission, and that he was afraid of being looked on as a deserter. 'I will undertake all responsibility with his Majesty,' I replied. And that is all I did in the matter."

Why there was such pressing haste to carry out this transaction does not appear, but in consequence King Charles's enemies to this day make out that he was degraded in the Prussian service as a deserter. This is untrue.

For reasons also not quite obvious, the Prince mistrusted the Austrian police. He therefore travelled *incognito* and second-class across the realms of Francis Joseph, assuming the common name of Lehmann, the same name, curiously enough, that the late Emperor William I. of Germany had taken when flying from Berlin in 1848. It was not until he had disembarked from the Austrian company's steamer that the young Lehmann, commercial traveller, dropped his disguise and appeared as his Royal Highness Prince Karol I. of Roumania.

This was in 1866. The fine soldierly bearing, the personal courage, the dark skin, eyes, and beard of Prince Charles, who, strange to say, though a Hohenzollern, is not fair, impressed his subjects favourably, and so did the energy he at once displayed in setting his realm in order. Still after a while the people fretted a little under his Prussian rigidity, and it was felt instinctively that a softer influence was needed to mitigate the monarch's involuntary harshness, which springs from no innate hardness, but from inborn northern inflexibility of temperament.

After three and a half years of struggles with great political difficulties, struggles in which he was nobly victorious, Prince Charles set forth to woo, in order that the softer elements might also be introduced into his reign. His aim was to obtain the hand of one of the most highly gifted princesses in all Europe, who years before had fallen involuntarily into his arms. If it be true to say *cherchez la femme* wherever a domestic tragedy occurs, may it not be equally true to apply the saying when we see a country well ruled, content, and prosperous? The moral and social development of a country is largely due to woman, especially in these latter days. Queen Elizabeth of Roumania has certainly proved the good genius of her country, so much so indeed that her renown has almost swamped that of her husband. When the world speaks of Roumania, it thinks rather of its Queen than of its King.

And the truth of this is beyond question. That the Prince of Hohenzollern, an alien, an unimaginative and inflexible Prussian, has been able to retain the throne, that he has overthrown intrigues, confounded conspiracies, that he has gained, if not the love, at least the sincere respect of his subjects, is due in great part to the lady who sits beside him, and who, a queen in the best and richest sense of the word, has made his paths smooth, and has won the hearts of all that come in contact with her. A lovable woman truly; one of those magnetic presences to whom our hearts go out at first sight, we know not why; in whom a true and noble womanhood rises above the factitious dignity of royalty.

Nor is it only her qualities of heart that make Queen Elizabeth remarkable. Under the pseudonym of Carmen Sylva she has made for herself a certain position in German literature as poet and novelist. The story of her life is full of interest.

Born in 1843, a daughter of Prince Hermann of Wied and his wife, a princess of Nassau (a couple of very superior intelligence), the little Elizabeth belonged to one of that innumerable class of petty German princes whose estates are often invisible. Her father, however, was regarded as a ruler, his realm the little area of Wied-neu-Wied upon Rhine, where his kindliness and culture had made him and his clever wife much beloved.

Their only daughter was a robust, bright-eyed little girl, who had to be taught to read at the age of three in order to keep her occupied, and whose alert intelligence was afterwards trained with care both by her cultivated parents and by able tutors. She early distinguished herself by her knowledge of languages, her passion for poetry and music, and her genuine love of the fine arts. Nor were the strictly feminine branches of education neglected. Princess Elizabeth learned to ply her needle as deftly as her pen, her cooking-spoon as well as her drawing-pencil. But she was by no means a merely studious child. Her lively animal spirits needed constant vent, and many a time would she manage to get outside the park, gather the village children about her, and prove the ringleader of wild and merry games. From the age of five it was her ardent desire—her ideal—to be a national schoolmistress; and when she was not romping with them it was her delight to gather the village children around her and teach them what she had just learned herself. There was not much etiquette in her father's little Court, where sorrow and sickness had early taken up a permanent abode. The father was a chronic invalid, and the mother was prostrated for five years, while during the whole period of Princess Elizabeth's intellectual development, for eleven years, her youngest brother struggled wearily with a life of pain to which death hourly held out hopes of release.

To succour those in distress—to aid the poor and nurse the sick—was early taught her by precept and example, and with her ardent temperament, which is apt to exaggerate everything, there seemed at one time some danger that she would not have a dress to her back, so liberally did she dispose of her wardrobe to all who asked. Meanwhile, to roam the woods that surrounded the country seat of the family—if possible accompanied only by her big dogs, so that she might dream her dreams undisturbed — remained the chief pleasure of the little girl. Day by day her German home grew dearer to her, and even among the more stately

Carpathians she has not forgotten the vine-clad hills of the Rhine. She too has given her poetical tribute to that much-sung river, and in introducing her translations of Roumanian folk-songs to her native land she invokes the stream in terms of endearment, while with a certain regal pride she presents to Father Rhine her battalion of Roumanian poets, all citizens of the land over which she reigns. Her very *nom-de-plume* is compounded from her fondness for song and forest.

This open-air life, this rustic simple training, united to a refined intelligence and careful mental nurture, has produced an original and charming result. To this day the Queen retains some of the unsophisticated directness of the tiller of the soil, while there is an aroma of the woods and fields in her poetry and her speech. As a mere child her instincts were towards independence and freedom, and to this day conventionality irks her. Many are the tales told of her wild exploits while in her Rhenish home.

Journeys to the Isle of Wight, to various German towns, and even to Paris, for the purpose of seeking change of air and surgical aid for her invalid brother, had broken the monotony of the Princess's life, but not until she was seventeen did she make acquaintance with the great world. She then paid a visit of several months to the Court of Berlin. Here an adventure befell her, and if (as Lord Beaconsfield asserts) adventures are to the adventurous, it was but right and proper that a romantic accident should befall the mercurial Princess

Elizabeth. Rushing down the stairs one day with her usual impetuosity, she slipped, and would have fallen to the bottom had not a gentleman who was ascending at the same moment caught her in his arms. It was a fall laden with unexpected consequences, for she had fallen into the arms of her future husband. But as yet she was not to rest in them for good. The young Princess evinced an almost savage dislike to matrimony, and in response to all proposals of marriage made to her replied, "I do not want to marry unless I can be Queen of Roumania, for down there there is still something left for me to do." This remark was meant to silence her friends, for at that time there was no Kingdom of Roumania.

A sad time were the next years, in which Death was busy in the household, removing the brother, the father, and Elizabeth's most intimate girl-friend. Music and the writing of verse were the Princess's only sources of consolation in these bitter trials. Little note did she take of the changing aspect of European events which were nevertheless so powerfully to affect the "wild rosebud of Wied," as her friends loved to call her. We cannot know if she ever gave a thought to the gallant cavalier who was the hero of her staircase adventure, and who had been suddenly called to fill the one throne she professed to covet. But Prince Charles had not forgotten her, and three years after his election as ruler (in October, 1869) he unexpectedly appeared at the castle on the Rhine and reminded Princess Elizabeth of the desire once expressed to reign over Roumania. If she still cherished that wish, it was in her power to gratify it—his hand and heart were hers. Thus it came about that one of Princess Elizabeth's fairy tales assumed real shape. But even so, though she had long felt sympathy for the Prince, and though he offered her the kingdom she had predicted, she hesitated a while before she could consent to resign her fiercely-cherished independence.

"Yours will be a noble mission," Prince Charles said to her on the day of their betrothal. "You must comfort tenderly when I have been too harsh, and you may petition for all."

These words show that the King knows that his uprightness is coupled with Hohenzollern lack of sympathy — that hence he often offends against the prejudices of his less sternly moulded subjects, even when it is his desire to act purely for their good. He rightly divined that his wife would furnish the emotional element to his excellent but rigid deeds.

"Ours is not an easy throne to fill," she once said to a friend. "We are not old and firmly rooted, but have to try and gain the general favour and good-will."

A short engagement was theirs, for the Prince could not long be absent. Two months after the engagement the wedding was quietly celebrated at Neu Wied. Four times over were the couples married—that is, according to the German civil code, according to the Lutheran (her) religion, according to the Roman Catholic (his), and according to the rites of the Greek Church, which is the creed of their kingdom.

Three days after the marriage the pair left for Roumania. They entered their kingdom, as the commercial traveller Lehmann had done, on board a common steamer, and, like that traveller, *incognito*. The first thing that struck the Princess as they passed the confines of her new home were the coastguards, resembling in feature and dress those Dacian prisoners depicted upon Trajan's column in Rome. It made her feel she had indeed come into a strange land—a land in which barbarism has overlaid ancient culture, but of which the foundations were good—foundations, she resolved, it should be her task to disinter and vivify into new life.

At the same spot where Prince Charles had landed three years before the bridal pair descended, and vast was the amazement of all on board the steamer to behold a large crowd eagerly greeting the quiet handsome tourists, acclaiming them as their sovereigns, and offering them the traditional bread and salt upon silver platters, while on a velvet cushion were presented the keys of the town.

From here to Bucharest the entry of the royal couple was a joyous progress, in which Princess Elizabeth was dazzled and interested by the Oriental splendour, barbarism, *naïveté*, and grace of her new subjects, and during which she already won the hearts of these people.

instinctively averse to foreigners, by her sweet smiles and pleasant words.

Arrived in her new home, the Princess at once threw herself with native ardour into all her new duties. She learned to read and write Roumanian, she made herself acquainted with the needs and requirements of the land, and soon saw that she had not been wrong when, years ago, she had aspired after this throne as one which would give her a noble work to do. While keeping herself aloof from the entanglement of politics, the result of her endeavours was soon felt more beneficially than those of cannon or diplomatists. She founded schools, hospitals, soup kitchens, convalescent homes, cooking schools, and *crèches;* she encouraged popular lectures; she inculcated respect for sanitary laws, most needful in an Eastern land; she founded art galleries and art schools. These institutions now bear practical testimony to the Queen's energetic love for her nation and her kind. It was her endeavour from the first to be a mother to her people in the best sense of the word, and "little mother" has long been the tender name by which her people call her.

To give but one instance, a small matter and yet one that has had much influence and greatly contributed to her popularity. It seems that Roumanian women have ever been famed for spinning and weaving, and their deftness in embroidery; but the new Queen found that a love for tawdry West-European clothes and Parisian fashions threatened to extinguish their national art, and to render the picturesque costume of the country a thing of the past. Out of her own private purse she founded a school of embroidery, in which the old Byzantine patterns were carefully reproduced. She encouraged the peasants to bring to her the robes they had embroidered, and when in the country she donned the national costume, and made her ladies wear it too, the only difference between her dress and that of peasants being that she wears the veil, which in old Greek costume, as we may learn from the story of Helen, is the mark of queenly dignity. She further made it obligatory that at the annual charity balls in Bucharest the national costume should be worn.

In 1870 the Queen became a mother, and though her child was only a little girl, and hence of no value to the land as heir, she was none the less precious to her mother's heart. For four years—four precious years— all the Queen's happiness was centred in this child; in her babe's beaming eyes she forgot all grief, all worries. Joy, of which she had known so little in her life, had taken up its abode beside her, and for a time banished sorrow, her too faithful attendant. There is a most charming portrait extant of the Queen, in all the pride and joy of young motherhood, carrying her child pick-a-back upon her shoulders.

Alas! her happiness was as short as it was intense. Death, who had already taken from her so much, dealt her the hardest, bitterest blow of all—a blow from which she will never recover. An epidemic of scarlet fever raged in Bucharest, and to this scourge the little princess fell a victim. "Other mothers had to give up all their treasures," said the Queen, "why should I hope to escape?" But it was her ewe lamb that had been taken.

"God gave me much," she wrote in a private letter about this date, "a father, mother, brother, husband, and child, such as are rarely seen."

And she strove to resign herself to the Divine will that had given and taken. True to her own doctrine, that "In work—in great rich work—must be sought the comfort for all sorrows," the Queen applied herself yet more strenuously to promote the welfare of her people. She now, too, first began to take up authorship seriously as a profession. From her childhood she had written verses in secret; her thoughts naturally took shape in metric speech, but she had never thought of publishing, or indeed of showing her verses except to near friends. Now, after this sore blow, her pen became her loved companion and trusted friend. She poured out her woe in song; she versified the tender sayings of her babe, she translated into German the favourite Roumanian folk-songs of her little one. This book she published, in the hope that what had given pleasure to her darling would also please the little ones in her distant German home among the vineyards and oak forests. All these early poems, as indeed her poesy in general, are characterized by a tone of deep melancholy. Expe-

THE KING OF ROUMANIA.

rience qualified her to write the cycle of "Sorrow's Earthly Pilgrimage," which is accounted one of the most charming and delicate of her works. After having years ago resigned all such hopes she was to find that sorrow had made her an artist, and that the world cared to listen to her speech.

It was not, however, until 1880 that the Queen first published, and meantime she had to make close acquaintance with the dread horrors of war. The Russo-Turkish campaign of 1877–8 broke out, and Roumania was deeply involved, taking part with Russia against the Turks. The country suffered cruelly. Its soldiers, the army organized and trained by King Charles, fought bravely, and he himself was ever at their head and in the thick of battle. Indeed, but for this Roumanian army, the creation of Prince Charles, great disaster might have overtaken the Russian arms. How Russia showed her gratitude for this timely and efficient help is a matter of history. Meanwhile, notwithstanding Russian faithlessness, the war had brought Roumania into knowledge. It proved to Europe that the country was self-sufficing, that it owned a ruler who was sagacious and steadfast, and an army that could make its deeds felt. To this war Roumania owes her emancipation from Turkish guardianship and Russian patronage.

While her husband fought thus bravely, it was the Princess's task to stay at home and succour the wounded and comfort the distressed. She maintained out of her private purse a lazaretto for a hundred patients, and was constantly found here or in the other hospitals, personally tending the patients; and often her persuasions alone induced the soldiers to submit to painful operations. Again and again was she present cheering and encouraging while the surgeon wielded the knife, and many a death-bed did she solace. No wonder the sick adored her as a saint; no wonder the coldly egotistical *haute société* of Bucharest were shamed out of their indifference, and accorded the Queen pecuniary and even personal aid in her noble work. There stands to-day, in the public place of Bucharest, a fine monument representing the Queen in the act of giving a drink of water to a wounded soldier. This statue was subscribed for by the wives of the Roumanian army as an enduring testimonial of their love and gratitude for her whom the popular voice now christened "the mother of the wounded."

What she did during this war is unforgotten—unforgetable by her subjects. "She is good, like the bosom of her mother," they say in their picturesque and Oriental imagery of speech. This is what she writes of it herself in a letter to her mother at the moment Prince Charles, the hero of Plevna, returned in triumph to Bucharest, the people singing in his honour a song composed by his wife—

"What a year draws to its close!"

"I had at first courage for all, and I sustained everybody by my confidence. I can assure you that it was a very difficult position for a lone woman. But work made me forget my anxieties. Thank God, Charles is here! I can retire back gradually into my shell—return to my flowers, my birds, my books, and my papers. I consider it an anomaly and a misfortune for a woman to be obliged to enter public life. . . . There were, however, some bright periods in these troublous times. May God soon grant a lasting peace to remove the gnawing anxiety from our hearts, and that these stirring times may belong to the past, which dims both our joys and sorrows, leaving only the bright impression of the results achieved! . . . Charles is splendid! . . . He shrugs his shoulders at ingratitude, and then forgives it. If people are unthankful it is all the same to him. When he is no more they will call him the Wise."

This pride in her husband reappears again and again in the Queen's letters to her old home. Meanwhile Prince Charles's warlike abilities, the complete independence he had obtained for his country, drew his people nearer to him and his good consort.

In 1881, by popular desire, the princedom was raised to a kingdom, and in May the couple were solemnly crowned, the royal diadem being fashioned out of iron made from Turkish guns taken at Plevna.

In graceful allegorical fashion Queen Elizabeth has told the story of her country—the struggles and difficulties it underwent before it could take its place among its jealous elder brethren. The little tale is called "Puiu!" that word being Roumanian for "My soul, my darling!" and is the name those proud Latins of the East give to their cherished country.

Nor are the struggles and difficulties of the land ended. It has ever to guard itself against Russian influence desirous of interfering with its national independence, and to be attentive lest the party of the pretender Couza, the dissolute former ruler of the State, regain preponderance. King Charles has lain on no bed of roses, especially in these latter years. The question of an heir, too, had to be considered, since further children were denied the couple. The successor chosen is Prince Ferdinand, second son of King Charles's elder brother, Prince Leopold, a prince now twenty-three years of age, who has been educated almost entirely in Germany. He is now about to take up his abode at Bucharest among his future subjects. That he did not do so before, so long as any hope remained of direct heirs, was due to a certain delicacy of feeling. Latterly, however, the agitations of the anti-dynastic party in Roumania have shown it to be a necessity of State that Prince Ferdinand should reside in the country.

The life led by the royal couple is one of constant hard work. In winter they live in Bucharest, in summer they retire to Sinaïa, a health resort in the Carpathians that combines the grand scenery of Switzerland with the more lovely and romantic features of the Italian Alps. Here they have built for themselves, after their own designs, a quaint castle, whose architecture is a fantastic medley of the Roumanian and mediæval German styles. But even here they get little rest. The conditions of the land require that the sovereigns should always be *en évidence*, at the beck and call of any one who likes to ask for them. In this semi-Oriental country Oriental customs prevail; the sovereign cannot live in peaceful seclusion.

The Queen usually rises early—often as early as four—and works until eight, the only hours in the course of the day when she can be, as she phrases it, " woman and author;" the rest of the time she must be Queen. Both sovereigns have often to talk for twelve, or even fifteen hours at a stretch, and from this cause the Queen once temporarily lost her voice. When she and the King sit down to dinner they are sometimes so tired they cannot speak a word. Yet early sleep is not theirs. Bucharest, it is said, is a very gay capital—the City of Pleasure it has been called—and a very late one. Gala performances, for example, do not begin till ten or twelve at night.

The strain upon the physical and mental organizations of the sovereigns is great, and especially upon the Queen, who is indefatigable. "Whirlwind" was the nickname she had at home, and which she has not lost. Never inactive herself, she will permit no idlers about her. She loves to surround herself with young girls, and incites them to utilize their talents by precept and example. In her *salon* a republican spirit reigns; she admits of but one aristocracy—that of the heart and mind.

Such are these rulers of Roumania, both in their way out of the common run—he for the clearness of his intellect and the sterling qualities of his character, she for her genius, her sweetness and elevation of soul. Between them they have developed the institutions and internal resources of their land, and raised it to an honoured place among the nations.

We have now brought to a close our series dealing with the European royal houses. It is true there are yet a few other kings of whom we have not spoken, but they are kings more in name than in influence. Of the old German petty States, now all incorporated under the collective style of Germany, a few remain, but their rulers have no influence on European politics, and even within the limits of their own States their autonomy is a restricted one. Sooner or later these also will cease to exist, and the more probably seeing that in all the three kingdoms the rulers are childless. On the throne of Bavaria sits a hopeless maniac, whose days are passed in strict confinement, and who is not even conscious of his dignity. The King of Wurtemberg, a well-intentioned but weak and colourless character, has no direct heirs. The same applies to King Albert of

Saxony, a brave soldier, a mere cypher as an administrator. In Eastern Europe kingdoms and principalities may be made and unmade with great frequency, but these lands have less influence upon the general course of politics by reason of the rulers who occupy their thrones than by reason of their geographical position. This, for example, is notably the case with Servia, which plays the part of a pawn upon the European chessboard, but a pawn whose position might at any moment bring about a check to some of the greater Powers. On this throne sits a poor little boy King, ruled over by three regents of mind and character little refined, abandoned by his father, forcibly separated from the mother he adores. In Bulgaria especially rulers succeed each other with rapidity. Prince Alexander of Battenberg, kidnapped and deposed by order of Russia, has been followed by Prince Ferdinand of Coburg, whom Russia and all the other European Powers refuse to recognize as legitimate sovereign. In Montenegro there commands a warlike chieftain, Prince Nicholas, a mountaineer, a mighty hunter before the Lord, a man whom the Czar of Russia has honoured with the distinction of calling him publicly "his only friend," but who outside his territory exerts no power over the councils of nations or the general course of events.

The future of Continental Europe is certainly for the moment in the hands of those countries which form the Triple Alliance, its far distant future perchance in the hands of the peoples, who will beyond question put down the crushing burdens of standing armies and of giant navies, and who under a federation of allies will inaugurate a more peaceful and civilized era than that in which we now live. But that day is not yet. Even the first signs of its dawn are barely seen upon the horizon. And until these indications are stronger the rulers of the various lands must and will exert a great influence over their respective countries, as indeed we can daily judge for ourselves from even the most superficial study of contemporary events. Even in the brief space that has elapsed since these papers were commenced, various important changes have taken place, notably in the actions of the German Emperor, that aspiring personality whose unexpected metamorphosis of character may go far within a decade towards changing the aspect of European affairs. These matters still "lie upon the knees of the gods," to use Homeric phraseology. But, as we said at the outset of our series, the time has not yet entirely gone by for kings to play a large part in making the story of their times.

THE KING OF SERVIA.

THE KING OF SERVIA.

NO European land has made itself so much talked of, of late years, as the little kingdom of Servia. It has attracted an attention quite out of proportion to its size or its status of civilization. This is in part due to the clamorous scandals existent between its sovereigns with which all Europe has rung, and to which no modern parallel exists, save the case of George IV., and Caroline of Brunswick, his wife. In part, however, the attention Servia has received is thanks to its geographical site. The little Balkan States find themselves called on in our century to play a European *rôle* quite out of proportion to the extension of their territories and their degree of culture. They are like the pawns at chess, who at a certain juncture may, by the position they occupy, acquire a decisive importance in settling the game. The kingdom, or rather principality of Servia, for its creation into a kingdom is quite a recent matter, has been ruled alternately by the rival houses of Karageorgévitch and Obrénovitch. The latter house raised themselves from cattle dealers to their present position, an origin which has given colour to Queen

Nathalie's reproach in reply to one of her husband's gross insults, that nothing better could be expected of him, seeing that in his veins ran not the blood of princes, but of swineherds. It was in 1868 that Michael Obrénovitch, then, sitting on the Servian throne, was murdered by a faction of his subjects—no rare occurrence in that semi-Oriental more than semi-barbarous land. Milan, his great-nephew, then a boy of fourteen, was called upon to be his successor—a fate no person had ever dreamed would befall his lot. The lad scarcely knew his parents, who died early. His guardians sent him to school in Paris, to the Lycée Louis le Grand, where neither masters nor companions could assimilate with or hold in check the wild, obstinate boy from the barbarian East. He was considerd an ill-tempered, malicious, stubborn child, not lacking withal in native parts. In Paris all too early the boy came in contact with vice. He was corrupted in mind before ever he was mature, this waif thrown without guide into the waters of life. An orphan, it has been the great misfortune of Milan's life that he has been entirely educated by men, and these men professional politicians. Of moral training he received none. Clever, not ill-read, in the main kind-hearted, King Milan never learnt the elementary lessons of self-control, purity, and respect for others. In short, it was a miserable training he had, and accounts for many of his failings. He knew this himself. It is told that a minister once respectfully remonstrated with him for some piece of duplicity, upon which the King answered, "Well, gentlemen, I am what you have made me; if you wanted a higher morality in your King you should have brought me up otherwise."

Responsible for at least the political part of his education was M. Ristitch, and the world naturally wonders whether he will profit by the unique hazard which has made him Regent for the second time, and do better by the son than he did by the father.

It was in October, 1875, that Milan, then but twenty-one years old, married Natalia Kechko, herself but sixteen. The present Queen was the daughter of a Russian officer and of the Princess Pulckerie Stourdza. She, as little as her husband, had been born with a likelihood to sit upon the throne, and a quiet burgher education had been hers at Odessa. But even here her great beauty attracted notice, as also her abilities, her ambition and her wealth. She brought as her dowry no less a sum than £18,000 a year—a goodly help towards the impecunious and extravagant household of King Milan. It is noteworthy, however, that the Queen with a rare shrewdness insisted from the first that her fortune should remain under her own control and administration. Fortunately for her, or she would to-day find herself penniless, for no monarch in Europe is more heavily in debt than King Milan.

The marriage really seems to have been a love match, for Mdlle. Kechko with her millions could have aspired higher than this princeling. It is related that when they were engaged, an old servant who had lived with Nathalie all her life and loved her fondly, said to the King, as he one day left the hotel at Vienna where they had met, "Sir, yours is an imperious nature, and so is Nathalie's; neither of you can bend. Listen to an old woman's advice and abandon this marriage." But Milan would not listen. Worse still, in a weak moment he confided the incident to Nathalie, who dismissed the servant. The poor old soul died broken-hearted some while after in Russia.

At first all went well, to outward appearance at least, for Milan was deeply enamoured of his beautiful wife, who soon became the idol of the Servians, on account of her beauty and her amiability. This affection was but increased when, a year after her marriage, she presented her subjects with an heir. But from that hour the domestic discords began. The Queen had been ill long and seriously after her boy's birth; Milan had sought distractions elsewhere. Scenes of jealousy and recrimination grew frequent. Further, Servia was then passing through a difficult political crisis: the Turkish war was in full swing. Milan, little beloved ever since he began to reign, brought home no wreaths from this conflict, although his subjects distinguished themselves by their valour. Then followed in 1882 the raising of the principality into a kingdom—a fact which left the Servians very indifferent, and in which they merely beheld the prospect of increased taxes, a prevision that was realized. As time went on, and troubles increased,

King Milan became somewhat of a despot, who was sustained solely by the army, itself undermined by factious intrigues.

Meantime the Queen, now doubtless grown somewhat callous to her husband's infidelities, aspired to comfort herself by assuming a political *rôle*, for which she believed herself to have great aptitude. Such pretensions did not, however, fit in with Milan's entirely Oriental views as to the mission of the fair sex in life—an immense mission according to him, but which had nothing to do with politics. *Inde iræ*, as she could not influence the decisions of the Prince, the lady entered into opposition to him, and made it her aim to oppose all his projects. The quarrel spread throughout the entire Palace, and two inimical factions were formed, that of the King and that of the Queen. This became the basis of the discussions, the enmities, the quarrels which year by year grew but more bitter and acute. Things even came to such a point that the rival parties never spoke except at official receptions. Under such circumstances life in the Servian *Konak* was certainly not attractive.

Meantime Milan got deeper and deeper into debt, so that after a time he had almost mortgaged his territory to the Austrian Laenderbank, a land for which nature has done everything, but of which politics have been the curse. The Irishman's dream of a peasant proprietary is realized here, since there is not a holding of less than nine acres; but the Servian, from a habit contracted under the Turks, works only just enough to support himself and family, which means that three or four days in the week he loafs about or betakes himself to the winehouse and talks politics. The country might feed four millions more than its present population but for this plague of politics. The greasy Pope who ambles by on his mule is a politician; so is the schoolmaster, who poses over a Radical newspaper in his empty class-room; so is the village ne'er-do-weel, who comes out strong at election time with a bludgeon for cracking Progressist heads. In such a country, as one of its Generals well said, it is particularly necessary that the King should set a pattern of manners and morals.

"We are only just emerging from Orientalism, and the vices of the East will cling to the nation so long as they are seen in its ruler."

Was Milan the man fitted for the task? Surely not. Of Orientalism there are traces enough in Servia—much more than in Bulgaria, where the people, although more recently emancipated, have shown a much greater aptitude for self-government, and a much more decided taste for civilization. Sofia in ten years has made more progress than Belgrade in sixty. The Servian has land in plenty, and is too idle to turn it to account. His rulers are politicians whom ignoble party quarrels have rendered silly, and who devote such energies as they have to ridiculous political speechifying. As an acute observer has remarked, "Servia has not the vestige of a claim to the sympathies of Europe, for it has no grievances which are not of its own making; and it has not the right to beg for a shilling of foreign capital towards carrying out public works, for it is only poor because its people will not work." Like master, like man. These were Milan's subjects; of these people Milan was the ruler.

While husband and wife were thus quarrelling and going their own ways, grave events were maturing in neighbouring Bulgaria. The *coup de tête* of Fillippopoli, which annexed Eastern Roumelia to the principality, enlarged it in such wise that Servia henceforth had to cut a sorry figure in the Balkans. Milan roused himself, or pretended to rouse himself, and war was declared against Bulgaria. The truth is, he found himself in that most perilous situation for a sovereign, the need to create for his subjects' attention diversions from home affairs. Milan's policy was identical with that of Napoleon III. in 1870. The results of a war conducted in such fashion, with troops disaffected and indifferent, with equipments insufficient and incomplete, was what might have been foreseen. It is true that the first success in arms was for the Servians, and then Nathalie evinced a re-awakening of interest in her spouse. Perchance she already saw him in her mind's eye entering Belgrade as victor. But, alas! it was all a mere flash in the pan. There followed the crushing defeat of Slivitza, in which Prince Alexander of Battenberg carried off such laurels, and the Servians had to beat a disgraceful and precipitate retreat. Far from proving himself the hero Nathalie had dreamed, Milan was never more vile and abject than on this occasion. No pettifogging little shopkeeper could have been more afraid of the effects of war, or shown his fear more plainly. Utterly dejected, he telegraphed to the Queen, busied with tending the wounded, that he intended to abdicate forthwith. This cowardly conduct gave the death-blow to any feeling the Queen might have retained for the King. Henceforth she despised him, and took no pains to hide the fact. She merely replied to his abdication projects that, if he persisted in carrying them into effect, she hoped he would apprise her in time, that she might make her arrangements in order to constitute a regency in favour of her son.

After this reply matters grew worse and worse between the couple. It is even said that Milan one day raised his hand to beat Nathalie. They no longer hid their discords in public. Nathalie openly insulted a lady friend of the King's; she ridiculed his weaknesses in the face of the courtiers. Meanwhile Milan's temper, always choleric, grew worse and worse, and he could not spend it as his uncle, Milosch, had done, by whipping his ministers in public and in person in front of the *Konak*. Servia had advanced a little since those days, and demanded a little more outward decency of conduct.

Since clearly the couple could not live in peace together, it was needful one should go, and, as the King could not leave his kingdom, it fell to the lot of the Queen. In 1887 the pair parted without outward scandals, the Queen taking with her the Crown Prince, who by the father's consent was to remain with his mother till he was of age, even Milan recognizing that a child could learn little that was good at the Court of Belgrade. And, indeed, no one who has once seen King Milan's face, with his bloodshot eyes, heavy jaw, and coarsened mouth, which have entirely destroyed the good looks of his younger days, could consider him as a fit guardian for any boy during the most crucial years of youth. On parting the couple duly exchanged at the station those royal embraces whose number and length are immediately telegraphed the length and breadth of Europe, to spread the notion of a complete intimacy and affection among persons who often despise or hate each other.

Florence was the goal of the Queen's wanderings, and here she spent a quiet winter, much admired and respected, while Milan continued his profligate career, polite to women, rude to men, spending beyond his means, carrying on a method of government which has been called a nervous policy, in order to cover by a phrase its entirely unstable and vacillating character. It may be that he was well-intentioned politically, but he lacked the stamina to change his intentions into acts. It is true he found himself between hammer and anvil, between Russia and Austria. He would have stood well with the latter; his people would stand well with the former, their Liberator, as they called the Czar, their co-religionist.

Things were in this state when, the winter ended, Nathalie desired to return to Belgrade. Milan would not hear of it. The Emperor of Austria patched up a compromise; the Queen went to Wiesbaden in consequence. While residing there Milan professed to be suddenly taken with a paternal craving to see his son, and demanded he should be returned to him without his mother. The Queen very properly would not hear of this, and appealed to Milan's written promises. Milan turned for help to the German Government, and to the shame of the German Government, be it said, they lent their hand to abducting an only child from his mother, who, relying upon German hospitality, had sought shelter in German territory. The act was an outrage upon civilization. Prince Bismarck might, if he had chosen, have expelled both mother and child as politically dangerous, though it would have been difficult to make out that they were so to Germany; but to expel the child and refuse to let the mother accompany him was an act worthy of kidnappers and slave-dealers. "C'est un homme nerveux, il faut à tout prix l'apaiser," was Bismarck the younger's cynical remark when remonstrated with on the matter. It should, however, be added that the first time Milan applied to Bismarck for his help in this matter he was courteously but firmly refused. At that time the chivalrous Emperor Frederick still sat on the throne, and he would not lend his hand to strike a woman and a mother. After his death Milan appealed again, and with the less chivalrous and rougher nature of the son proved more successful. Nor was the vileness of the act rendered less odious by the choice of the emissary who was to carry off the little Prince, being no other than General Protitch, husband of the potential Queen of Servia. "In sending Protitch to Wiesbaden," wrote the Queen to an intimate friend, "Milan has offended my honour as a woman, showing how absolutely he lacks tact or any finer sentiment."

And before ever the excitement about this act could subside in Europe, Milan prepared another dastardly insult for his wife. He petitioned the Servian Synod for a divorce on the ground of "irreconcilable mutual antipathy." Neither by canonical nor civil law was this possible, and the Queen refused her consent, challenging her enemies to prove a single offence against either her public or private character. Nor could the divorce have been obtained but for the servile complaisance of the Servian Metropolitan Theodore, who by a quibble made possible, or plausible, what the Greek Church pure and simple would not have allowed and does not recognize.

Nathalie accepted the situation with as much dignity as she best could, pleading only to be allowed from time to time to see her son—a request harshly refused.

Quick vengeance, however, was in store for Milan. The internal affairs of Servia had grown more and more disturbed. It was needful to dissolve the National Assembly; it was needful to vote a new and more liberal constitution; but nothing availed to restore order into disorder. The King, perplexed, afraid, storm-tossed between divided counsels, highly irritable, and deeply impressed by Rudolf of Hapsburg's recent suicide, suddenly announced his intention to abdicate in favour of his son. "No, I can't any more; I can't any more," he was heard to say after reading a letter from the Emperor of Germany urging him to reconsider his decision. And he held firm. Without regret his people saw depart from among them a man who at thirty-five years of age was already decrepit, and who had not the pluck or ambition to try and overcome a difficult political crisis. They felt things could not well be worse, so at least there were hopes they might prove better under the new reign. How far Milan did his duty by his boy in thus abandoning him fatherless and motherless in a perilous situation is another question. One would be led to suppose that his parental affection is not so great as at one time he chose to flaunt in the face of Europe.

After kneeling down before his son and swearing fidelity to him as a subject, Milan betook himself off to tour through Europe and enjoy himself, leaving the little boy and his guardians to extricate themselves out of a complicated position as best they could. "Now I can see mamma again," were the first words of the boy King on hearing of his elevation. For he had yearned after his beloved mother, and at one time had sunk into such a state of melancholy that the doctors feared for his health, and urged his father to yield to the child's legitimate desires. But on this point Milan remained obdurate. It is his *idée fixe* that his wife is his mortal enemy, and he is afraid of her influence over the boy.

Three Regents are appointed to aid the King during his minority, the Ristitch who corrupted his father, the Protitch who is an instrument of King Milan's, and a certain Joan Belimarkowitch, an insignificant person. To such people is confided a well-disposed, but rather weak and impressionable lad! How much he ever clung to his mother's memory various anecdotes prove. Thus once at dinner, when receiving the officers of his battalion, he raised his glass to propose a toast. "To my beloved mother," he said. The officers were embarrassed what to reply, fearing to pronounce the word Queen and yet not desiring to shock the boy. Then one who had more presence of mind than the rest, replied, "To the mother of our Prince."

In order to make his son's throne surer Milan insisted that he should be anointed—a ceremony which was supposed to proclaim the young King as a legitimate successor to the old Servian Czars, thereby commending him to the loyalty of the faithful. It was a most impressive ceremony—this of anointing the tiny King with the holy oil. No wonder that the sacredness of the rite and the peculiar circumstances attending it should have deeply moved the child. He bore up manfully through the first part of the ceremony, but after the general homage, when his father's telegram was put into his hands, he changed colour and looked so faint that the Regent Protitch led him out of the church. He remained absent three-quarters of an hour, returning later to take the Holy Communion fasting, as the laws of his church require. It was then eleven o'clock, and he had not eaten since the previous day.

It is much to be hoped that King Alexander will grow up to be a strong, well-taught, clear-headed man, that he may make a good ruler to a land that sorely needs good ruling. But as everything depends on his training during the next years, it is difficult not to have misgivings. The boy's father has left him, and his mother is not allowed to live with him; it is even said that some of the men who have a political interest in keeping Queen Nathalie out of the country have been working upon the young King's vanity to persuade him that he does not need to be "tied to a mother's apron strings." They have said to him, "You are a King now, and don't require to be governed by a mamma;" to which the boy has been heard to answer, "Oh yes, I am a King now, and can take care of myself." King Alexander is not yet fourteen years old; but he is precociously developed. It seems but a short while ago that he was being photographed in sailor's dress and knickerbockers, but now, in his colonel's uniform, he stands as tall as the three Regents, and has acquired a good deal of self-possession. He has bright features, but not an intellectual face. His forehead is low, and little of it would be seen if he did not wear his hair close cropped. He has large, soft eyes and a quick, pleasing smile; but a physiognomist would say that the mouth and nose showed indecision of character. The boy looks as though he could easily be led, and most easily by those who would let him have his own way a great deal. His tutor is a Dr. Dogitch, a medical man who was for some time his body-physician, and for whom he feels affection. Dr. Dogitch has a kind face and pleasant manners, but is not reported to have much firmness, and certainly looks as though the task of educating a King were one which he could only discharge by constantly humouring his pupil.

The life led by the young King cannot be considered either happy or enviable. It is true his mother now lives at Belgrade, but he is not allowed to be with her even for one whole hour during the week, and even then not alone. The Regents keep him in strict seclusion in the Konak where his parents once lived, with no outlook save over the dreary Hungarian plain spread beyond the Danube. His time is spent between his studies and his rare and solitary amusements. A young French tutor teaches him French, and from outside come masters in history, geography, Servian language and literature, and in military science. His sole distractions are lawn tennis and a ride on horseback in the morning in the military riding-school. Verily a sort of regal imprisonment, and not a regimen calculated to make either a happy childhood or to develop a strong manly character fitted to deal with the struggle of life.

Who can tell, however, whether King Alexander will

ever really sit upon the throne and rule over the Servians? Mutations of rulers, changes of territory are frequent in Eastern Europe, not to mention revolutions and the assassin's dagger.

THE KING OF SAXONY.

THE KING OF SAXONY.

MIDSUMMER of 1889 the people of Dresden, and, indeed, of all Saxony, were busy celebrating on a grand scale the octocentenary of their ruling house of Wettin. The commemorative *fêtes*, besides the customary illuminations, reviews, and religious services, included a monster procession of several thousand costumed characters illustrating the history of the kingdom of Saxony and of its royal house. This celebration was probably a unique festival of its kind. The Wettins claim to be the oldest sovereign family, not only in Germany, but also in Europe; older by more than three centuries than the Hohenzollerns, older than the Hapsburgs, and older than the Wittelsbachs of Bavaria, who in 1888 celebrated the seventh centenary of their rule over that country.

As Prussia developed into what it now is from the Mark of Brandenburg, as a territorial seed-kernel, so the origin of Saxony was the Marquisate of Meissen, which was conferred by the Emperor Henry IV. on Henry of Eilenberg, or Wettin, the latter title derived from a schloss still extant on the banks of the Saale.

Later on the Marquisate of Meissen, now famous for its china, expanded into Kursachen, the primary Electorate of the Empire, and afterwards, by the favour of Napoleon I., into the kingdom which it is now. True, the Guelphs are of even more ancient date than the Wettins, but the Guelphs, though still directly represented in the male line by the Duke of Cumberland, have ceased to be a ruling dynasty in Germany. In England, however, their line still survives, intertwined as it now is with that of the Wettins in the person of the Prince of Wales, who, through his father, is related to the founder of the House of Saxony, and thus in his person forms the meeting-point of all the streams of family history that have wandered down the field of events both in Germany and in England.

The *rôle* which has been played by Saxony in German history by no means presents a very clean record, and some of her rulers were the possessors of qualities not altogether calculated to strengthen the bonds between them and their people. Still, some of the Wettins were superior men, and there certainly was a time when Saxony was a refuge for the cause of enlightenment and freedom of thought. The names of Leipzig and Wittenberg alone recall those of two towns whence went forth a flood of light over Europe. Besides, it takes a great deal to undermine the intense monarchical feelings of most Germans, and if ever the loyalty of the Saxons was in danger of being shaken by the faults and follies of their sovereigns, that danger was for the time over when the crown descended on its present wearer, who is at once a brave and efficient soldier, as he proved himself to be in the war against France, a worthy, warm-hearted man, and an enlightened ruler, nor any the less tolerant of other men's creeds for being a Roman Catholic himself. What the old Emperor William was in Prussia, King Albert is fast growing to be in Saxony, and therefore his subjects, especially those of his capital, profited by this occasion to pour out upon him all the cornucopia of their love and loyalty.

The present King of Saxony, who is before all else a soldier, was born at Dresden in April, 1828, son of King John and Princess Amelie of Bavaria. After being carefully educated under his learned father's eye and direction, he was sent at the age of nineteen to the University of Bonn, where studied at the same time the then Prince Frederick William of Prussia, with whom he knit close friendship—a friendship many common battle-fields in after years were to cement yet closer. His studies were, however, interrupted by the revolution of 1848, it being held desirable that the Prince should be in his own home, and should devote himself rather to military than literary studies. The war with Denmark in 1849 gave him his "baptism of fire," and he distinguished himself on this occasion by personal bravery. From that time forward he rose higher and higher in military rank, until at last he took command of the whole Saxon infantry.

It was in 1853 that the then Prince Albert married

the Princess Caroline of Wasa, a union that proved childless. The following year the reigning King of Saxony died quite suddenly, owing to a carriage accident while driving in Tyrol; and thus King John ascended the throne, and his son became Crown Prince. This King was one of the best Dante scholars Germany can boast. He also made the best metrical translation of the "Divine Comedy," with critical and historical notes, that the same language possesses. As might be expected, he proved himself an enlightened monarch, and introduced several reforms of great benefit to his country. To his son, less literary in his tastes, was entrusted the military command of the land. It was an anxious time politically, and that the Crown Prince saw as clearly as he did whither events were tending speaks well for his intelligence. Thus he was convinced of the hopelessness of the Austrian cause. Nevertheless, he and his land were bound by treaty to hold to the Austrians. In 1866, therefore, Prussia declared war upon Saxony, overran the land with its troops, and exacted from it, after the peace of Prague, a large sum of money and the cession of its chief fortress. In this war again Prince Albert distinguished himself by military prowess, and after the peace, when the Saxon army had to become a portion of the military force of the North German federation, a leading position was accorded to him by the Prussian chief.

The brief years of peace that elapsed between 1866 and the great Franco-Prussian struggle were utilized by the Prince to perfect the corps under his command, and generally to improve the army. The good results of his training made themselves felt on the battle-fields of France, where the Saxon division fought bravely under the headleadership of the Red Prince, Frederick Charles of Prussia. At Sedan it was a Saxon bomb that wounded Marshal MacMahon. Crown Prince Albert visited the sick man as he lay on his couch at Sedan, and both generals recalled the fact that they had met last in Königsberg on the occasion of the crowning of William I. as King of Prussia. What events had occurred since then!

After Emperor William and his son returned home it fell to the lot of Prince Albert to command the allied armies still left behind in France. He was merely allowed a brief vacation, which he employed in hurrying to Saxony and fetching his wife to keep him company at Compiègne, Napoleon III.'s favourite country residence having been assigned to the Saxon commander-in-chief for his abode while on French soil. When the disorders of the Commune broke out in Paris, Prince Albert hurried to the Parisian forts then manned by Germans, and rendered effective service. When the victorious German troops held their triumphant entry, first into Berlin, then into Dresden, the Crown Prince of Saxony rode proudly at the head of his men, feeling he had earned the enthusiastic applause that everywhere greeted his appearance. King William had created him General Field-Marshal on this occasion, and it is interesting to note that he carried in his hand that day the marshal's staff which the Polish King John Sobieski had borne on his entry into Vienna in 1683. Through the ancient connection between Saxony and Poland this baton had come to Dresden, and King John bestowed it on his son on that festive day in honour of his bravery.

In October, 1873, King John's earthly career ended, and King Albert ascended the throne. He at once gave the same energy and attention to his country's internal affairs as he had given to the army, and under his rule Saxony has increased in prosperity both as to its commerce and industry. He and his wife have known how to make themselves popular and beloved among their people, and when, five years after their accession, they celebrated their silver wedding, it was an occasion of real rejoicing in the land.

THE MINOR GERMAN SOVEREIGNS.

THE MINOR GERMAN SOVEREIGNS.

UNDOUBTEDLY the making of Germany was an historical necessity, an event which under any circumstances would have taken place, the current of things, the evolution of history, rendering it imperative. But it is also beyond question that the task of the makers of new Germany was rendered much easier than it might otherwise have been, thanks to the insignificant character of most, if not all the rulers who sat upon the various thrones of the various minor States. Only one uprose above the average, and that was King Louis of Bavaria, but his ambition was to be before all else an artist and a musician, and to retire as much as possible from the burdens of kingcraft. The heads of the various States who still retain a modified autonomy are much reduced in number since 1870. Hanover was annexed to Prussia. The realm of Brunswick was deprived by death of heirs. Of kings, properly speaking, there remain but three: those of Wurtemberg, Saxony, and Bavaria, all titles of young lineage, created as they were by Napoleon I., and none of them, either from the character of their rulers or of the ruled, likely ever to form an opposition to the present order of things in Prussianified Germany.

THE KING OF WURTEMBERG.

King Charles Frederick Alexander of Wurtemberg was born March 6, 1823, at the royal castle of Stuttgart, the first and only son of his parents, King William of Wurtemberg, and his wife, a Princess of Nassau. A careful early education was given to this much-cherished heir, who soon evinced a liking rather for the arts of peace than those of war, and he reckons the years spent at the Universities of Tübingen and Berlin among the happiest of his life. After attaining his majority, at the age of eighteen, after the manner of princes, who for some occult reason are held to grow mature earlier than common mortals, he made a tour of Europe. At Palermo he met his future wife, the Grand Duchess Olga, daughter of the Czar Nicholas of Russia, whom he married at Peterhof in July, 1846. After a triumphal entry into Stuttgart the young couple led a very quiet life. Both were fond of music and art and literature, and both encouraged the society of artists and professors at their house. The outer world did not hear much of them, but to the Wurtembergers the Princess soon became a beloved figure, her deeds of charity, her interest in education, and in the welfare of the people endearing her to her future subjects. For eighteen years their life sped on thus uneventfully; their only sorrow of which the outer world knew aught was the childlessness of their union. The death of his father, King William, in his eighty-second year, called the son to the throne in June, 1864.

It was a difficult moment in German history. The Schleswig-Holstein question was strongly foreshadowing itself. King Charles held an attitude of reserve and tact, but when the victories over the Austrians made it no longer doubtful who would in future hold the regency of Germany, he and his land openly professed themselves with the Prussians. Not, however, in time. The Wurtembergers had sided first with the Austrians, and the result was that their land was occupied by Prussian troops, and a heavy indemnity was claimed. From that day forward Prussia encroached more and more upon the internal administration of Wurtemberg affairs, until the army at least became a mere appendage of the Prussian, though the people hated the Prussian system, and would have preferred the Swiss form of military service. But Prussia was too strong for them, and King Charles could not even afford to protest. Like all the southern German States, he had to bow to the will of the strongest, and to accede *bon gré mal gré* to a defensive and offensive alliance with Prussia— an alliance that at first, however, was kept most secret, for the people of Southern Germany still retained a tender place in their hearts for the more amiable, less rigid, Austrians. But the declaration of war by France on Prussia in 1870 brought matters to a climax, and all Northern and Southern Germany mobilized its troops and marched together upon Paris. Wurtemberg, too, sent in a mighty contingent, of which, however, the King did not take personal command. He contented himself with superintending affairs at home, and visiting his Wurtembergers only at Versailles in 1871, after William I. of Prussia had been proclaimed German Emperor.

The land of Wurtemberg celebrated in close succession the triumphal entry of its troops and its royal master's silver wedding. The latter was celebrated quietly by the couple in their summer residence of Friedrichshofen on the Lake of Constance, in the company of their adopted daughter, Grand Duchess Vera, the Princess whose twin daughters, Elsa and Vera, are now the joy of their adopted grandparents. A number of charitable institutions were founded to celebrate the event. Meanwhile the royal couple continued the quiet retired life they had ever led; the King, helped by his ministers, occupied in furthering the interests of his land, especially in the matters of education and agriculture; the Queen incessantly busy with the welfare of the less fortunate among her subjects. Both are amiable, unobtrusive personalities, who neither seek publicity, nor have character enough to support it. Both are popular in their land, the Queen perhaps most so of the two. The King of late years at least has forfeited a little of his popularity owing to his liking to dabble in spiritualism, which caused him to encourage around him a band of American adventurers, who, the Wurtembergers thought, exploited this foible of his Majesty's in a manner the reverse of justifiable. Perhaps it is the King's weak health that has made him a victim to this weak-minded and pernicious form of amusement. For it is some years now that he is far from strong, and obliged to live more and more in retirement, spending his winters either in the South of France or in Italy, where the Queen always accompanies him.

The King of Bavaria.

During the past decade the hand of Fate has borne heavily upon the royal Houses of Europe, and tragedies have occurred among their members such as to arouse the sympathies of all peoples and parties, whether Royalists or Republicans. The very fact of the exalted station of the sufferers but helped to emphasize the well-worn adage that sorrow enters into cottage and palace alike, that riches bring with them no exemption from care. Tragic among the tragic was the fate of Louis II., King of Bavaria.

We are all familiar with the history of this handsome, gifted youth, the patron of Wagner, enamoured of pomp and splendour, whose rage for building castles ruined his own and his country's finances, and whose eccentricities, at first gently smiled at by his Court, assumed gradually such proportions that it was needful to place him under medical restraint—a restraint from which he escaped four days after by means of suicide, dragging down with him into the Lake of Starenberg the doctor who was to watch over his life.

Was there ever a sadder tale in public or private life than this of this descendant of Kings, who, perchance, expiated in his own person the physical sins and extravagances committed by the forbears, who had introduced into the family of the Wittelsbach that strain of insanity a touch of which reveals itself in a more or less acute form in each of its members.

King Louis of Bavaria was the son of Maximilian II., himself the son of King Louis I., famous throughout Europe for his desire to prove a German Mæcenas, and for his connection with the Spanish dancer, Lola Montes.

In the romantic castle of Hohenschwangen, perched upon a wooded eminence in a rocky defile of the lovely Bavarian Alps, there lived, in the early thirties, Crown Prince Max of Bavaria with his wife, a Prussian Princess, and their two little boys, Louis and Otto. These boys' education was a somewhat strange one. The mother, desirous that the children should be simple, denied them many little luxuries and pleasures common to wealth and rank, so much so that King Louis, for example, who passionately desired a horse, never had one to ride until he was a monarch, with the result that the young sovereign, able at last to give free scope to his desires, in the early days of his accession playing at riding as a child of ten might do. The same applied to toys. Brought up thus in a wild mountain district, away from their kind, deprived of the natural pursuits of boyhood, endowed by heredity with a morbid strain, is it wonderful that the younger early became a hopeless maniac, while the elder contracted that love of solitude, that tendency to jealous and sombre reverie, that proclivity towards the bizarre, the exaggerated, which finally stranded him among the ranks of men bereft of reason? It was a long, a sad decline of intelligence, commencing with what appeared mere oddities and ending in hopeless folly.

And when there occurred the tragedy of Berg, depriving Bavaria of the mad sovereign, with whom the nation had borne so patiently, it was but to place yet another lunatic upon the throne, for Prince Otto's hopeless mental condition did not exclude him from assuming his birthright.

The reigning King of Bavaria, therefore, is Otto I., a man whose state of mental alienation is dark and terrible. He lives since his accession, as he lived before, shut up in the small palace of Fürstenreid, about two hours distant from Munich. Of late his malady has taken the form of stupor, though there are still occasional outbreaks of violence. There is no prospect of recovery, or even of improvement, in his case, although his merely animal existence may continue a long time. He occupies a suite of apartments on the ground floor, the doors of which, as well as the outside door leading into the garden, are always left open in the daytime, as a closed door immediately excites his rage. He seems suspicious of restraint, and his attendants hide as much as possible all appearance of authority over his movements.

Once he broke all the front windows of his apartment, and since then the glass has been protected by wire; but otherwise there is nothing to indicate that a lunatic inhabits the premises. The rooms are handsomely furnished, and everything that can amuse the patient is promptly supplied.

Not long ago some one tried the experiment of setting a small musical box to playing in the King's vicinity. He listened with evident pleasure, and soon afterwards a large instrument of the same kind was furnished at a cost of five thousand marks. But he was indifferent to the louder tones, and began to show a dislike to the instrument, which was speedily taken out of his sight.

The King is always dressed in black. His beard is very long and thick, and he will not allow it to be trimmed. He often washes his hands and face, but can seldom be persuaded to take a full bath. He is extremely fond of cigarettes, and smokes more than thirty a day—enough in itself to make him crazy and keep him so! Every time he lights a cigarette he burns a whole box of matches, and seems to enjoy the noise and the flame. He has a good appetite, and eats heartily of the food allowed by his physicians. He drinks several glasses of beer at dinner, and often calls for champagne, which is brought to him whenever the physician gives an assenting sign to the waiter. He is allowed a knife and fork, and eats in a decent manner, excepting that he sometimes neglects his napkin and wipes his mouth upon his coat-sleeve. He sits alone at one end of the table, and his physician, with the Court-Marshal and the adjutant, occupy places at some distance. The King does not wish to be spoken to while he is eating, and never says anything to his attendants except to call for what he wants. He often walks out in the park, but is very unwilling to drive out—probably because it annoys him to be looked at by people on the road.

The sensational reports concerning King Otto which appear occasionally in the papers are for the most part false. He is said to long to return to his " dear Munich," and to beg to be allowed to drive thither. But the truth is he has no desire for anything. His gaze is generally fixed on vacancy, and he does not appear to recognize even his servants, excepting an old woman who has charge of the silver. He has known her all his life; she used to carry him in her arms when he was a baby, and it is touching to see how the last faint rays of his fading intelligence rest upon her alone. When he sees her, he calls her name in a loud voice, and orders her to bring him a glass of beer or whatever he may happen to think of; but he soon forgets what he has said, and relapses into his usual state of apathy.

Two of the most prominent physicians of Munich are in attendance on alternate weeks, and every Sunday the Director of the Insane Asylum visits the Palace to examine the medical report. At rare intervals the King speaks coherently to his attendants, and it is said that soon after his accession to the throne he remarked to a lackey: "Henceforth you must address me as 'Your Majesty.'" But this story does not appear to be well founded, and it is certain that when Princess Thérèse went from the deathbed of the Queen-Mother to apprise her son of his loss, he showed no sign of comprehension, and was unmoved by the grief of the Princess, whose tears were, doubtless, more for the living than for the dead.

In a word, Bavaria has a King but in name, it is a Regent that rules over her. Obviously in an ordinary country such a state of things would be quite impossible; but Bavaria, like other lands absorbed by Prussia in 1870, exists but nominally. It has a mere semblance of independence. In reality it is only a fraction of the vast empire which Bismarck organized. Hence the inconveniences that would otherwise arise are minimized.

The Regent of Bavaria is Prince Luitpold, a man of seventy, youngest son of Louis the Extravagant, and brother of the deposed King Otto of Greece. Prince Luitpold has held the reins of government for some time, for at Louis II.'s express wish his uncle performed all onerous state functions, thus leaving the King free to seek the solitude he loved. And it is his children who must succeed to the throne of Bavaria when Otto shall at length be released from his sufferings—a release which does not seem likely to be immediate, as the King is but forty-three and strong in every respect, except mentally.

The Prince is a widower, sincerely mourning the

death of his wife, to whom he was deeply attached. His daughter, Princess Therese, takes the place of her mother as presiding lady at the Palace. She is the Abbess of a religious order, but has returned to the world in order to be of use to her father. Her piety and charity are proverbial. It is whispered that in her youth she cherished an unrequited love for her cousin, King Ludwig II., who was then beautiful and interesting enough to attract the affection of any sensitive spirit. If this is true, how deep must have been her sorrow as she watched the gradual ruin of all the hopes built upon the promise of his early years!

The Prince Regent is a devout Catholic, and when he took the reins of government there was great rejoicing in the camp of the Ultramontanes, and corresponding depression among the ranks of the Liberals and Protestants. But thus far he has justified neither the hopes of the one nor the fears of the other party. He has displayed complete impartiality respecting all questions affecting the general welfare of the people, and has steered clear of all attempts to entrap him into compromising situations. His sincere wish to be just is shown on private occasions, as well as in matters of State policy, wherein he is guided by the advice of his ministers and the decisions of Parliament.

The Prince Regent, although over sixty years old, has shown himself active and diligent in the duties of his station since the first moment of his assumption of office. His earliest undertaking was to make a tour of the kingdom, visiting the principal towns, inquiring into long neglected wants and grievances, and expressing interest in all useful progress. He was received everywhere with the warmest enthusiasm; it was plain that the Bavarians felt hurt by the total indifference of King Ludwig towards his subjects, and were happy in the thought that they had again a friend and well-wisher on the throne.

The Prince has moved from his private palace to the royal residence, which is frequently the scene of magnificent entertainments, while almost every day during the season his dinner-table is surrounded by guests invited on account of their worthy work in art, or literature, or science, or business affairs. It will certainly be an awkward moment for Bavaria should Prince Luitpold, as is probable, die before the King, as a regency is necessarily not hereditary. Of heirs there is no lack. Prince Luitpold has three sons and one daughter, and these, again, all married, by the way, to scions of the House of Hapsburg, have upreared a large family around them, Prince Louis, the probable heir, having already no less than ten descendants. Of this Prince all that is known is in his favour. He seems a man who prefers the arts of peace to those of war, is devoted to agriculture, and loves the fine arts.

Still, for the present his hour has not come, and who knows whether it ever will, in these revolutionary days, when the tendency is to collect nationalities into huge empires, in lieu of dividing them into small States. In any case Bavaria is a mere dependency of the strong German Empire, and as such its anomalous present condition in no wise disturbs the course of either European or internal affairs.

QUEEN VICTORIA OF ENGLAND.

QUEEN VICTORIA OF ENGLAND.

A TRAVELLER who, in the late bleak days of March, 1819, traversed the high roads that lie between Amorbach, the capital of the tiny principality of Leiningen, and the Dutch sea-coast, might have encountered an old-fashioned, heavy travelling-coach, driven by a tall, stout, bald-headed, red-faced, elderly gentleman. He would scarcely, however, have imagined that this coachman was no less a personage than His Royal Highness the Duke of Kent, fourth son of the then reigning English Sovereign, George III. If he was indiscreet enough to peep into the carriage he would have seen that its occupant was a lady who still possessed much youthful grace and beauty, though she had passed her prime, and he might further have observed that she was about to become a mother. This lady was Victoria of the house of Saxe-Coburg, widow of the Prince of Leiningen, and wife of her amateur coachman, who was driving her thus carefully himself for fear of those untoward accidents not rare in pre-railway days. The Duke was anxious that his expected offspring should be born on English soil, for it was by no means improbable that this unborn child would some day sit upon the throne of England. The journey was indeed accomplished in safety, though hampered by serious pecuniary difficulties.

It seems strange that this should have been the case with a royal Prince, but the Duke was no favourite with his family, and, moreover, jealousy and ill-feeling of all kinds were rife among the royal brothers of England on account of this expected child, each desiring to be the father of the future sovereign. For, notwithstanding the fact that George III. and his royal spouse, Queen Charlotte, had been most prolific, the younger members of the family were few. The long Continental war, and the Royal Marriage Act passed by the King himself, had kept the younger princes unmarried till they were middle-aged men. The heir to the throne in those days was first George, Prince of Wales, for some time Regent, owing to his father's insanity, and then his only daughter Charlotte, who in 1816 married Leopold, afterwards King of the Belgians. But when in the winter of 1817 Princess Charlotte was laid in eternal rest, her still-born infant in her arms, it was perceived with consternation that there was no young heir to the throne. Immediately the royal princes who were still unmarried hurried to look around them for suitable connections, and early the next year the Dukes of Clarence, Kent, and Cambridge married three princesses. Indeed, the two former were married on the same day. The Duke of

Kent, however, had stolen a march upon his brother, for he had a few months previously married his bride in Germany, the English ceremony being merely a formula to render yet more legal the possible fruit of the union. For all these men were far advanced in the fifties, had led dissipated lives, and offspring was no certainty. The Duke of Kent was by far the best and most moral of the royal princes, though it can scarcely be said that he was popular. He had not been a favourite child with his parents, and had thus perhaps escaped the evil effects of Court flattery and home indulgence. His leanings were Liberal—at that time an object of loathing to royalty, and on this account he was cut off with a niggardly allowance quite unfitting his rank. His tastes were Continental rather than English—another cause for unpopularity, the nation in those days having a great distaste for everything not insular. The coarseness of the age preferred the home-bred extravagances and even vices of his brothers to his more decorous and moral conduct. It was therefore not quite seen with favour that he might be the father of the future sovereign. And, indeed, the Duke of Clarence, his elder, who had forestalled him by a few weeks in becoming a father, might yet have other children, though his baby had died ere the Duke of Kent's saw the light. Still, when his own little daughter was born, the Duke regarded her high destiny as such a settled thing, that he was wont to hold her up in his arms and say, "Look at her well;

she will yet be Queen of England." And, indeed, the sickly Clarence Princess who followed her sister also faded in babyhood into an early grave.

It was when the horsechestnut trees, for which Kensington Gardens are famous, were in full snowy bloom, that there was born (May 24, 1819) in the old red-brick, Dutch-looking abode of Kensington Palace, London, the infant whom her German relations loved to call the "May blossom." The baby's birth was a matter of no small national moment; it was to inaugurate a reign that has proved one of the longest, noblest, most prosperous, and most stirring in England's proud story. Yet when those blue eyes first opened to the light of day, matters looked anything but halcyon for Britain. True, Napoleon, the great disturber of the peace of nations, was enjoying ample leisure on the rock of St. Helena to meditate upon the seas of blood with which he had iniquitously deluged Europe, and it was England that, almost unassisted, had withstood him and pinned him captive; but as inevitable reaction after a long war, there was misery in the land; taxes were high, food was dear, trade was at a standstill. The reigning King was old, blind, and crazy; the Regent an elderly profligate. No brilliant outlook truly.

It was a month after her birth that the small Royal Highness was baptized with all pomp in the grand saloon of Kensington Palace. The royal gold font, long unused, was brought from the Tower on purpose, and Archbishops and Bishops performed the ceremony.

There was some little trouble about finding a name for the baby. The father wished to call her Elizabeth, thinking that from its glorious tradition, that would prove a name to please people should she occupy the throne. But the Prince Regent, who was godfather together with the Emperor of Russia, gave only the name of Alexandrina to the clergy. The father pleaded that another name be added, and proposed the feminine form of the Regent's own name, Georgina. But the Regent said his name could not come in the second place, and as the Emperor's must take precedence, if the baby had to have another name, "give her her mother's." So the Princess came to be called Alexandrina Victoria, and in infancy was known as the Princess Drina, a name she dropped after her accession.

It was the first winter after her birth that the baby Princess went with her parents to pass the cold months in the pretty seacoast town of Sidmouth in Devonshire. The visit was to have a fatal termination. The father, who was devoted to his child, came in one day wet after walking in a storm, and instead of changing his clothes, lingered to play with the baby. A chill struck him, inflammation set in, and in January, 1820, he died, leaving his six months' old child an orphan in poor circumstances, under the sole guardianship of her mother. Prince Leopold, brother of the widow, and ever after the faithful friend and guide of mother and daughter, came at once to be beside his sister in the hour of her sorrow. It was he who advised that the Duchess should stay on in England, that her child might have an English education—expedient, seeing how near she stood to the crown. Two days after the death, therefore, the Duchess and her babe returned to London. The infant held up at the carriage-window, to bid farewell to the assembled population of Sidmouth, laughed joyously and patted the glasses with her dimpled hands, in utter unconsciousness of her bereavement. On the very day the party arrived in London (January 29, 1821) George III. was at last gathered to his fathers, and the worst, and happily last, of the Georges ascended the throne. Knowing the impurity of his Court, the Duchess of Kent resolved from the first to keep herself absent from it, for her daughter's sake, and for this her widowhood and her very restricted pecuniary means gave her a good pretext. The position of the Duchess was certainly a sad and difficult one. She had resigned her German home and jointure, and was now alone in a foreign land, the language of which she could hardly speak, with the charge of bringing up its probable heir. Kensington Palace was assigned to her as a residence, and here she received the official deputation of condolence that waited upon her. To spectators the contrast was painful between the tear-stained face of the mother and the smiling baby face of the child. Here, in Kensington, with frequent changes of scene in the summer, the infant years of the Princess Victoria were passed, in company of her mother and her half-sister Feodore. It was no infrequent sight to see the two in the gardens, the elder drawing the younger in a little carriage, or walking beside her donkey chair. The baby liked to be noticed, and answered all who spoke to her, holding out her soft dimpled hand to be kissed. Life passed quietly and somewhat monotonously at the Palace. The Queen herself has told us that her childhood was lonely and sad. Simplicity and regularity were the marked features of her early life, that had one great want, that of a companion of her own age. There was plenty of out door exercise as well as of good teaching and study. The child rather objected to regular instruction at first, and was inclined to ask, after the style of her grandfather, George III., "What good this? what good that?" but was at last convinced of the need of learning. Of her governess, a wise and excellent woman, who remained with her till after her marriage, the after Queen wrote: "I adored her, though I was greatly in awe of her." At the age of five she was entrusted to an English tutor—very needful, as both mother and governess were Germans. This tutor related how the Princess had always a most strict regard for truth. "I remember when I had been teaching her one day she was very impatient for the lesson to be over—once or twice rather refractory. The Duchess of Kent came in and asked how she had behaved. Lehzen said, 'Oh, once she was rather troublesome.' The Princess touched her and said, 'No, Lehzen, twice, don't you remember?'" French, Italian, Latin, Greek, mathematics, music, and drawing were the chief studies pursued. In the two latter especially she made good progress. The Queen is a fair musician and draughtswoman, and to this day employs her leisure in these accomplishments. A tender consideration for others was also inculcated in the Princess, as well as strict economy and the habit of cash payment. This was all the more remarkable in an age when spendthrift extravagance was held a princely virtue. She was also taught to finish whatever she was doing before she began anything else— a rule that was applied even to her amusements. Indeed it would have been difficult for her mother to have educated her with more prudence and wisdom, and she grew up submissive to authority and happy in the pleasures of her age. All knowledge of her probable future dignity was carefully kept from her. As she grew old enough to notice it, it puzzled her that when she and her sister were out together the gentlemen took off their hats to her (Victoria) and not to the elder lady. But when it was explained to her that she was a royal Princess of England, and her half-sister a German and of lower rank, she was satisfied.

Yet even the most careful training cannot make children angels. The Princess Victoria had her faults like other children, and these faults have remained with her through life, though in changed form—that is to say, she was impulsive, and sometimes not a little wilful and imperious. But as the affections are strong and the head well trained, these matters always righted themselves. She has an ingrained sense of justice which can always redress the balance.

In 1830 William IV. ascended the throne, and it was then that both mother and governess held that the Princess Victoria ought to be informed of her high rank. One day, therefore, the genealogical table of England, till then carefully kept from her, was purposely put into her lesson book. The Princess opening it and seeing the additional paper, said—

"I never saw that before."

"It was not held necessary you should, Princess," replied Fraulein Lehzen.

"I see I am nearer the throne than I thought."

"So it is, Madam."

The young girl was quiet awhile, and then said—

"How many a child would boast! But they don't know the difficulty. There is much splendour, but there is more responsibility."

The Princess, having lifted up the forefinger of her right hand while she spoke, gave that hand to her governess, saying—

"I will be good. I understand now why you urged me so much to learn, even Latin. My Aunts Augusta and Mary never did, but you told me Latin is the foundation of English grammar and of all the elegant expressions, and I learnt it, as you wished it, but I understand all better now." Again she repeated, "I will be good."

"But your Aunt Adelaide is still young," said the governess, "and may have children, and of course they would ascend the throne after their father, William IV., and not you, Princess."

To which the girl replied—

"And if it was so, I should never feel disappointed, for I know by the love Aunt Adelaide bears me how fond she is of children."

It now became needful for the little Princess, as acknowledged heiress, to be seen sometimes at Court and in public, but her mother took care that these interruptions to her studies should be as rare as possible. Nor was the Court of the coarse-languaged William a more fit place for a young girl than that of his dissipated brother. Certainly few maidens have been reared so quietly. At sixteen she went to her first ball, and even then was sent off to bed after one dance.

It was in 1836 that the destined Prince came first to the quiet shades of Kensington. Albert of Saxe-Coburg was first cousin to the Queen on her mother's side, and both their common uncle Leopold and his intimate adviser, Baron Stockmar, had formed the idea of uniting these two cousins in marriage from the time they were babies. They were born within three months of each other, nursed by the same nurses, reared on the same system. It is true that it seemed something of a *mésalliance* for the Queen of England to marry a petty German prince, but as the youth grew up he gave such evident signs of superior mental capacity that it was felt that he would make up in wisdom what he lacked in birth. It was, however, agreed that neither should know of the plan, but that as soon as possible the young people should meet and see if they could love each other before making any other arrangements. Shrewd Baron Stockmar, who gave this advice, was well aware of the potency of the spell the young Prince bore about with him, namely, that of great personal beauty and simple, charming manners. So in 1836 Prince Albert and his brother Ernest, lads of sixteen and seventeen, were sent to England to see the country and visit their relations. A pleasant month passed, during which the cousins saw much of each other, singing and drawing together, and visiting the sights. They evidently came to some understanding, for among the rings the Queen wears to this day is one, a small enamel with a tiny diamond in the centre, given her by Prince Albert when he first came to England as a lad of seventeen. Still nothing was settled, and nothing, it seems, was said to the Prince, who returned to his studies at Bonn University. The King of the Belgians, however, had confided his pet scheme to his niece, who, in a letter to him (June 7, 1836), acknowledges her affection for her cousin. "I have only now to beg you, my dearest uncle," it concludes, " to take care of the health of one now so dear to me, and to take him under your special protection. I hope and trust that all will go on prosperously and well on this subject, now of so much importance to me."

In consequence of this letter, of which Prince Albert, however, was ignorant, a turn was given to his studies that should prepare him for his future exalted position.

Meantime, in May, 1837, the Princess came of age; for royal folk, for reasons unexplained, are allowed this privilege three years earlier than common people. There were great national rejoicings, and a State ball was given; but at this neither King nor Queen were able to be present, for rough-spoken William IV. lay upon what was to prove his death-bed. He had, however, attained his desire—to see the Princess of age ere his death, for he did not wish that the sister-in-law he most unjustly hated should hold the reins of government. The festivities over, the Princess Victoria returned once more to the privacy of her life at Kensington Palace. But it was not to be of long duration. In the early dawn of June 20th, the gate porter was roused by a knocking which, like that in "Macbeth," was significant of a king's death. A coach and four had dashed full speed up the great central avenue, its occupants grave men who listened not to the birds' morning songs, nor noticed the sweetness of the flower-scented morning air. They heeded only the importance of their solemn errand. "They knocked, they rang, they thumped for a considerable time before they could rouse the porter at the gate; they were again kept waiting in the courtyard; then turned into one of the lower rooms, where they seemed to be forgotten by everybody. They rang the bell, and desired that the attendant of the Princess Victoria might be sent to inform Her Royal Highness that they requested an audience on business of importance. After another delay and another ringing to inquire the cause, the attendant was summoned, who stated that the Princess was in such a sweet sleep that she could not venture to disturb her. Then they said, 'We are come on business of State to the *Queen,* and even her sleep must give way to that.' It did; and to prove that she did not keep them waiting, in a few moments she came into the room in a loose white nightgown and shawl, her nightcap thrown off, and her hair falling upon her shoulders, her feet in slippers, tears in her eyes, but perfectly collected and dignified." She listened to the news they communicated with tender sympathy for her Aunt Adelaide, and it is said that she asked the Archbishop to pray with her.

Her first act after the announcement of her accession was to write to her aunt, Queen Adelaide, a tender letter of condolence, begging her to remain at Windsor as long as she pleased. She addressed it "To Her Majesty the Queen" at Windsor Castle. Told that she ought to write, "To Her Majesty the Queen-Dowager," she answered, "I am aware of that, but I will not be the first to remind her of her altered position."

Only after this was done was the girl Queen at liberty

to go and finish her toilet and talk over her changed fortune with her beloved mother. At nine, however, she had to see the Prime Minister, and at eleven her first council was held. The crowds of peers and high officials who came to that council was almost incredible, for all were curious to see how the young girl, of whose inner nature so little was known, would demean herself. England had seen women mount the throne before, but then they had never been so young. Even Mr. Greville, present on this occasion, and who has left behind him an acid diary in which he abuses most things, has only words of praise to bestow. The simple dignity with which she went through the long ordeal of this multitude of men swearing allegiance and kissing her hand, the charm of voice and delivery with which she read her first speech, earned her the praise of all present. Indeed, the beauty of her voice, the clearness of her enunciation in public speaking, have ever been a theme of praise. When her aged uncles knelt to do her homage, she was visibly affected, and blushed up to the eyes, as though she felt the contrast between their civil and natural relations. But this was the only sign of emotion she evinced.

Next day the ceremony of Proclamation took place, when, according to custom, the Queen had to appear at the open window of the Presence Chamber in St. James's Palace, surrounded by her great nobles in their State robes. She herself, and her mother who stood beside her, were simply dressed in mourning. Below were heralds and trumpeters ready to proclaim to all men: "The King is dead! Long live the Queen!" Hundreds of guns repeated the record, and loud acclamations from the populace rent the air. The last sovereigns had not gained the love or esteem of the people; it was hoped, and not in vain, that this new ruler would prove more constitutional, and would obliterate all unhappy recollections.

One result of the Queen's accession was that the connection of the English Crown with Hanover, so hated by the English people, and which in later times would have drawn the country into Continental troubles, was severed, since in that little kingdom the Salic law was in force. The crown was therefore assumed by the Queen's uncle, the unpopular Duke of Cumberland.

Busy weeks full of State functions followed. The Queen entered fully into all business matters brought before her, and the then Prime Minister, Lord Melbourne, once said that he would rather have ten kings to manage than one Queen. He could not place a single document in Her Majesty's hand for signature but she first asked an infinite variety of questions respecting it, and she not infrequently ended her interrogations by declining to put her name to the paper in question till she had taken further time to consider its merits. Once when Melbourne urged the expediency of an Act he was stopped short by the Queen with: "I have been taught, my lord, to judge between what is right and what is wrong; but expediency is a word which I neither wish to hear nor to understand." And another time when he pleaded paramount importance for the matter in hand, he was met with: "It is with me a matter of paramount importance whether or not I attach my signature to a document with which I am not thoroughly satisfied." The truth was the Queen knew well that public business had been neglected by her predecessors, and was resolved this should not be the case in her reign. And to this resolve she has kept to this day. In times of private sorrow, of sickness, of difficulty, the Queen of England has never shirked her business duties, has never put her name to a document whose import she has not weighed and considered. That is why she has proved so good a sovereign, why her subjects are so justly proud of her reign.

Into all the gaieties and pleasures of her new position the Queen entered with zest, removing her Court to London, her youthful spirits, and perhaps also the reaction from her quiet and secluded life, making her prefer the city to the country's solitude. After all the young sovereign was little more than a child, though a very wise one. From the first she arranged and ordered her household with great judgment and economy, ruling it with gentle authority and consummate tact. Here, like in public business, she would insist on knowing everything.

The early months of her reign were not easy. Each great party, Whig and Tory, tried to get her into their power. They thought because she was a woman they could mould her as they chose, that she would be as wax in their hands. They proved mistaken. True, she had been reared in Liberal principles, and had most of her friends on that side, but she knew what was due to her as a constitutional sovereign, and even later, in moments of yet greater difficulty, when her private views were in discord with the will of the nation expressed through Parliament, she never swerved from her duty. Her first Minister was Lord Melbourne, a man of fascinating manners, but of easy morals. Yet such was the charm her innocence exerted over him, that to her he was unblemished chivalrous devotion. With singular patience he taught her the formulæ of her position, shielded her, advised her, and amused her. No wonder she liked to have him about her, no wonder she feared a change of parties might deprive her of him.

On June 28, 1838, the Queen was formally crowned in Westminster Abbey. It was the most imposing spectacle of her reign; indeed, the same ceremonial, splendour, and public rejoicing had never before been witnessed. Ancient traditions were adhered to, quaint old customs revived. Only one was abolished, namely, that the Peers should do homage by kissing their sovereign's left cheek. To the girl Queen it was an appalling prospect that six hundred men should have the right to salute her. The manner in which she conducted herself on this trying and most fatiguing occasion—for the ceremonial is long, the crown, the robes, and the regalia heavy to wear and carry—once more won her all praise. It is said that when she knelt for a moment in silent prayer, before seating herself upon the throne, there were many who shed tears at the sight of this simple maiden, the centre of so much splendour, the cynosure of a whole empire. Her sex and her tender years combined helped to gain her all hearts. The only incident that occurred during the ceremony helped to endear her but more. Lord Rolle, an infirm peer of nearly ninety, when going up the steps of the throne to do homage, slipped and fell to the bottom, encoiled in his robes. The Queen half rose, and when the old man again and in vain tried to approach her, she rose entirely and advanced to him—an act of kindness that caused a great sensation. As Mr. Greville wrote on this occasion: "It is in fact the remarkable union of *maïveté*, kindness, nature, good-nature, with propriety and dignity which makes her so admirable and so endearing to those about her as she certainly is. . . . She never ceases to be a Queen, but is always the most charming, cheerful, obliging, unaffected Queen in the world."

Foreign writers have never failed to inform their readers that the Lords Rolle hold their title on the condition of performing this feat at every coronation!

The five weary hours of coronation over, the Queen, crown on head and sceptre in hand, returned in pomp to her Palace. When the State coach drove up to the steps the first thing the young girl noticed was the glad bark of her pet dog, from whom she had been separated longer than usual. "There's Dash!" she exclaimed, and was in a hurry to doff her crown and royal robe, and lay down the sceptre and orb, to go and give Dash his bath.

The first important incident in the Queen's reign was one that for a time endangered her popularity, and became known as the Bedchamber Plot. It is the constitutional custom that on a change of Ministry the ladies in closest connection with the sovereign should abandon their posts and give place to those whose political views are in accord with the party in power. Lord Melbourne's Cabinet had to resign, the Tories came into office, and Sir Robert Peel informed the Queen that her ladies would have to leave her. At this she flared up in imperious anger, saying her lords might go, but that she would not part from her ladies, and she wrote a letter to the Cabinet which Elizabeth might have penned, but whose strain was no longer permissible in an era of constitutional monarchy. The blame of the whole matter must be laid on the Queen's advisers. Her own action was that of a warm-hearted, high-spirited child, and had the matter been explained to her fully she would no doubt have yielded to constitutional demands, as she ever after did when similar occasions arose. As it was the matter made an immense hubbub: the Tories would not form a Ministry under these circumstances, the Whigs could not get the confidence of the land, evil tongues set themselves a-clacking, confusion and strife were rife. Of course they smoothed down at last, as things always do, but meantime wise King Leopold and astute Stockmar were growing uneasy. They saw that the young inexperienced Queen needed guidance and protection, and they came to the conviction that the hour was ripe to send the destined Prince to the rescue of the maiden Princess whom he had loved from boyhood. Stockmar was convinced that evil enchantments, and the plots of self-interested courtiers, would all vanish at the touch of that Ithuriel's spear—true love. The Queen, it is true, had told her uncle that she did not intend to marry for years to come, that she was too young, and the Prince also, and that he had better study English longer. Nevertheless the two Saxe-Coburg brothers were once more sent to England, though Prince Albert himself felt far from certain if the sort of half engagement entered into was still supposed to hold good. Moreover there were other and, from a worldly point of view, more eligible suitors in the field.

The Coburgs arrived in the autumn of 1839, and were received at Windsor Castle by the Queen in person at the head of the staircase. She almost failed to recognize in the tall, stately young man of rare beauty, the stripling of three years before. The next day she wrote to her anxious uncle: "Albert's beauty is most striking, and he is most amiable and unaffected—in short, very *fascinating*. The young men are very amiable, delightful companions, and I am happy to have them here."

A pleasant month followed, during which the cousins saw much of each other, and in which the Queen showed Prince Albert many marked attentions. At last one evening at a Court Ball she presented him with her bouquet. This flattering indication of her favour might have involved a less quick-witted lover in an awkward dilemma, for his uniform jacket was fastened up to the chin after the Prussian fashion, and offered no button-hole wherein to place the precious gift. But the Prince, in the very spirit of chivalry, seized a penknife and immediately slit an aperture in his dress next his heart, and there triumphantly deposited the royal flowers.

The next day he was told that the Queen wished to speak to him, and it was then that she formally proposed to him—a most nervous thing to do, as she herself has since told the world in the simple naïve account of her courtship and marriage, which she has given to her subjects. But etiquette demanded that she should take the initiative. This was what the Prince wrote at once after to his grandmother at Gotha : " The Queen sent for me alone to her room, and declared to me in a genuine outburst of affection that I had gained her whole heart, and would make her intensely happy if I would make her the sacrifice of sharing her life with her, for she said she looked on it as a sacrifice; the only thing which troubled her was that she did not think she was worthy of me. The joyous openness with which she told me this enchanted me, and I was quite carried away by it."

Meantime the Queen wrote to Stockmar, to whom she had said but a while before that she should not marry yet a while: "I do feel so guilty, I know not how to begin my letter; but I think the news it will contain will be sufficient to ensure your forgiveness. Albert has completely won my heart, and all was settled between us this morning. I feel certain he will make me happy. I wish I could feel as certain of my making him happy."

The Queen felt much, and repeatedly dwelt on the sacrifice the Prince made for her. Although many would have regarded him as only to be envied, in one sense the Queen was quite right. She was not called upon to surrender anything, while she received the love and devoted care of a good husband. He, on the other hand, left his native home to dwell amongst strangers, with whom he had yet to make his way He parted from his much-loved brother, and took upon himself a portion of the burdens of the English sovereign, without taking equal rank with her in the rights and privileges of sovereignty. It was a difficult position, and they both knew it, and only Prince Albert's rare tact, integrity, and honesty enabled him to carry it through. If he sometimes made mistakes, he certainly made fewer than might have been expected from one in his delicate situation. As the Prince himself subsequently expressed it, he resolved "to sink his own individual existence in that of his wife, to aim at no power, by himself or for himself, to shun all ostentation, to assume no separate responsibility before the public; continually and anxiously to watch every part of the public business in order to be able to advise and assist her at any moment in any of the multifarious and difficult questions brought before her—sometimes political, or social, or personal—as the natural head of the family, superintendent of her household, manager of her private affairs, her sole confidential adviser in politics, and only assistant in her communications with the affairs of the Government." And since the couple were in deep sympathy with each other, and since love, trustful and unfeigned, was the moving spring of both, difficulties were overcome instead of becoming themselves insurmountable. For of few royal marriages can it be said, as of this one, that it was a marriage of profound happiness and mutual trust, that it was a real union of souls. But we are anticipating. The Queen had yet another trying ordeal to go through, namely, to announce her engagement to her Privy Council. She tells us that to give her courage she wore a bracelet containing the Prince's portrait. "Precisely at two I went in. The room was full, but I hardly knew who was there. Lord Melbourne I saw looking kindly at me with tears in his eyes, but he was not near me. I then read my short declaration. I felt my hands shook, but I did not make one mistake. I felt most happy and thankful when it was over. Lord Landsdowne then rose, and in the name of the Privy

Council asked that this most gracious and most welcome communication might be printed. I then left the room, the whole thing not lasting above two or three minutes."

The next embarrassing task was to tell the news to her faithful Parliament, and ask them to make a proper provision for her husband and household. The tidings proved acceptable to the Queen's subjects, who already felt anxiety as to her union and the need for heirs, but very unpleasant discussions arose as to the Prince's religion, some people having spread the report that he was a Catholic, as to the sum he should receive for his household, as to his precedence. Indeed the last point was never settled, and only courtesy and good feeling ensured that the Queen's husband enjoyed place and precedence beside her. As, however, the Prince's rank was but a petty one, and as on the Continent the due courtesy as husband was not accorded to him, the Queen herself in after years cut the Gordian knot, creating him Prince Consort as well as a Royal Highness, and declaring it as her royal will that he should take precedence next to her. She would have liked to have given him the rank of king, on the same principle that the consort of a king takes rank as queen, but of this the English would not hear, although there was precedent in the case of William of Orange and Queen Mary.

On February 10, 1840, a wet, chilly day, the royal couple were married with great pomp at St. James's Palace, and after enjoyed one day of perfect seclusion at Windsor Castle. For if royalty has its privileges, it has also its penalties: they belong to the public, and honeymoon retirement cannot be theirs. Addresses of congratulation without end, tedious ceremonials required their presence. But they managed to be very happy all the same, as the Queen's letters and journals of the period testify. Indeed, the home life of the royal lovers proved most serene. Their tastes were alike, and their characters assimilated, each being most truly the complement of the other. Yet, nevertheless, even theirs could not be a path only of roses. The Prince had his way to make still into the hearts of the people, who mistrusted him as a foreigner; there was much friction in quarters ruled by old Court principles; it was not always seen with favour that the young couple determined to discountenance the lavish extravagance, the lax manners of their predecessors. Looked back upon, many of their annoyances seem of a trifling character, but they caused real trouble at the time, much heart-burning, much evil-speaking and slandering. But the Prince's tact and good sense, aided by the Queen's love and perfect confidence, overcame these difficulties, though some years elapsed before they all were vanquished. Her Majesty has, since her widowhood, thus described her domestic life, which in essential features remained unaltered from first to last. They breakfasted at nine, and took a walk every morning soon afterwards. Then came the usual amount of business (far less heavy, however, than now), besides which they drew and etched a great deal together, which was a source of great amusement, having the plates "bit" in the house. Luncheon followed at the usual hour of two o'clock. Lord Melbourne (the Prime Minister at the time) came to the Queen in the afternoon, and between five and six the Prince generally drove her out in a pony phæton. If the Prince did not drive the Queen, he rode, in which case she took a drive with the Duchess of Kent or the ladies. The Prince also read aloud most days to the Queen. The dinner was at eight o'clock, and always with the company. The Prince often played double chess of which he was fond, of an evening. The hours were never late, and it was very seldom that the party had not broken up at eleven o'clock. The practice in English homes for gentlemen to remain at table for a considerable time after dinner was never favourably viewed by the Queen, and in this she had a seconder in her husband, who was a very temperate man, and not addicted to the pleasures of the palate. Thus between them they helped to break down a pernicious custom that led to much drunkenness. Indeed, the decrease in the national vice of drunkenness during the Queen's reign is one of its many noteworthy high moral features.

November of the year of marriage saw the birth of the Queen's first child, the Princess Royal, now the widowed Empress Frederick. Prince Albert feared that the people might be disappointed at the sex of the child, whereupon the Queen reassured him by saying, "Never mind, the next shall be a boy," and adding that she hoped she might have as many children as her grandmother, Queen Charlotte. She kept her word in both respects. In less than a year after the Prince of Wales was born. How happy things were in the home life is proved by a passage written by the Queen in her journal a few days after her confinement. "Albert brought in dearest little Pussy (the Princess Royal) in such a smart white merino dress trimmed with blue, which mamma had given her, and placed her on my bed, seating himself near to her, and she was very dear and good; and as my precious, invaluable Albert sat there, and our little love between us, I felt quite moved with happiness and gratitude to God." Things were, however, not so ideal outside the house; in her regal capacity the Queen had many anxieties. Discontent and disturbance were rife in the country, great distress prevailed. England was in difficulties in Canada, India, and China; there were even two attempts to assassinate the sovereign. Still, as she herself wrote in a letter of the period, "We all have our trials and vexations; but if one's home is happy, then the rest is comparatively nothing." That same year the Queen went to France, the first visit of an English sovereign to that country since Henry VIII. and Francis I. met on the Field of the Cloth of Gold. In this year the Queen first visited Scotland, and from that time dates the too partial preference she has given to one portion of her dominions over the others, exciting thus some jealousy and ill-feeling. It is more than possible that had she shown some of the same partiality for Ireland, the world would have heard less of Irish discontent.

An episode in this summer was the visit of Mendelssohn to the Queen and Prince at Buckingham Palace. A graphic account of this visit was given by the composer in a letter to his mother, which, though lengthy, we reproduce, as nothing can better illustrate the inner domestic life of the Queen and her husband. Such glimpses are deeply interesting, as revealing the personal aspects of a monarch's nature.

". . . Prince Albert had asked me to go to him on Saturday at two o'clock, so that I might try his organ before I left England. I found him alone, and as we were walking away the Queen came in, also alone, in a simple morning dress. She said she was obliged to leave for Claremont in an hour; and then, suddenly interrupting herself, exclaimed, 'But goodness! what a confusion!' for the wind had littered the whole room, and even the pedals of the organ (which, by the way, made a very pretty feature in the room), with leaves of music from a large portfolio that lay open. As she spoke she knelt down and began picking up the music. Prince Albert helped, and I, too, was not idle. Then Prince Albert proceeded to explain the stops to me, and she said that she would meanwhile put things straight.

"I begged that the Prince would first play me something, so that, as I said, I might boast about it in Germany; and he played a chorale by heart, with the pedals, so charmingly and clearly and correctly that it would have done credit to any professional; and the Queen, having finished her work, came and sat by him, and listened and looked pleased. Then it was my turn; and I began my chorus from *St. Paul*, 'How lovely are the messengers.' Before I got to the end of the first verse they both joined in the chorus; and all the time Prince Albert managed the stops for me so cleverly, . . . and all by heart, that I was really quite enchanted. Then the young Prince of Gotha came in, and there was more chatting; and the Queen asked if I had written any new songs, and said she was very fond of singing my published ones. 'You should sing one to him,' said Prince Albert; and after a little begging she said she would try the *Früklingslied* in B flat—'if it is still here,' she added, 'for all my music is packed up for Claremont.' Prince Albert went to look for it, but came back saying it was already packed. 'But one might perhaps unpack it,' said I. 'We must send for Lady ——,' she said. (I did not catch the name.) So the bell was rung, and the servants were sent after it, but without success; and at last the Queen went herself, and while she was gone Prince Albert said to me, 'She begs you will accept this present as a remembrance,' and gave me a little case with a beautiful ring, on which is engraved—'V. R., 1842.'

"Then the Queen came back and said, 'Lady —— is gone, and has taken all my things with her. It really is most annoying.' (You can't think how that amused me.) I then begged that I might not be made to suffer for the accident, and hoped she would sing another song.

After some consultation with her husband, he said, 'She will sing you something of Gluck's.'

"Meanwhile the Princess of Gotha had come in; and we five proceeded through various corridors and rooms to the Queen's sitting-room, where there was a gigantic rocking-horse standing near the sofa, and two big bird-cages, and pictures on the walls, and bound books on the table—music on the piano. The Duchess of Kent came in too; and while they were all talking I rummaged about amongst the music, and soon discovered my first set of songs. So, of course, I begged her rather to sing one of those than the Gluck, to which she very kindly consented; and which did she choose?—*Schöner und Schöner schmückt sich!*—sang it quite charmingly: in strict time and tune, and with very good execution. Only in the line ' Der Prosa Lasten und Müh,' where it goes down to D, and comes up again chromatically, she sang D sharp each time; and as I gave her the note both times, the last time she sang D, and there it ought to have been D sharp. But, with the exception of this little mistake, it was really charming, and the last long G I have never heard better or purer or more natural from any amateur. Then I was obliged to confess that Fanny had written the song (which I found very hard, but pride must have a fall), and begged her to sing one of mine also. If I would give her plenty of help she would gladly try, she said; and then she sang the *Pilgerspruch*, 'Lass dich nur,' really quite faultlessly, and with charming feeling and expression.

"I thought to myself one must not pay too many compliments on such an occasion; so I merely thanked her a great many times; upon which she said, 'Oh, if only I had not been so frightened. Generally I have such long breath.' Then I praised her heartily, and with the best conscience in the world; for just that part with the long G at the close she had done so well, taking the three following and connecting notes in the same breath, as one seldom hears it done; and therefore it amused me doubly that she herself should have begun about it.

"After this Prince Albert sang the *Erndte-lied*, '*Es ist ein Schnitter;*' and then he said I must play him something before I went, and gave me as themes the chorale which he had played on the organ, and the song he had just sung. If everything had gone as usual, I ought to have improvised most dreadfully badly—for it is almost always like that with me when I want it to go well—and then I should have gone away vexed the whole morning. But, just as if I was to keep nothing but the pleasantest, most charming recollection of it, I never improvised better. I was in the best mood for it, and played a long time, and enjoyed it myself; so that between the two themes I brought in the songs that the Queen had sung, naturally enough; and it all went off so easily that I would gladly not have stopped; and they followed me with so much intelligence and attention that I felt more at ease than I ever did in improvising to an audience. She said several times she hoped I would soon come to England again and pay them a visit; and then I took leave. And down below I saw the beautiful carriages waiting, with their scarlet outriders; and in a quarter of an hour the flag was lowered, and the *Court Circular* announced, 'Her Majesty left the palace at twenty minutes past three.'"

1843 saw the birth of Princess Alice, and 1844 that of Prince Alfred. Indeed, a child every year seemed to become the Queen's rule, but this never hindered her either from fulfilling all the duties of her station, or from having time and strength to spare for gaieties, charities, home occupations, and general kindnesses. Habits of early rising, strict punctuality, and careful method enabled her to find time for everything, and in this, as in all things, she was more than seconded by Prince Albert. She was ever in the foreground of the national life, affecting it always for good, and making an example of purity and virtue. The changed tone and character of the Court from what it had been in the time of the Georges excited universal admiration and respect.

The year 1848, that year of great upheaval in all Europe, had a faint revolutionary echo also in England. There occurred the abortive chartist demonstration which, thanks to the national good sense, aided by the national wet weather, came to nothing. Treason under an umbrella had a somewhat ludicrous air, and the mob dispersed without troubling the police. During the course of these troubled months, however, the Queen read no less than twenty-eight thousand despatches sent out or received at the Foreign Office—an amount of work which few of the Queen's male subjects would have accomplished without complaints of overwork, not to mention that she had besides given birth to a child, the Princess Louise. No wonder a holiday was required; and Balmoral was for the first time visited. A visit paid to Ireland in 1849 ought to have convinced her that here, too, she had loyal, warm-hearted subjects. The royal children in especial pleased the people, and an old woman in the crowd shouted, "Oh, Queen, dear, make one o' them darlings Prince Patrick, and all Ireland will die for ye." And the next royal baby was indeed called Patrick, but unfortunately the Duke of Wellington's name, Arthur, which preceded it, was the one by which he became known, so even this innocent little satisfaction was denied the Irish people. This was the seventh child. Here is the Prince's announcement of birth to his grandmother:—"May Day, 1850. This morning, at about a quarter-past eight, . . . a little boy glided into the light of day, and was received by the sisters with *jubilates*. 'Now we are just as many as the days of the week,' was the cry, and a struggle arose as to who was to be Sunday. Out of well-bred courtesy the honour was accorded to the new-comer."

The end of 1851 saw the *coup d'état* of Napoleon III., and a good deal of ill-feeling resulted in England, with fear of war between the two countries. But before long the nation and its rulers resigned themselves to the changed state of things. Napoleon and his wife visited the English Court, and were received as equals, the Queen and Prince Albert returning their visit the same year. After seeing on this occasion the tomb of the Great Napoleon, the Queen writes: "... It seems as if in this tribute of respect to a departed and dead foe, old enmities and rivalries are wiped out, and the seal of Heaven placed upon that bond of unity which is now happily established between two great and powerful nations." The little Prince of Wales, who was with his parents then, acquired that love for the French capital which has since distinguished him. He tried hard to persuade the Empress to keep him and his sister in Paris after the departure of his parents. The Empress said she could not do so, as the Queen and Prince could not spare them. "Oh, yes," was the reply, "they can, there are six more of us at home."

Foreign politics had meantime become embroiled and difficult. The Crimean War broke out, and though England was prosperous at home this embroilment caused anxiety. "Albert," the Queen wrote to King Leopold, "grows daily fonder and fonder of politics and business, and is wonderfully fit for both—showing such perspicuity and courage!—and I grow daily to dislike them more and more. We women are not made for governing, and if we are good women we must dislike these masculine occupations. But there are times which force one to take an interest in them, *mal gré, bon gré*, and of course, therefore, I feel this interest *now intensely*."

. Yet with all this dislike for politics, her Majesty never failed in her duty of studying them carefully.

In 1853 another child was born, Leopold, after Duke of Albany, who died at Cannes in 1884. He was sickly from his birth, and hence a special favourite with his mother. Besides, he was the only one of the Queen's sons who had inherited some of his father's intellectual tastes. His mantle in this respect rather fell upon the females, most of them gifted women, than the males. The sons are more descendants of the grosser House of Hanover. Yet certainly few royal children have been more anxiously and carefully reared and educated. Their parents strove to make of them not only ladies and gentlemen, but worthy men and women, apt and able in all things. Thus at Osborne, a house built entirely by Prince Albert, and a favourite residence of the Queen's, the Prince had made his sons— no doubt to their great delight—build a fort entirely with their own hands, even to making the bricks. The royal children had gardens and garden tools appropriated to each. They worked under a gardener, and their father paid them the same sum for their labour that an ordinary gardener would receive. The Swiss Cottage, so well known at Osborne, was built and furnished for them, and in it the Princesses practised all household and domestic duties, cooking themselves, and giving the food thus prepared to the poor, except when her Majesty and the Prince dined with them at the cottage—a great occasional honour. The Princes also had a museum in it of curiosities and specimens collected by themselves. One can imagine no happier or fuller life for their age than that of the children of the Queen, at Osborne and Balmoral.

The Queen took a profound and pained interest in the Crimean War, so much so, indeed, that a royal child remarked to one of the generals, "You must hurry to Sebastopol and take it, else it will kill mamma." And when the fortress was at last taken, her joy and relief was great.

Together with this news there came, as guest to Balmoral, where the Queen was then staying, Prince Frederick William of Prussia, a youth of twenty-four, of whom Prince Albert writes: "His prominent qualities are great straightforwardness, frankness, and honesty." A possible marriage with one of the English Princesses was the object of his visit, and indeed he felt soon attached to the eldest, but as she was only fifteen, her parents desired him not to speak as yet. Still, one day, ascending a mountain together, he could not resist picking a piece of white heather, the emblem of good luck, and telling her his wishes. An informal engagement was then entered upon, but the wedding, it was resolved, should not be for another two years. Thus the young people could see more of each other and make sure they were really suited. For the Queen, happily married herself, broke down for all her children the royal custom of *mariages de convenance*. How successful that marriage proved, how mournful its end, all the world knows. The heart of the Queen, tenderly responsive to all domestic incidents, was deeply moved by this first wooing in her family, she herself so young, her daughter almost a child.

The Indian Mutiny of 1857 was another terrible trial to the monarch. That same year saw the birth of her last child, Princess Beatrice, while the next witnessed the gorgeous marriage and State departure of the Princess Royal.

In 1861 the Queen and Prince celebrated what they playfully termed "the coming of age of their wedding day." On this occasion her Majesty wrote to King Leopold: "Very few can say with me that their husband, at the end of twenty-one years, is not only full of the friendship, kindness, and affection which a truly happy marriage brings with it, but of the same tender love as in the very first days of our marriage."

Very rare were their separations, and the Queen, could bear them as little in after years as in the earliest days of their union, and when the circumstance occurred she was almost in despair. To her faithful Uncle Leopold she tells, much about the same date: "You cannot think how much this costs me [her husband's absence], nor how completely forlorn I am and feel when he is away, or how I count the hours till he returns. All the numerous children are as nothing to me when he is away. It seems as if the whole life of the house and the home were gone." She little thought, poor woman, how soon she was to lose him for ever, how the trials, that had hitherto been spared her singularly happy life, were to come upon her, so thickly, so severely, as never to permit her to recover from the successive shocks.

Early in 1861 the Duchess of Kent, now in her seventy-sixth year, died rather unexpectedly. This was the first time the Queen had lost a person dear to her, and the way she bore a grief, which was after all to be anticipated in the course of nature, proved how ill adapted her character was to cope with the crushing sorrows of our common humanity. Very probably royal life and royal education fails to temper the spirit, and causes men to think that even nature must bend to their decrees. Prince Albert was seriously alarmed at the manner in which the Queen was overwhelmed by her sorrow. He sent for the eldest daughter from Germany to comfort her, and did all he himself could to rouse her. To King Leopold he wrote: "Victoria is greatly upset and feels her childhood rush back on her memory with the most vivid force. . . . For the last two years her constant care and occupation has been to watch over her mother's comfort, and the influence of this upon her own character has been most salutary. . . . She remains almost entirely alone."

This sorrow was lightened a little later by the engagement of Princess Alice to Prince Louis of Hesse Darmstadt, also a love marriage, and by the first tentatives with regard to the union of the Prince of Wales—an anxious business, seeing he was the heir to the crown. All these matters meant increased work for Prince Albert. The Duchess of Kent had further instituted him her executor—no small labour. Then Prince Leopold was ailing with the illness that finally killed him. He had to be sent to Cannes to winter, and it was no small anxiety for the Prince and Queen that the worthy gentleman to whom the child was entrusted should have died on the journey out.

And besides all these private troubles, there were public ones. The United (?) States of America were at civil war, the South had tried to implicate England. It was an imbroglio that might easily have proved serious, and would probably have done so, but for the unremitting efforts of the Queen and Prince, and especially of the latter, upon whom the chief burden of this business fell. This peaceful settlement of what came to be known as the "Trent affair," was the last public service rendered to England in the beneficent life of him whom his grateful fellow-citizens have surnamed "Albert the Good." But these loads all came upon him at a time when his nervous system was much weakened, and depressed him greatly. Whether a presage of death pursued him or no, certain it is that about this time the

Prince spoke often and seriously to the Queen of the problems of life and mortality. "I do not cling to life," he told her one day. "You do; but I set no store by it. If I knew that those I love were well cared for, I should be quite ready to die to-morrow."

It has never been accurately ascertained how the fever originated under which the Prince sank. Certain it is that it had been for some time hanging about him, but that even those nearest and dearest to him failed to notice how ailing he was, and in lieu of sparing his strength, fresh masses of work were put upon him. How bitterly the Queen repented this in after years her own journals prove. He himself bore all in his usual unselfish, uncomplaining fashion, but he wrote in his diary that he was full of rheumatic pains, and that he had scarcely closed his eyes for a fortnight. Still, though very ill, he continued to go out as usual, and on December 1st attended divine service and insisted upon going through all the kneeling. It was at last whispered to the Queen that the Prince was suffering from low fever. She was terribly disturbed at this, remembering how this fever had lately decimated the royal family of Portugal, but the Prince tried to reassure her, saying it was not fever, and adding that if it were he was sure it would prove fatal to him. So the days went on. At last Lord Palmerston, not one as a rule to take gloomy views, grew so alarmed by all he saw and heard, that he insisted that a second physician should be called in. The case was pronounced grave, but not hopeless. Unfortunately, however, the Prince lost strength daily, and there was often a strange wild look in his face. Only his pet child, Princess Beatrice, could extract a smile from him. His constant companion was Princess Alice, whose fortitude and firmness upheld both father and mother. She played to him, read to him, prayed with him, the Queen herself going about all her duties, as she said, "in a dreadful dream." The Prince recognized his state and spoke openly of it, expressing his last wishes. He could not speak thus to the Queen herself, for she could not bear to listen, and shut her eyes to the danger. It was a trying time for the young daughter, but one in which she proved of what excellent metal she was made. To the doctors who expressed hopes of his recovery the Prince said, "No, I shall not recover; but I am not taken by surprise; I am not afraid; I trust I am prepared." On the afternoon of Saturday, December 14th, the end came. "Gutes Frauchen" (good little wife) were the last loving words he said to the Queen as he kissed her and laid his head on her shoulder. He dozed and wandered, and did not seem to know the children, who had been summoned. But when the Queen once more bent over him and whispered, "Est ist kleins Frauchen" (it is your little wife) he bowed his head in answer. A quarter before midnight the noble spirit passed to "where beyond these voices there is peace."

Few were prepared for the event, for the Prince's serious state had been kept secret, and all hearts went out to the widowed sovereign. For some days great solicitude was felt for her life, so strong was her grief, so abject her dejection. She was removed almost by force from Windsor, where the Prince died, to Osborne, and here once more the Princess Alice showed herself in all the greatness of her character. For months it was she who sustained the Queen, she who was her right hand, she who was the chief means of communication between the sovereign and her ministers. "There is no one near me to call me Victoria now," was the Queen's piteous exclamation, often reiterated, and this touching expression strongly illustrates her great loneliness.

The Queen had now to learn, like to her humblest subject, how true it is that—

> "It is to live without the vanished light—
> That strength is needed."

Slowly she roused herself to perform once more her high duties, but from this time forward she shirked as much as possible all State ceremonials and the mere splendours of royalty, and has lived almost entirely in seclusion. Much serious inconvenience has at times arisen from the sovereign's inaccessibility, but on this point sons and daughters, ministers and advisers, have argued with her in vain, and the death, in 1865, of Leopold, King of the Belgians, removed the last person who had power to turn her counsels.

That the effect of this withdrawal of the sovereign has been pernicious for England politically, it would be false to maintain. Where the effect has been felt banefully is socially. It is true the Prince of Wales has taken his mother's place in this respect, but he cannot replace the pure, high influence exerted by his father and mother. His aims, his sympathies are less exalted and intellectual than theirs; he loves pleasure for its own sake; he does not strive as they did to elevate the general tone of the nation. In consequence the Court has grown less pure, its tone more flippant; democratic and socialist feelings have increased among the people; some of the old English integrity has been lost. It may, perhaps, be that these changes are the natural result of growth, of inevitable modification and mutation, but even so the Queen's pure influence, had it been exercised, could but have acted for good in stemming the tide of a too rapid transition from the old *régime* to the new, always pernicious and more than the ordinary mind can bear up against with safety. It has been held by some, and not without justice, that the Court itself has but little direct connection with the life of the people; and in one sense this is true. During the fifty and odd years of the Queen's reign the Court has altered little in this respect, that then, as now, it neither attracts nor attempts to attract the leaders in art, science, and literature. It is strange that royalty in England, at least—and we notice the same phenomenon elsewhere—seems only to have the power to attract round it second-class people. The best class of all, those who are continually advancing the country in science or keeping alight the flame of letters, who are its scholars, architects, engineers, artists, poets, authors, teachers, and preachers. As an English writer has well said, for these persons "the Court simply does not exist. One states the fact without comment. But it should be stated and clearly understood. The whole of those men who in this generation maintain the greatness of our country in the ways where alone greatness is desirable or memorable, the only men of this generation whose memories will live and adorn the Victorian era, are strangers to the Court. It seems a great mistake—for the Court."

Very brilliant indeed is the Victorian age in great men and great discoveries, and it will ever rank among the most prominent in English story.

But to return to the monarch herself, whose life story was thus sadly and sharply severed from its past tranquil course by the Prince's sudden death. It has been since, with few exceptions, of the most strictly private nature, and traversed by many sorrows. She has lost friend upon friend, has seen children and grandchildren pass away before her, but quite recently had the great grief to lose the noblest, most eminent of her sons-in-law. True, there have also been joys to lighten that widowed darkness, and they have come to her also through her children, and above all her grandchildren, for the Queen is devoted to young children, whom she knows admirably well how to rear and manage.

Still, it was not at once that she resigned herself to live thus on a lower plane of happiness. Princess Alice tells in her letters of the terrible sufferings of the first three years of the Queen's widowhood, but adds that after the long storm came rest, so that the daughter could tenderly remind the mother, without re-opening the wound, of the happy silver wedding that might have been this year, when the royal parents would have been surrounded by so many grandchildren in fresh young households. Henceforward the public *rôle* Queen Victoria has enacted towards her people has been rather to be a comforter to those in distress, a helper to the needy, than a brilliant, conspicuous show-figure. Rarely has she, for example, opened Parliament in person since the Prince's death, and never since that event have her "Lords and faithful Commons" heard the royal speech read by her in that clear voice which penetrated into every corner of the vast hall. She sits mute, and generally sorrowful, clad in the widow's weeds she has never discarded, while the Lord Chancellor delivers her oration. Even at the weddings of some of her children, even at that of the heir to the throne, she was present only informally, regarding the ceremony from a distance. Her greatest private interest for years was preparing for print the "Life of the Prince Consort," which was compiled under her personal direction. She followed it by two volumes of extracts from her private journals, the object of all these publications being solely that of making known to the world at large how noble a character had vanished from the earth in the shape of Prince Albert. And even in the portions of the journals written after her widowhood it is made manifest how closely every enjoyment, as well as every care, was connected in her mind with the Prince. If she sees a lovely view, it is to regret that he is not there to see it too. If she gazes on fine trees, it is to think how he would have admired them. In her heart the Prince is always living.

The year 1870, with its terrible war, was a trying one to the Queen, and the next year gave her a fresh sorrow in the form of the Prince of Wales's serious illness. His life was despaired of, when, on December the 14th, the anniversary of his father's death, and a date which was, seven years later, to note the death of Princess Alice, who nursed him tenderly, as she had his father, he took a sudden turn for the better. A national Thanksgiving Day was held the following year, at which the Queen appeared in full State, though never dropping her mourning dress.

Her next great State appearance was on her Jubilee, marking the conclusion of her fifty years' rule over her people. This fell in June, 1887, and was kept as high festival, not only in Great Britain itself, but in every colony and dependency of the land, in every spot on earth where two or three English were gathered together. The rejoicings, the gladness, were truly spontaneous, and had every right to be, for the English have reason to be proud of their Queen and her long reign. Notwithstanding the "fierce light that beats upon a throne," the character of the English sovereign has borne the test of that light, and has entwined itself in the hearts of her people, not one of whom but echoes with sincerity the words of the national hymn, "God bless the Queen." A better, more virtuous, and more conscientious sovereign, one whose character is above suspicion and unblemished by reproach, is not likely ever to sit upon the throne of Great Britain, Ireland, and India.

D. APPLETON & CO.'S PUBLICATIONS.

A FRIEND OF THE QUEEN. By PAUL GAULOT. With Two Portraits. 12mo. Cloth, $2.00.

"M. Gaulot deserves thanks for presenting the personal history of Count Fersen in a manner so evidently candid and unbiased."—*Philadelphia Bulletin.*

"There are some characters in history of whom we never seem to grow tired. Of no one is this so much the case as of the beautiful Marie Antoinette, and of that life which is at once so eventful and so tragic. . . . In this work we have much that up to the present time has been only vaguely known."—*Philadelphia Press.*

"A historical volume that will be eagerly read."—*New York Observer.*

"One of those captivating recitals of the romance of truth which are the gilding of the pill of history."—*London Daily News.*

"It tells with new and authentic details the romantic story of Count Fersen's (the friend of the Queen) devotion to Marie Antoinette, of his share in the celebrated flight to Varennes, and in many other well-known episodes of the unhappy Queen's life."—*London Times.*

"If the book had no more recommendation than the mere fact that Marie Antoinette and Count Fersen are rescued at last from the voluminous and contradictory representations with which the literature of that period abounds, it would be enough compensation to any reader to become acquainted with the true delineations of two of the most romantically tragic personalities."—*Boston Globe.*

THE ROMANCE OF AN EMPRESS. Catharine II, of Russia. By K. WALISZEWSKI. With Portrait. 12mo. Cloth, $2.00.

"Of Catharine's marvelous career we have in this volume a sympathetic, learned, and picturesque narrative. No royal career, not even of some of the Roman or papal ones, has better shown us how truth can be stranger than fiction."—*New York Times.*

"A striking and able work, deserving of the highest praise."—*Philadelphia Ledger.*

"The book is well called a romance, for, although no legends are admitted in it, and the author has been at pains to present nothing but verified facts, the actual career of the subject was so abnormal and sensational as to seem to belong to fiction."—*New York Sun.*

"A dignified, handsome, indeed superb volume, and well worth careful reading."—*Chicago Herald.*

"It is a most wonderful story, charmingly told, with new material to sustain it, and a breadth and temperance and consideration that go far to soften one's estimate of one of the most extraordinary women of history."—*New York Commercial Advertiser.*

"A romance in which fiction finds no place; a charming narrative wherein the author fearlessly presents the results of what has been obviously a thorough and impartial investigation."—*Philadelphia Press.*

"The book makes the best of reading, because it is written without fear or favor. . . . The volume is exceedingly suggestive, and gives to the general reader a plain, blunt, strong, and somewhat prejudiced but still healthy view of one of the greatest women of whom history bears record."—*New York Herald.*

"The perusal of such a book can not fail to add to that breadth of view which is so essential to the student of universal history."—*Philadelphia Bulletin.*

New York: D. APPLETON & CO., 1, 3, & 5 Bond Street.

D. APPLETON & CO.'S PUBLICATIONS.

THE GILDED MAN (EL DORADO), and other Pictures of the Spanish Occupancy of America. By A. F. BANDELIER. 12mo. Cloth, $1.50.

"Every paper in this volume is wonderfully interesting, and the collection is of such historical value as to make it a necessary part of every library in which American history is represented."—*Boston Herald.*

"One of the most entertaining of recent historical works, and, besides its novelty and freshness has the great merit of being original historical research."—*Philadelphia Times.*

"Mr. Bandelier's work under the auspices of the Archæological Institute of America and on the Hemenway Survey entitles him to rank as the leading documentary historian of the Southwest. . . . The book possesses genuine historical value, and is a necessary part of the annals of our country."—*Philadelphia Ledger.*

"Just such a work as Mr. Bandelier has done has long been needed. . . . A contribution of the first order of value to a part of American history that deserves to be more fully studied."—*Literary World.*

WARRIORS OF THE CRESCENT. By W. H. DAVENPORT ADAMS, author of "Battle Stories from English History," etc. 12mo. Cloth, $1.50.

"A work without a rival in its particular field. . . . All the gorgeousness of the barbaric East invests this glowing pageant of kings and conquerors. . . . This is a remarkably able book in thought and in manner of presentation."—*Philadelphia Ledger.*

"A lively, carefully prepared chronicle of the careers of quite a number of the Mohammedan rulers in Asian regions who made their marks, one way or another, in the development of the peculiar civilization of the East. . . . This author has selected from the long chronicle the salients likely to be most interesting, and has obviously taken much pains to sift the fact carefully out of the rather confused mass of fact and fable in the Moslem chronicles."—*New York Commercial Advertiser.*

"Nowhere in history are there to be found such records of conquest, such frightful tales of blood, such overwhelming defeats or victories, as in the lives of the Asiatic sovereigns. . . . The author is a historian who tells his story and stops. He has done his work faithfully and well."—*Cincinnati Commercial Gazette.*

PICTURES FROM ROMAN LIFE AND STORY. By Professor A. J. CHURCH, author of "Stories from Homer," "Stories from Virgil," etc. Illustrated. 12mo. Cloth, $1.50.

"Prof. Church is a tried and approved master of the art of interesting young people in historical themes. The present work, while too thoughtful to be called strictly juvenile, treats of the great emperors and families of Rome in a simple narrative style certain to captivate youth and older people fond of historic lore."—*The Chautauquan.*

"The material for these sketches is drawn partly from the inexhaustible riches of Plutarch, partly from contemporaneous history, and partly from letters, edicts, etc.; and, well chosen and briefly related, are interesting, whetting the appetite of the studiously inclined. . . . Various illustrations add to the interest of the work.'—*Springfield Republican.*

"Each of the chapters presents some striking scene or personality in the period from Augustus to Marcus Aurelius. . . . Several of the chapters are thrown into the form of contemporary letters. The plan of the book is well conceived, and the subjects are those of general human interest."—*New York Critic.*

New York: D. APPLETON & CO., 1, 3, & 5 Bond Street.

D. APPLETON & CO.'S PUBLICATIONS.

LIFE IN ANCIENT EGYPT AND ASSYRIA. By G. MASPÉRO, late Director of Archæology in Egypt, and Member of the Institute of France. Translated by ALICE MORTON. With 188 Illustrations. 12mo. Cloth, $1.50.

"A lucid sketch, at once popular and learned, of daily life in Egypt in the time of Rameses II, and of Assyria in that of Assurbanipal. . . . As an Orientalist, M. Maspéro stands in the front rank, and his learning is so well digested and so admirably subdued to the service of popular exposition, that it nowhere overwhelms and always interests the reader."—*London Times.*

"Only a writer who had distinguished himself as a student of Egyptian and Assyrian antiquities could have produced this work, which has none of the features of a modern book of travels in the East, but is an attempt to deal with ancient life as if one had been a contemporary with the people whose civilization and social usages are very largely restored."—*Boston Herald.*

A most interesting and instructive book. Excellent and most impressive ideas, also, of the architecture of the two countries and of the other rude but powerful art of the Assyrians, are to be got from it."—*Brooklyn Eagle.*

"The ancient artists are copied with the utmost fidelity, and verify the narrative so attractively presented."—*Cincinnati Times-Star.*

THE THREE PROPHETS: Chinese Gordon; Mohammed-Ahmed; Araby Pasha. Events before, during, and after the Bombardment of Alexandria. By Colonel CHAILLE-LONG, ex-Chief of Staff to Gordon in Africa, ex-United States Consular Agent in Alexandria, etc., etc. With Portraits. 16mo. Paper, 50 cents.

"Comprises the observations of a man who, by reason of his own military experience in Egypt, ought to know whereof he speaks."—*Washington Post.*

"The book contains a vivid account of the massacres and the bombardment of Alexandria. As throwing light upon the darkened problem of Egypt, this American contribution is both a useful number of recent facts and an estimate of present situations."—*Philadelphia Public Ledger.*

"Throws an entirely new light upon the troubles which have so long agitated Egypt, and upon their real significance."—*Chicago Times.*

THE MEMOIRS OF AN ARABIAN PRINCESS. By EMILY RUETE, *née* Princess of Oman and Zanzibar. Translated from the German. 12mo, Cloth, 75 cents.

The author of this amusing autobiography is half-sister to the late Sultan of Zanzibar, who some years ago married a German merchant and settled at Hamburg.

"A remarkably interesting little volume. . . . As a picture of Oriental court life, and manners and customs in the Orient, by one who is to the manner born, the book is prolific in entertainment and edification."—*Boston Gazette.*

"The interest of the book centers chiefly in its minute description of the daily life of the household from the time of rising until the time of retiring, giving the most complete details of dress, meals, ceremonies, feasts, weddings, funerals, education, slave service, amusements, in fact everything connected with the daily and yearly routine of life."—*Utica (N. Y.) Herald.*

New York: D. APPLETON & CO., 1, 3, & 5 Bond Street.

D. APPLETON & CO.'S PUBLICATIONS.

MEMOIRS. By CHARLES GODFREY LELAND (Hans Breitmann). With Portrait. 12mo. Cloth, $2.00.

"From first to last a very entertaining book, full of good stories, strange adventures, curious experiences, and not inconsiderable achievements, instinct with the strong personality of the writer."—*London Times.*

"A book that no one who wants to be entertained as he has not been entertained in many a long day can afford to let go unread."—*New York Herald.*

"Mr. Charles G. Leland's 'Memoirs' may be reckoned among the autobiographical successes of the day. . . . Mr. Leland's experiences were out of the common run, and his book is a fair reflection of the exceptional character of his life. . . . This volume will add to his fame, not lessen it."—G. W. S., *in New York Tribune.*

"In a way Mr. Leland's 'Memoirs' carry with them the same joy as Sir Richard Burton's, in that they combine the charms of the man of intellect and the man of action. Happily they differ in that Mr. Leland is still alive. Mr. Leland's stories about the American war are interesting. If anything were needed to enlarge one's ideas of that tremendous struggle, Mr. Leland's stories would do it."—*Pall Mall Gazette.*

THE STORY OF MY LIFE. By GEORG EBERS, author of "Uarda," "An Egyptian Princess," "A Thorny Path," etc. With Portraits. 16mo. Cloth, $1.25.

"It is written with a charming frankness that is peculiarly German, and an appreciation of the incidents of his life that is peculiar to the novelist. Few of his stories afford more agreeable reading."—*The Critic.*

"To those who know Dr. Ebers chiefly as an Egyptologist, and whose interest lies in his imaginative work, the early chapters of this autobiography will prove a source of illumination, for it is in them that we are let into the secrets of those experiences which not only molded his character but were potent in shaping the bent of his mind."—*Philadelphia Bulletin.*

"One of the most delightful books which Georg Ebers, the German Egyptologist and novelist, has written, and this is saying a great deal. . . . It is the picture of the life of a bright, active, happy boy in a German home of the most worthy sort, and at German schools mostly of conspicuous excellence. There is neither undue frankness nor superfluous reticence, but the things which one wishes to be told are recorded naturally and entertainingly."—*The Congregationalist.*

PERSONAL RECOLLECTIONS OF WERNER VON SIEMENS. Translated by W. C. COUPLAND. With Portrait. 8vo. Cloth, $5.00.

"This volume of straightforward reminiscence reflects new credit on its author, and deserves a high place among the records of great inventors who have made a name and a fortune in ways which have been of immense public benefit."—*Literary World.*

"The full account of Siemens's work will be most interesting to the engineer and to the man of science; but even the reader who may choose to skip all this will find it one of the most charming publications of the year."—*The Nation.*

"The general reader need not be deterred from taking up the book by the fear that he will have to wade through chapters of long technical terms which he does not understand. Whether he is describing his simple home life or his scientific career and its manifold achievements, Von Siemens writes plainly, unaffectedly, and in a uniformly attractive fashion. The whole work is, as the publishers of the translation say with truth, 'rich in genial narrative, stirring adventure, and picturesque description,' and stamped throughout with the impress of an original mind and a sterling character."—*London Times.*

New York: D. APPLETON & CO., 1, 3, & 5 Bond Street.

D. APPLETON & CO.'S PUBLICATIONS.

*THE COUNTRY SCHOOL IN NEW ENG-
LAND.* By CLIFTON JOHNSON. With 60 Illustrations from Photographs and Drawings made by the Author. Square 8vo. Cloth, gilt edges, $2.50.

"An admirable undertaking carried out in an admirable way. . . . Mr. Johnson's descriptions are vivid and lifelike and are full of humor, and the illustrations, mostly after photographs, give a solid effect of realism to the whole work, and are superbly reproduced. . . . The definitions at the close of this volume are very, very funny, and yet they are not stupid; they are usually the result of deficient logic."—*Boston Beacon.*

"A charmingly written account of the rural schools in this section of the country. It speaks of the old-fashioned school days of the early quarter of this century, of the mid-century schools, of the country school of to-day, and of how scholars think and write. The style is animated and picturesque. . . . It is handsomely printed, and is interesting from its pretty cover to its very last page."—*Boston Saturday Evening Gazette.*

"A unique piece of book-making that deserves to be popular. . . . Prettily and serviceably bound, and well illustrated."—*The Churchman.*

"The readers who turn the leaves of this handsome book will unite in saying the author has 'been there.' It is no fancy sketch, but text and illustrations are both a reality."—*Chicago Inter-Ocean.*

"No one who is familiar with the little red schoolhouse can look at these pictures and read these chapters without having the mind recall the boyhood experiences, and the memory is pretty sure to be a pleasant one."—*Chicago Times.*

"A superbly prepared volume, which by its reading matter and its beautiful illustrations, so natural and finished, pleasantly and profitably recall memories and associations connected with the very foundations of our national greatness."—*New York Observer.*

"It is a point not yet decided whether the text or illustrations of this 'Country School' give the most pleasure. Both are original, and removed from the beaten track of conventionality."—*Philadelphia Ledger.*

"One of the finest and most fitting of all the Christmas books likely to appear."—*Hartford Times.*

THE BRONTËS IN IRELAND. By Dr. WILLIAM WRIGHT. With Portraits and numerous Illustrations. 12mo. Cloth, $1.50.

"A striking contribution to biographical literature and a significant confirmation of the doctrine of hereditary genius has been made by Dr. William Wright in his wonderfully entertaining narrative. . . . The book is admirably written, and is in itself as interesting as a romance. It has a number of valuable illustrations, plans, etc., and will be of the most intense fascination to all who have read and thrilled over 'Jane Eyre' and 'Shirley,' or puzzled over the mystery of the wild and erratic Branwell."—*Boston Beacon.*

"Dr. Wright has faithfully traced the current of Brontë life and thought back to the hidden sources. The biography has some surprises in store for the reader. It is fully illustrated, and presents a varied and romantic tale without a touch of the commonplace."—*Philadelphia Ledger.*

"One of the most curious pages which have lately been added to literary history."—*Boston Traveller.*

"A new and thrilling chapter in the history of the Brontë sisters."—*Boston Advertiser.*

New York: D. APPLETON & CO., 1, 3, & 5 Bond Street.

D. APPLETON & CO.'S PUBLICATIONS.

COLONIAL COURT-HOUSE,
PHILADELPHIA, 1707.

"This work marks an epoch in the history-writing of this country."—*St. Louis Post-Dispatch.*

THE HOUSEHOLD HISTORY OF THE UNITED STATES AND ITS PEOPLE. FOR YOUNG AMERICANS. By EDWARD EGGLESTON. Richly illustrated with 350 Drawings, 75 Maps, etc. Square 8vo. Cloth, $2.50.

FROM THE PREFACE.

The present work is meant, in the first instance, for the young—not alone for boys and girls, but for young men and women who have yet to make themselves familiar with the more important features of their country's history. By a book for the young is meant one in which the author studies to make his statements clear and explicit, in which curious and picturesque details are inserted, and in which the writer does not neglect such anecdotes as lend the charm of a human and personal interest to the broader facts of the nation's story. That history is often tiresome to the young is not so much the fault of history as of a false method of writing by which one contrives to relate events without sympathy or imagination, without narrative connection or animation. The attempt to master vague and general records of kiln-dried facts is certain to beget in the ordinary reader a repulsion from the study of history—one of the very most important of all studies for its widening influence on general culture.

"Fills a decided gap which has existed for the past twenty years in American historical literature. The work is admirably planned and executed, and will at once take its place as a standard record of the life, growth, and development of the nation. It is profusely and beautifully illustrated."—*Boston Transcript.*

"The book in its new dress makes a much finer appearance than before, and will be welcomed by older readers as gladly as its predecessor was greeted by girls and boys. The lavish use the publishers have made of colored plates, woodcuts, and photographic reproductions, gives an unwonted piquancy to the printed page, catching the eye as surely as the text engages the mind."—*New York Critic.*

INDIAN'S TRAP.

GENERAL PUTNAM.

"The author writes history as a story. It can never be less than that. The book will enlist the interest of young people, enlighten their understanding, and by the glow of its statements fix the great events of the country firmly in the mind."—*San Francisco Bulletin.*

New York: D. APPLETON & CO., 1, 3, & 5 Bond Street.

D. APPLETON & CO.'S PUBLICATIONS.

THE REAR-GUARD OF THE REVOLUTION. By JAMES R. GILMORE (Edmund Kirke). With Portrait of John Sevier, and Map. 12mo. Cloth, $1.50.

"The Rear-Guard of the Revolution" is a narrative of the adventures of the pioneers that first crossed the Alleghanies and settled in what is now Tennessee, under the leadership of two remarkable men, James Robertson and John Sevier. The title of the book is derived from the fact that a body of hardy volunteers, under the leadership of Sevier, crossed the mountains, and by their timely arrival secured the defeat of the British army at King's Mountain.

JOHN SEVIER AS A COMMONWEALTH-BUILDER. A Sequel to "The Rear-Guard of the Revolution." By JAMES R. GILMORE (Edmund Kirke). 12mo. Cloth, $1.50.

John Sevier was among the pioneers who settled the region in Eastern Tennessee. He was the founder of the State of Franklin, which afterward became Tennessee, and was the first Governor of the State. His innumerable battles with the Indians, his remarkable exploits, his address and genius for leadership, render his career one of the most thrilling and interesting on record.

THE ADVANCE-GUARD OF WESTERN CIVILIZATION. By JAMES R. GILMORE (Edmund Kirke). With Map, and Portrait of James Robertson. 12mo. Cloth, $1.50.

This work is in a measure a continuation of the thrilling story told by the author in his two preceding volumes, "The Rear-Guard of the Revolution" and "John Sevier as a Commonwealth-Builder." The three volumes together cover, says the author in his preface, "a neglected period of American history, and they disclose facts well worthy the attention of historians—namely, that these Western men turned the tide of the American Revolution, and subsequently saved the newly-formed Union from disruption, and thereby made possible our present great republic."

THE TWO SPIES: Nathan Hale and John André. By BENSON J. LOSSING, LL. D. Illustrated with Pen-and-Ink Sketches. Containing also Anna Seward's "Monody on Major André." Square 8vo. Cloth, gilt top, $2.00.

Illustrated by nearly thirty engravings of portraits, buildings, sketches by André, etc. Contains also the full text and original notes of the famous "Monody on Major André," written by his friend Anna Seward, with a portrait and biographical sketch of Miss Seward, and letters to her by Major André.

New York: D. APPLETON & CO., 1, 3, & 5 Bond Street.

D. APPLETON & CO.'S PUBLICATIONS.

ABRAHAM LINCOLN: The True Story of a Great Life. By WILLIAM H. HERNDON and JESSE W. WEIK. With numerous Illustrations. New and revised edition, with an introduction by HORACE WHITE. In two volumes. 12mo. Cloth, $3.00.

This is probably the most intimate life of Lincoln ever written. The book, by Lincoln's law-partner, William H. Herndon, and his friend Jesse W. Weik, shows us Lincoln the man. It is a true picture of his surroundings and influences and acts. It is not an attempt to construct a political history, with Lincoln often in the background, nor is it an effort to apotheosize the American who stands first in our history next to Washington. The writers knew Lincoln intimately. Their book is the result of unreserved association. There is no attempt to portray the man as other than he really was, and on this account their frank testimony must be accepted, and their biography must take permanent rank as the best and most illuminating study of Lincoln's character and personality. Their story, simply told, relieved by characteristic anecdotes, and vivid with local color, will be found a fascinating work.

"Truly, they who wish to know Lincoln as he really was must read the biography of him written by his friend and law-partner, W. H. Herndon. This book was imperatively needed to brush aside the rank growth of myth and legend which was threatening to hide the real lineaments of Lincoln from the eyes of posterity. On one pretext or another, but usually upon the plea that he was the central figure of a great historical picture, most of his self-appointed biographers have, by suppressing a part of the truth and magnifying or embellishing the rest, produced portraits which those of Lincoln's contemporaries who knew him best are scarcely able to recognize. There is, on the other hand, no doubt about the faithfulness of Mr. Herndon's delineation. The marks of unflinching veracity are patent in every line."—*New York Sun.*

"Among the books which ought most emphatically to have been written must be classed 'Herndon's Lincoln.'"—*Chicago Inter-Ocean.*

"The author has his own notion of what a biography should be, and it is simple enough. The story should tell all, plainly and even bluntly. Mr. Herndon is naturally a very direct writer, and he has been industrious in gathering material. Whether an incident happened before or behind the scenes, is all the same to him. He gives it without artifice or apology. He describes the life of his friend Lincoln just as he saw it."—*Cincinnati Commercial Gazette.*

"A remarkable piece of literary achievement—remarkable alike for its fidelity to facts, its fullness of details, its constructive skill, and its literary charm."—*New York Times.*

"It will always remain the authentic life of Abraham Lincoln."—*Chicago Herald.*

"The book is a valuable depository of anecdotes, innumerable and characteristic. It has every claim to the proud boast of being the 'true story of a great life.'"—*Philadelphia Ledger.*

"Will be accepted as the best biography yet written of the great President."—*Chicago Inter-Ocean.*

"Mr. White claims that, as a portraiture of the man Lincoln, Mr. Herndon's work 'will never be surpassed.' Certainly it has never been equaled yet, and this new edition is all that could be desired."—*New York Observer.*

"The three portraits of Lincoln are the best that exist; and not the least characteristic of these, the Lincoln of the Douglas debates, has never before been engraved. . . . Herndon's narrative gives, as nothing else is likely to give, the material from which we may form a true picture of the man from infancy to maturity."—*The Nation.*

New York: D. APPLETON & CO., 1, 3, & 5 Bond Street.

D. APPLETON & CO.'S PUBLICATIONS.

APPLETONS' CYCLOPÆDIA OF AMERICAN BIOGRAPHY.

Complete in six volumes, royal 8vo, containing about 800 pages each. With sixty-one fine steel portraits and some two thousand smaller vignette portraits and views of birthplaces, residences, statues, etc.

APPLETONS' CYCLOPÆDIA OF AMERICAN BIOGRAPHY, edited by General JAMES GRANT WILSON, President of the New York Genealogical and Biographical Society, and Professor JOHN FISKE, formerly of Harvard University, assisted by over two hundred special contributors, contains a biographical sketch of every person eminent in American civil and military history, in law and politics, in divinity, in literature and art, in science and in invention. Its plan embraces all the countries of North and South America, and includes distinguished persons born abroad, but related to American history. As events are always connected with persons, it affords a complete compendium of American history in every branch of human achievement. An exhaustive topical and analytical Index enables the reader to follow the history of any subject with great readiness.

"It is the most complete work that exists on the subject. The tone and guiding spirit of the book are certainly very fair, and show a mind bent on a discriminate, just, and proper treatment of its subject."—*From the* Hon. GEORGE BANCROFT.

"The portraits are remarkably good. To any one interested in American history or literature, the Cyclopædia will be indispensable."—*From the* Hon. JAMES RUSSELL LOWELL.

"The selection of names seems to be liberal and just. The portraits, so far as I can judge, are faithful, and the biographies trustworthy."—*From* NOAH PORTER, D. D., LL. D., *ex-President of Yale College.*

"A most valuable and interesting work."—*From the* Hon. WM. E. GLADSTONE.

"I have examined it with great interest and great gratification. It is a noble work, and does enviable credit to its editors and publishers."—*From the* Hon. ROBERT C. WINTHROP.

"I have carefully examined 'Appletons' Cyclopædia of American Biography,' and do not hesitate to commend it to favor. It is admirably adapted to use in the family and the schools, and is so cheap as to come within the reach of all classes of readers and students."—*From* J. B. FORAKER, *ex-Governor of Ohio.*

"This book of American biography has come to me with a most unusual charm. It sets before us the faces of great Americans, both men and women, and gives us a perspective view of their lives. Where so many noble and great have lived and wrought, one is encouraged to believe the soil from which they sprang, the air they breathed, and the sky over their heads, to be the best this world affords, and one says, 'Thank God, I also am an American!' We have many books of biography, but I have seen none so ample, so clear-cut, and breathing so strongly the best spirit of our native land. No young man or woman can fail to find among these ample pages some model worthy of imitation."—*From* FRANCES E. WILLARD, *President N. W. C. T. U.*

"I congratulate you on the beauty of the volume, and the thoroughness of the work."—*From* Bishop PHILLIPS BROOKS.

"Every day's use of this admirable work confirms me in regard to its comprehensiveness and accuracy."—*From* CHARLES DUDLEY WARNER.

Price, per volume, cloth or buckram, $5.00; sheep, $6.00; half calf or half morocco, $7.00. Sold only by subscription. Descriptive circular, with specimen pages, sent on application. Agents wanted for districts not yet assigned.

New York: D. APPLETON & CO., 1, 3, & 5 Bond Street.

D. APPLETON & CO.'S PUBLICATIONS.

THE STORY OF WASHINGTON. By Elizabeth Eggleston Seelye. Edited by Dr. Edward Eggleston. With over 100 Illustrations by Allegra Eggleston. A new volume in the "Delights of History" Series, uniform with "The Story of Columbus." 12mo. Cloth, $1.75.

"One of the best accounts of the incidents of Washington's life for young people."—*New York Observer.*

"The Washington described is not that of the demigod or hero of the first half of this century, but the man Washington, with his defects as well as his virtues, his unattractive traits as well as his pleasing ones. . . . There is greater freedom from errors than in more pretentious lives."—*Chicago Tribune.*

"The illustrations are numerous, and actually illustrate, including portraits and views, with an occasional map and minor pictures suggestive of the habits and customs of the period. It is altogether an attractive and useful book, and one that should find many readers among American boys and girls."—*Philadelphia Times.*

"A good piece of literary work presented in an attractive shape."—*New York Tribune.*

"Will be read with interest by young and old. It is told with good taste and accuracy, and if the first President loses some of his mythical goodness in this story, the real greatness of his natural character stands out distinctly, and his example will be all the more helpful to the boys and girls of this generation."—*New York Churchman.*

"The book is just what has been needed, the story of the life of Washington, as well as of his public career, written in a manner so interesting that one who begins it will finish, and so told that it will leave not the memory of a few trivial anecdotes by which to measure the man, but a just and complete estimate of him. The illustrations are so excellent as to double the value of the book as it would be without them."—*Chicago Times.*

THE STORY OF COLUMBUS. By Elizabeth Eggleston Seelye. Edited by Dr. Edward Eggleston. With 100 Illustrations by Allegra Eggleston. "Delights of History" Series. 12mo. Cloth, $1.75.

"A brief, popular, interesting, and yet critical volume, just such as we should wish to place in the hands of a young reader. The authors of this volume have done their best to keep it on a high plane of accuracy and conscientious work without losing sight of their readers."—*New York Independent.*

"In some respects altogether the best book that the Columbus year has brought out."—*Rochester Post-Express.*

"A simple story told in a natural fashion, and will be found far more interesting than many of the more ambitious works on a similar theme."—*New York Journal of Commerce.*

"This is no ordinary work. It is pre-eminently a work of the present time and of the future as well."—*Boston Traveller.*

"Mrs. Seelye's book is pleasing in its general effect, and reveals the results of painstaking and conscientious study."—*New York Tribune.*

"A very just account is given of Columbus, his failings being neither concealed nor magnified, but his real greatness being made plain."—*New York Examiner.*

"The illustrations are particularly well chosen and neatly executed, and they add to the general excellence of the volume."—*New York Times.*

New York: D. APPLETON & CO., 1, 3, & 5 Bond Street.

D. APPLETON & CO.'S PUBLICATIONS.

A HISTORY OF THE UNITED STATES NAVY, from 1775 to 1894. By EDGAR STANTON MACLAY, A. M. With Technical Revision by Lieutenant ROY C. SMITH, U. S. N. In Two Volumes. Volume I. With numerous Maps, Diagrams, and Illustrations. 8vo. Cloth, per volume, $3.50.

This is the only complete history of the American Navy. There are many books dealing with phases of naval history, but no comprehensive narrative has been published since the days of Cooper, and Mr. Maclay's book, which tells the story of our navy from 1775 to 1894, has the field to itself.

For nine years the author has devoted himself to the task of supplying the want of a complete history of our navy. His researches in France, with the assistance of Admiral Aube, Minister of the Colonies and the Marine, and in England with the aid of the late Sir Provo Wallis and others, together with the use of private papers and unpublished documents in this country, the aid of descendants of naval heroes and the suggestions of naval officers who have taken part in some of the events described, render the results of his diligent labor complete and authoritative. The appearance of this standard history is a peculiarly happy accompaniment of the development of our new navy.

In addition to the spirited illustrations of Mr. J. O. Davidson, who has earned the title of the artistic historian of our navy, there are many carefully prepared diagrams of important battles, showing the respective positions of the ships throughout the contest, and there are many small maps of the scenes of naval operations.

⁎⁎ Volume II, containing the naval history of the Rebellion, revised by Rear-Admiral Jouett and other distinguished naval officers, will be published within a few weeks.

OUTLINE OF CONTENTS, VOLUME I.

PART FIRST.—THE WAR OF THE REVOLUTION.

Chapter I. The United States a Maritime Nation. II. Development of Naval Warfare. III. Outbreak of the Revolution. IV. The American Navy in Europe. V. The Struggle in American Waters. VI. Second Cruise of Captain John Paul Jones. VII. The Bonhomme Richard-Serapis Fight. VIII. Closing Naval Actions of the Revolution.

PART SECOND.—WARS WITH FRANCE AND TRIPOLI.

Chapter I. Outbreak of the War with France. II. A Vigorous Naval War against France. III. The War with France in 1800. IV. The Beginning of the War with Tripoli. V. The War in the Mediterranean. VI. The Frigate Philadelphia. VII. Bombardment of Tripoli. VIII. Conclusion of the War with Tripoli.

PART THIRD.—THE WAR OF 1812.

Chapter I. The Outbreak. II. First Naval Efforts of 1812. III. First Frigate Action. IV. Second Frigate Action. V. The Constitution-Java Fight. VI. First Sloop Actions. VII. The Chesapeake and the Shannon. VIII. Operations on the Great Lakes. IX. Battle of Lake Erie. X. Active Naval War of 1813. XI. Captain Porter's Cruise in the Pacific. XII. Heroic Defense of the Essex.

(*War of 1812 continued in Volume II.*)

New York: D. APPLETON & CO., 1, 3, & 5 Bond Street.

APPLETONS' LIBRARY LISTS.

Libraries, whether for the school, home, or the public at large, are among the most important and wide-reaching educational factors in the advancement of civilization. Modern intellectual activity, keeping pace with modern invention, has added to the earlier stores of literature myriads of books, and a still greater mass of reading matter in other forms. Unfortunately, much of the material put into print is not of an educational or elevating character. It is important, then, in the selection of books for public use, especially for the young, that great care be exercised to secure only such kinds of reading as will be wholesome, instructive, and intrinsically valuable.

For more than fifty years Messrs. D. APPLETON & Co. have been engaged in the publication of the choicest productions from the pens of distinguished authors of the past and present, of both Europe and America, and their catalogue of books now comprises several thousand volumes, embracing every department of knowledge. Classified lists of these publications have been prepared, affording facilities for a judicious selection of books covering the whole range of LITERATURE, SCIENCE, and ART, for individual bookbuyers or for a thorough equipment of any library.

LISTS A, B, and C are of books selected especially for School Libraries.

List A.—*For Primary and Intermediate Grades.*

List B.—*For Grammar and High School Grades.*

List C.—*For College and University Libraries.*

The other lists are of books grouped according to subjects, and include the above.

The classifications are as follows :

List D.—HISTORY.
" E.—BIOGRAPHY.
" F.—PHYSICAL SCIENCE.
" G.—MENTAL AND MORAL SCIENCE.
" H.—POLITICAL AND SOCIAL SCIENCE.
" I.—FINANCE AND ECONOMICS.
" K.—HYGIENE AND SANITARY SCIENCE.
" L.—PHILOSOPHY AND METAPHYSICS.
" M.—TECHNOLOGY AND INDUSTRIAL ARTS.
" N.—ANTHROPOLOGY, ETHNOLOGY, ARCHÆOLOGY, PALÆONTOLOGY.

List O.—LANGUAGE, LITERATURE, AND ART.
" P.—REFERENCE BOOKS.
" Q.—POETRY AND ESSAY.
" R.—TRAVEL AND ADVENTURE.
" S.—PEDAGOGY AND EDUCATION.
" T.—FICTION.
" U.—AMUSEMENT AND RECREATION.
" V.—EVOLUTION.
" W.—RELIGION.
" X.—LAW.
" Y.—MEDICINE.
" Z.—JUVENILE BOOKS.

AA.—UNCLASSIFIED. BB.—SCHOOL AND COLLEGE TEXT-BOOKS.
CC.—SPANISH PUBLICATIONS.

We respectfully invite the attention of public and private book-buyers everywhere to these lists, confident that they will be found of interest and profit. Single lists mailed free. Complete set, 18 cents to cover postage.

D. APPLETON & CO., PUBLISHERS,
New York, Boston, Chicago.

www.ingramcontent.com/pod-product-compliance
Lightning Source LLC
Chambersburg PA
CBHW021426300426
44114CB00010B/673